Contemporary Translation Theories

Translation Studies
General editors: Susan Bassnett and André Lefevere

In the same series:

Translation, Rewriting, and the Manipulation of Literary Fame
André Lefevere

Translation, Poetics and the Stage
Six French *Hamlets*
Romy Heylen

Translation/History/Culture
A Sourcebook
Edited by André Lefevere

Translation as Social Action
Russian and Bulgarian Perspectives
Edited by Palma Zlateva

Contemporary Translation Theories

Edwin Gentzler

London and New York

First published 1993
by Routledge
11 New Fetter Lane, London EC4P 4EE

Simultaneously published in the USA and Canada
by Routledge Inc.
29 West 35th Street, New York, NY 10001

Typeset in 10 on 12 point Baskerville by
Computerset, Harmondsworth, Middlesex
Printed in Great Britain by Clays Ltd, St Ives, plc

British Library Cataloguing in Publication Data
A catalogue record for this book is available from the
British Library.

Library of Congress Cataloging in Publication Data
Contemporary translation theories/Edwin Gentzler.
    p.   cm. — (Translation studies)
    Includes bibliographical references and index.
    1. Translating and interpreting. I Title. II. Series:
Translation studies (London, England)
P306.G44 1993
418'.02—dc20   92-28822

ISBN 0–415–09171–3
    0–415–09172–1 (pbk)

To Paul Engle

Contents

General editors' preface

The growth of Translation Studies as a separate discipline is a success story of the 1980s. The subject has developed in many parts of the world and is clearly destined to continue developing well into the twenty-first century. Translation Studies brings together work in a wide variety of fields, including linguistics, literary study, history, anthropology, psychology, and economics. This series of books will reflect the breadth of work in Translation Studies and will enable readers to share in the exciting new developments that are taking place at the present time.

Translation is, of course, a rewriting of an original text. All rewritings, whatever their intention, reflect a certain ideology and a poetics and as such manipulate literature to function in a given society in a given way. Rewriting is manipulation, undertaken in the service of power, and in its positive aspect can help in the evolution of a literature and a society. Rewritings can introduce new concepts, new genres, new devices, and the history of translation is the history also of literary innovation, of the shaping power of one culture upon another. But rewriting can also repress innovation, distort and contain, and in an age of ever increasing manipulation of all kinds, the study of the manipulative processes of literature as exemplified by translation can help us towards a greater awareness of the world in which we live.

Since this series of books on Translation Studies is the first of its kind, it will be concerned with its own genealogy. It will publish texts from the past that illustrate its concerns in the present, and will publish texts of a more theoretical nature immediately addressing those concerns, along with case studies illustrating manipulation through rewriting in various literatures. It will be comparative in nature and will range through many literary traditions both Western and non-Western. Through the concepts of rewriting and manipulation, this series aims to tackle the problem of ideology, change, and power in literature and society and so assert the central function of translation as a shaping force.

Susan Bassnett
André Lefevere

Preface

The formulation of this project began in the early 1980s at the International Writing Program (IWP) at the University of Iowa, where I worked on translations of poems and short stories and helped arrange panel discussions on the literary situation in various countries around the world. Because Iowa houses not only outstanding English and foreign language departments, but also the famed Writers' Workshop, the IWP members were seldom at a loss for an audience. Fiction and poetry readings at local bookstores as well as the panel discussions at the school were invariably crowded. Yet while creative writers, graduate students, and faculty respectfully attended and listened to the IWP presentations, the international writers' work remained a curiosity rather than an integral part of the literary community, often referred to by students and professors alike as "minor" or "secondary" – separate and to a large degree unequal.

The reception of the foreign writers' work, in turn, did affect the nature of the International Writing Program's translation work. The desire of many international writers to be translated, published, and valued in English was enormous. While some measure of acceptability was gained in Iowa City and at certain university campuses in the United States, it was almost impossible to place translations in mainstream literary journals. The visiting writers reacted differently to such cultural disinterest. Some members, who had arrived in the United States eager to read, to talk, to exchange ideas and texts, withdrew because their work did not conform to the norms governing current literary taste in this country. Generally, these IWP participants returned to their home countries, wrote an essay about their stay in the USA, and continued with writing projects intended for native audiences, perhaps to return at a later date when conditions were more favorable. Other visiting writers recognized the problem and redirected their energies to conform to thematics and styles that might meet a more favorable reception – but at certain costs. By rewriting texts to "appeal" to Western audiences, certain themes, styles, modes of reference, and referents themselves were elided from the texts translated. Those "silences" in the text, often known only to the translator, were often not only the most interesting in terms of creativity, but also the most revealing with regard to cultural differences.

No matter how "good" our translations were, they would never conform to certain "literary" expectations of the audience, a "problem" that may be operative regardless of the originating and receiving cultures. After all, professors, editors, and creative writers make their living from perpetuating one set of literary values over another; as "objective" or as "open" as any literary establishment tries to be, tastes are conditioned, and certain economies predominate. Though language and cultural constraints in America seem enormous, the possibility of challenging norms and creating new forms of expression is always present. At those rare moments when cultural barriers disappear and an international writer meets with success, the "double constitution" of the act of translation becomes visible. Such a "theory" motivated the translation work at Iowa and led to my investigation of other "theories" of translation for this book.

Paul and Hualing Nieh Engle, Co-Founders and Directors of the International Writing Program, knew well the socio-political restrictions governing the context in which translations occur, and devoted their lives to breaking down such barriers. With their influence in mind, I attempt in this book to focus not just on various translation theories, but also on the "political realities" that surround the practice of literary translation, and include them in respective discussions. One of the goals of the book is to raise questions concerning the way literary translations are studied in the West and to help readers rethink conceptually how translations are defined and categorized. I thank the Engles, Peter and Mary Nazareth, Daniel Weissbort, the IWP staff, all the visiting writers, and the University of Iowa for their unswaying commitment to promoting translation and for their ongoing efforts to effect international communication.

Sincere thanks go to Hans-Joachim Shulz, Director of the Comparative Literature Program at Vanderbilt University, not only for allowing me to a large degree to create my own curriculum in pursuit of a fairly wide range of literary and theoretical interests, many of which form the basis for sections of the book, but also for his friendship and trust. Eugene Van Erven, a colleague in the Comparative Literature Program at Vanderbilt and former Director of McTyeire International House, shared my belief in the relevance of international creative writing, especially that of popular political poetry, to academic pursuits. His involvement in and support of many of my "extra-curricular" projects was invaluable. Much of the pleasure I had in the writing of this book was derived from the discussions I had with fellow students during the formative stages of each section; particular thanks go to those students in Charles Scott's seminars on Continental Philosophy at Vanderbilt, especially Gene DiMagno, and to those students in Donald Davie's Pound seminar. Professors Alice Harris and Frantisek Galan, from the Linguistics Department and Comparative Literature Program at Vanderbilt, provided valuable comments on the manuscript. English professors Jack Prostko, Phyllis Frus, and Mark Jarman, also at Vanderbilt, not only read and responded positively to the text, but also included me in their circle of friends, making Nashville a warmer place to work.

Special thanks go to Maria Tymoczko at the University of Massachusetts/Amherst for her meticulous reading of the original manuscript and for encouragement and intellectual companionship during revisions. Conversations with the staff and participants in the 1991 CERA Summer Seminar for Translation, Communication, and Cultures at the Catholic University in Leuven, Belgium, were also very helpful during the final stage. The lectures given by Susan Bassnett, 1991 CERA Professor and this series' co-editor, in Leuven proved very thought-provoking; she also gave me valuable feedback on some of the more controversial sections which follow. Series co-editor André Lefevere's unique interest in translation theory and his incisive suggestions made the entire publication process pleasurable. Publisher Janice Price supported the project from its earliest stage through to its final form.

Most importantly, Janet Gentzler Studer and Marianne Gentzler provided love and affection throughout the writing process.

Megan Gentzler's love, creativity, and companionship renewed my energy during critical phases. And finally, my gratitude for Jenny Spencer's love, intellectual engagement, and unwavering confidence, extends beyond words.

Chapter 1

Introduction

"Translation Theory" is and is not a new field; though it has existed only since 1983 as a separate entry in the *Modern Language Association International Bibliography*, it is as old as the tower of Babel. Some literary scholars claim never to have heard of it as a subject in and of itself; others, who may themselves translate, claim to know all that they need to know. Anyone working "monolinguistically" may purport no need for translation theory; yet translation inheres in every language by its relationships to other signifying systems both past and present. Although considered a marginal discipline in academia, translation theory is central to anyone interpreting literature; in an historical period characterized by the proliferation of literary theories, translation theory is becoming increasingly relevant to them all.

What is "contemporary translation theory"? Roman Jakobson breaks the field down into three areas: *intralingual* translation, a rewording of signs in one language with signs from the same language; *interlingual* translation, or the interpretation of signs in one language with signs from another language (translation "proper"); and *intersemiotic* translation, or the transfer ("transmutation") of the signs in one language to non-verbal sign systems (from language into art or music). All of Jakobson's fields mutually reinforce each other, and, accepting this definition, one can easily see how translation theory can quickly enmesh the student in the entire intersemiotic network of language and culture, one touching on all disciplines and discourses. I will be concerned mostly with the second aspect of Jakobson's definition – *interlingual* translation – but I hope to demonstrate as well that such isolation is impossible, and that even translation "proper" entails multiple linguistic, literary, and cultural aspects.

In recent years, translation theory has exploded with new developments. George Steiner characterized the history of translation theory until Jakobson as a continual rehashing of the same formal (consistent with the form of the original) versus free (using innovative forms to simulate the original's intent) theoretical distinction. "Modern" translation theory, like current literary theory, begins with structuralism and reflects the proliferation of the age. The following chapters focus on just five different approaches to translation that began in the mid-sixties and continue to be influential today: (1) the American translation workshop; (2) the "science" of translation; (3) early Translation Studies; (4) Polysystem theory and Translation Studies; and (5) deconstruction.

Given the marginal status of translation theory within literary studies, I have assumed that the reader has had little previous exposure to the theories presented here. The investigations themselves differ greatly, a fact reflected in the terminology specific to each field as well as in the ideas themselves. Literary translators, for example, distance themselves from the "jargon" of linguistic approaches; deconstructionists subvert the very "scientific" terminology demanded by semioticians; and the aggressive rhetoric of the deconstructionists alienates scholars from many of the other fields. Of necessity, each of the following chapters conforms in a gradual way to the preferred terminology within the branch of study, for certain ideas are dependent upon the terms used to describe them.

In addition to terminological differences, however, other barriers have impeded the exchange of ideas among scholars of various approaches. Despite the fact that proponents of "new" approaches such as Translation Studies have been developing their ideas and publishing their data for over two decades, their ideas remain foreign to more traditionally based approaches. Euro-American translators, for example, generally resist the suggestion that institutional manipulation influences translation. Translation Studies scholars do not relish the idea that their meticulously collected data may be interpreted by deconstructionists to reveal multiple gaps and literary repression rather than systematic literary evolution. Interdisciplinary translation conferences have been held, but many incompatabilities remain; one of the purposes of this study is to show how such problems in communication and exchange are grounded in the differing theoretical assumptions of each approach.

An attempt has also been made to read symptomatically, to look at the "discourse" of the given text, and to point out what can and cannot be said given the philosophical premises of the scholar. For example, after reviewing Eugene Nida's religious presuppositions and missionary goals, I find that his adoption of a deep structure/surface structure model derived from "modern" linguistics as a base upon which to found his "science" highly suspect. What he means by "deep" structure – something vague and related to the Word of God – and what Noam Chomsky intended – again, something vague, but related to innate structures of the human brain – are two different concepts. Often the theoretical assumptions are less overt than those of Nida, but still can be discerned by the terminology, rhetoric, and style chosen by a particular scholar. Thus when early Translation Studies scholars adopt concepts such as "literariness," "estrangement," "primary," and "secondary," I find the terms themselves reveal assumptions about the hierarchical nature of a culture. While such terms may help the translation scholar articulate the way translations function in a society, they may also serve to inhibit the nature of the investigation.

Given this methodology, original sources have proven more valuable than the secondary literature, most of which comes from "outside" a translation-oriented or even a comparative discipline, or, in other words, from within the particular discipline – be it literary theory, linguistics, or philosophy. Instead, by returning to the "original" source, I can analyze not just what the text explicitly says, but also what it does *not* say or says only by implication. For example, when Jonas Zdanys, Translation Workshop Director at Yale, says that he avoids "predetermined aesthetic theories" and then later talks about his commitment to "creative solitude," or, even more revealing, talks about his hoping to convert a linguistics student to his beliefs, I suggest that he has his own predetermined yet unspoken agenda. Or when I. A. Richards first argues in *Practical Criticism* that he is looking for a new theory allowing individuals to discover themselves and to discover new methods, and then turns around, dismisses the varied responses of his students as errors, and argues that the goal also is to achieve "perfect understanding" and a unified and correct response, I suggest his argument is less than consistent.

Some of the "precursors"' work may or may not have been intended for translation. Richards, for example, was clearly teaching students techniques for learning the English canon, yet translation workshops in the United States use New Critical methods to interpret and evaluate translations. Richards' approach – whether consciously or unconsciously – remains at the heart of classroom. Chomsky did not intend his model to be used for translation, but Nida and Wolfram Wilss – director of a translation institute in Saarbrücken – have incorporated, correctly or incorrectly, aspects of Chomsky's model in their work, and thus the translation scholar must ask those hard, and sometimes unfair, questions regarding the suitability of a particular model for translation theory. Others have spoken directly to issues of translation. Late Russian Formalists such as Jurij Tynjanov and Roman Jakobson allowed for translation as well as other cultural phenomena in their theory of art, but infrequently expanded upon specifics. Questions regarding the nature of translation are always underlying the movement of the thought driving Heidegger's and Derrida's work, and thus color a subsequent generation of "scholars." Yet in many ways some of Derrida's terminology seems dated in light of recent translation theory – such as his reference to the "impossibility" of translation – and the Translation Studies scholar must point out the progress which has been made.

In general, I am greatly encouraged by developments in the field of "modern" translation theory. The focus in translation investigation is shifting from the abstract to the specific, from the deep underlying hypothetical forms to the surface of texts with all their gaps, errors, ambiguities, multiple referents, and "foreign" disorder. These are being analyzed – and not by standards of equivalent/inequivalent, right/wrong, good/bad, and correct/incorrect. Such standards imply notions of substantialism that limit other possibilities of translation practice, marginalize unorthodox translation, and impinge upon real intercultural exchange. As is true in literary theory in general, a revaluation of our standards is well underway, and within the field of translation theory substantialist notions are already beginning to dissipate (though no doubt they will die slowly). For literary history, translation case studies are already proving a valuable resource showing how cultural ideology directly influences specific literary decisions. For literary theory, this may very well be an exciting time of renewed study of *actual* texts from a new discipline, which can only help us gain increased insight into not only the nature of translation, but the nature of language and (international) communication as well. Yet, my optimism is tempered by the feeling that all the translation theories discussed in this text reflect certain values and aesthetic assumptions about literature as understood by Western critics. As the translation theories outlined in this book become more and more complex, they seem to gain more and more support from academia, which, in turn, also enhances their power to exclude.

Chapter 2

The American translation workshop

THE BOOM IN LITERARY TRANSLATION

In many academic circles in America, literary translation is still considered secondary activity, mechanical rather than creative, neither worthy of serious critical attention nor of general interest to the public. Translators, too, frequently lament the fact that there is no market for their work and that what does get published is immediately relegated to the margins of academic investigation. Yet a closer analysis of the developments over the last three decades reveals that in some circles literary translation has been drawing increasing public and academic interest.

In the early sixties, there were no translation workshops at institutions of higher learning in the United States. Translation was a marginal activity at best, not considered by academia as a proper field of study in the university system. In his essay "The State of Translation," Edmund Keeley, director of translation workshops first at Iowa and later at Princeton, wrote, "In 1963 there was no established and continuing public forum for the purpose: no translation centres, no associations of literary translators as far as I know, no publications devoted primarily to translations, translators, and their continuing problems" (Keeley, 1981: 11; qtd. by Weissbort, 1983: 7). In this environment, Paul Engle, Director of the Writers' Workshop at the University of Iowa, gave the first heave; arguing that creative writing knows no national boundaries, he expanded the Creative Writing Program to include international writers. In 1964 Engle hired a full-time director for what was the first translation workshop in the United States and began offering academic credit for literary translations. The following year the Ford Foundation conferred a $150,000 grant on the University of Texas at Austin toward the establishment of the National Translation Center. Also in 1965, the first issue of *Modern Poetry in Translation*, edited by Ted Hughes and Daniel Weissbort, was published, providing literary translators a place for their creative work. In 1968, the National Translation Center published the first issue of *Delos,* a journal devoted to the history as well as the aesthetics of translation. Literary translation had established a place, albeit a small one, in the production of American culture.

The process of growth and acceptance continued in the seventies. Soon translation courses and workshops were being offered at several universities – Yale, Princeton, Columbia, Iowa, Texas, and State University of New York, Binghamton among them. Advanced degrees were conferred upon students for creative, historical, and theoretical work in the field of literary translation. This, in turn, led to the establishment of the professional organization American Literary Translators Association (ALTA) in the late seventies as well as the founding of the journal *Translation* for that organization. By 1977, the United States government lent its authority to this process with the establishment of the National Endowment of the Humanities grants specifically for literary translations. For a while in the late seventies and early eighties, it looked as if the translation workshop would follow the path of creative writing, also considered at one time a non-academic field, and soon be offered at as many schools as had writing workshops.

But despite the increase in translation activity and its gaining of limited institutional support in the sixties and seventies, the process of growth plateaued. Many assumptions about the secondary status of the field remained. Today, while many universities offer advanced degrees in creative writing, comparatively few offer academic credit for literary translation. One reason is surely the monolinguistic nature of the culture. However, such typecasting is also due to socio-economic motives: labeling translations as derivative serves to reinforce an existing status quo, one that places primary emphasis not on the process but on the pursuit and consumption of "original" meaning. The activity of translation represents a process antithetical to certain reigning literary beliefs, hence its relegation to marginal status within educational and economic institutions, and its position in this society as part of a counter-cultural movement.

Indeed, during the sixties and early seventies, the practice of literary translation became heavily involved in representations of alternate value systems and views of reality. While not taken seriously by academics, sales of translated literary texts enjoyed unprecedented highs on the open market. Perhaps no one articulated the political urgency and popular attraction of literary translations during this period better than Ted Hughes:

That boom in the popular sales of translated modern poetry was without precedent. Though it reflected only one aspect of the wave of mingled energies that galvanized those years with such extremes, it was fed by almost all of them. . . . Buddhism, the mass craze of Hippie ideology, the revolt of the young, the Pop music of the Beatles and their generation. . . . That historical moment might well be seen, as . . . an unfolding from inwards, a millennial change in the Industrial West's view of reality.

(Hughes, 1983: 9)

For Hughes, the translation boom of the sixties was simply one aspect of a generational movement that articulated itself in a variety of media. While his view of translation as anti-establishment may not have been true of all translation during this period, it did hold true for a large and influential group of contemporary American poets actively translating at the time: Robert Lowell, Robert Bly, W.S. Merwin, Gary Snyder, Denise Levertov, Galway Kinnell, Elizabeth Bishop, W.D. Snodgrass, and Lawrence Ferlinghetti, among the most important. These poets not only rebelled against traditional literary institutions, but also against the national and international policies of their government and Western society in general. A decade later, in the Foreword to *Writing from the World II* (1985), an anthology of literary translations from the late seventies and early eighties, Paul Engle summed up the socially active, politically urgent cause of translation in the contemporary world as follows:

As this world shrinks together like an aging orange and all peoples in all cultures move closer together (however reluctantly and suspiciously) it may be that the crucial sentence for our remaining years on earth may be very simply:

TRANSLATE OR DIE.

The lives of every creature on the earth may one day depend on the instant and accurate translation of one word.

(Engle and Engle, 1985: 2)

THE TRANSLATION WORKSHOP PREMISE

Despite the surge of popular interest in literary translation and the raising of important questions regarding the theoretical nature of language by American literary critics during the past several decades, few have paused to make connections between the two practices. One explanation for this lack of critical attention may be attributed to the "atheoretical" premises of those practicing and teaching translation as revealed in the numerous prefaces and introductions to texts containing translations. An essay by Jonas Zdanys of the Yale translation workshop illustrates the problem. In "Teaching Translation: Some Notes Toward a Course Structure" (1987), Zdanys talks about his initial ambivalence about teaching literary translation because he feels this creative process cannot be taught. He then overcomes his reluctance and agrees to do so, hoping to attract literature students interested in "exploring the theoretical and the practical aspects of poetic translation" (Zdanys, 1987: 10). Zdanys proceeds to review the course, the books taught, the structure of the seminar, and its successes, emphasizing especially the enjoyment of the poems and the students' translations. The article concludes with Zdanys changing his mind about the inappropriateness of teaching translation, arguing instead that the art of translation not only can be taught, but also can make the student more aware of aspects of poetry, language, aesthetics, and interpretation.

Zdynas' notes seem characteristic of prevailing assumptions regarding the teaching of translation in the United States. He shares the assumption that creative writing cannot be taught, that creative talent is something one is born with. Such a belief plagued creative writing for years before it was accepted as an university discipline. Secondly, Zdanys reveals a prejudice for teaching students how to enjoy the original poem, one which is in keeping with New Critical tenets. His conclusion is not altogether surprising – although he argues against conventional wisdom that translation can be taught at the university, he does it not for reasons Ted Hughes suggested – that it may lead to a change in the way the West views reality – but because it reinforces a fairly conservative humanistic ideology. This is nowhere better revealed than in a contradiction within the essay regarding the theoretical basis of the course. On the one hand, Zdynas hopes the course will attract students interested in theoretical questions; on the other hand, he argues that he himself opposes the restraints of "pre-

determined aesthetic theories." In addition, without telling us
why, Zdanys says that "this essay unfortunately cannot consider"
the contribution of deconstruction to the field, although, ironically, Yale itself houses numerous such critics who are in fact part
of the same department (a special interdepartmental program) in
which the course was offered. Despite claims to the contrary,
Zdanys reveals the aesthetic predispositions which underlie his
approach:

> Although I am not yet ready to surrender my commitment to
> creative solitude, I do believe that discussions of the various
> theoretical essays, the careful readings of original poems, first
> drafts, and finished translations, and the consideration of the
> various aspects of translation made workshop participants
> more fully aware of the dynamic process that is literature. By
> the end of the course, students certainly had a richer under-
> standing of literary complexity.
>
> (Zdanys, 1987: 11)

Zdanys clearly finds translation a subjective activity, subsuming
translation under the larger goal of interpreting literature. His
argument that the study of translation can lead to a qualitative
"richer" understanding reveals the humanistic agenda. His goal is
more clearly disclosed in a section of the same essay in which he
talks about the presence of a female linguistics student who,
despite Zdanys' "initial misgivings" about what she might contribute to the seminar, actually brought a "valuable and intriguing"
perspective to the aesthetic process he was teaching. Zdanys
contradicts his stated premise – a rejection of predetermined
aesthetic theories – when he concludes that although her
approach was a "refreshing" addition to the course, he "secretly
hopes" that he "converted" her during the course. The lingering
question is "converted her to what?"

That unarticulated "what" is the topic I wish to address in this
chapter. Scholars associated with the American translation workshop premise tend to claim that their approach is not theoretically
preconditioned; this chapter attempts to formulate the *non-dit*
present in their works, to analyze those underlying assumptions,
and to show how they either reinforce the existing literary edifices
or offer a counterclaim which deserves further consideration.
Through this approach, I hope to show that the translation

workshop approach actually does both, i.e., simultaneously reinforces and subverts, and that this dual activity, necessarily
operative because of the methodology, is in itself a contribution to
the ongoing investigation of not only translation phenomena, but
of language in general.

I. A. RICHARDS: THEORETICAL FOUNDATIONS

If there is one text which best exemplifies the theory of the
practice-oriented workshop approach to translation, it is I.A.
Richards' *Practical Criticism* (1929). The precursor to both the
creative writing workshop and the translation workshop, I.A.
Richards' first reading workshop took place at Harvard in the late
1920s. Richards' famous experiment was to give his best Harvard
undergraduates thirteen poems from authors ranging from
Shakespeare to Ella Wheeler Wilcox. The students received
poems with no further information (no title, author's name, or
biographical information) and had one week to respond, after
which Richards collected the "protocols." Richards' aims were
threefold: (1) to introduce a new kind of documentation into
contemporary American culture; (2) to provide a new technique
for individuals to discover for themselves what they think about
poetry; and (3) to discover new educational methods. With an
approach that cut both the student and the text off from society,
Richards hoped to introduce new documentation supporting his
aesthetic beliefs: that a unified "meaning" exists and can be
discerned and that a unified evaluative system exists by which the
reader can judge the value of that "meaning."

How does Richards' reading workshop of the twenties relate to
today's translation workshop? First, both introduce new documentation into the culture, often the responses of the not yet fully
formed literary critic. As Zdanys' article above indicates, subsequent translation workshops followed Richards' precedent,
taking pride in the fact that their students did not yet have any
predetermined methodology. While this freedom from constraint may seem to allow a "truer" investigation of the process of
translation, in practice, for Richards' and subsequent translation
projects in institutions of higher education, the effect is simply
that students conform to the existing tastes and prejudices of
those in control of the literary institutions. Secondly, although
Richards' emphasis on the individuals' "discovering themselves"

may seem magnanimous as well as democratic, it was not without a hidden humanist agenda. Richards' approach *appeared* open to multiple interpretations, to readings which were liberating, individual, and potentially anti-establishment as well as to those reinforcing traditional interpretation. In fact, the aim of his project was exactly the opposite: to establish new educational techniques that would lead to "perfect understanding" of the text and result in a unified and correct response. In his actual workshop, Richards did not seek variable responses, but rather unified solutions to communication problems, generating rules and principles by which individual interpretations could be made and properly judged:

> The whole apparatus of critical rules and principles is a means to the attainment of finer, more precise, more discriminating communication. . . . When we have solved, completely, the communication problem, when we have got, perfectly, the experience, *the mental condition* relevant to the poem, we still have to judge it, still to decide upon its worth.
>
> (Richards, 1929: 11)

Such a model presumed a primary poetic experience that can be exactly and completely communicated to another person, if one were properly educated. The evaluation of the poem was similarly determined, again by the consensus of those whose trained abilities allowed them to see the light and judge accordingly. Evaluative power settled into the hands of the elite, revealing Richards' didactic goals only too clearly: Richards' Harvard students learned to think and judge exactly the way he did. At one point, Richards argued that the deficiencies in the protocol writers were not "defects" in the human mind, but "mistakes" that could have been avoided with better training (Richards, 1929: 309).

Structurally, the translation workshop methodology has adopted certain aspects of Richards' reading workshop. First, the attempt to discover rules and principles which help attain that finer, "more discriminating" communication exists, the only difference being that translation workshop participants try to generate reading *and* writing rules. Secondly, the same goal – that of achieving primary experience and rearticulating it – exists, the only difference being the media in which that experience is expressed. Literary translation in America is often viewed as a form of close reading – some argue the closest form. Perfect rearticulation of the experience in a perfect interpretation/ translation is the goal. Richards' summary of the aim of his reading workshop might equally hold true for the translation workshop: "A perfect understanding would involve not only an accurate direction of thought, a correct evocation of feeling, an exact apprehension of tone and a precise recognition of intention, but further it would get these contributory meanings in their right order" (Richards, 1929: 332).

Thus far from being new, i.e., something unique and different which individuals, given their different backgrounds and ideological presuppositions, can bring to a text, Richards' reading model posits a unified "meaning" right where it was traditionally assumed to be, in a "precise recognition of [the author's] intention." Richards assumed *a fortiori* that readers can understand precisely what the author said, and that via interpretation they can recover that same meaning. It should come as no surprise that in *Practical Criticism*, Richards advocated a very stringent educational regime – increasing homework, improving maturity, controlling stock responses, and safeguarding readers from their own preconceptions – through which reading problems could be solved and consensus attained. The argument that initially appeared so democratic – teaching students to think for themselves – turned into a condemnation of the American educational system. René Wellek, writing in *A History of Modern Criticism: 1750–1950*, argues that Richards' solution failed because of its "highly concealed dogmas" and that his conclusions, based upon the "anarchic" variety of readers' responses, are "absurd" (Wellek, 1986: 229). Richards believed that the reader of good poetry was more valuable to society than one who did not read, and his political values got confused with his literary practice, resulting in a theory that posited the possibility of a perfect reader who could recover the author's original meaning. Far from offering anything new, Richards' approach actually reinforced conservative literary institutions and political structures.

In addition to his well-known contribution to American criticism of this century, Richards also made a foray into the field of translation theory. In "Toward a Theory of Translating," published in 1953, Richards refined his theory of meaning while discussing how one should compare translations to original texts. His initial project, attempting to resolve problems inhibiting perfect understanding, had been made increasingly problematic in light of three decades of theoretical inquiry, influenced largely by the theories of relativity and referentiality. Richards was not untouched by evolving critical theory:

> How can one compare a sentence in English poetry with one (however like it) in English prose? Or indeed any two sentences, or the same sentence, in different settings? What is synonymy?* A proliferous literature of critical and interpretive theory witnesses to the difficulty. It seems to have been felt more and more in recent decades.
>
> (Richards, 1953: 249)

Richards noted Quine after "synonymy" because meaning and its translation within one language or across two languages had become increasingly problematic for literary critics. For Quine and the Anglo-American philosophical tradition, the problem of synonymy – equating identity with semantic exactness – extended beyond the laws of logic.

A few years later in *Word and Object* (1960), Quine would use translation to demonstrate the complexity and indeterminacy of language. In the Preface he wrote, "Language is a social art. In acquiring it we have to depend entirely on intersubjectively available cues as to what to say and when. Hence there is no justification for collating linguistic meanings" (Quine, 1960: ix). In the chapter "Translation and Meaning," Quine switched to translation to make "more realistically" what was often an abstract point when viewing languages monolinguistically. He introduced the "scope" for "empirically unconditioned variation" by citing the example, "two men could be just alike in all their dispositions to verbal behavior under all possible sensory stimulations, and yet the meanings or ideas expressed in their identically triggered and identically sounded utterances could diverge radically" (Quine, 1960: 26). Quine's conclusion directly contradicted any theory of translation based upon notions of equivalence:

> Manuals for translating one language into another can be set up in divergent ways, all compatible with the totality of speech dispositions, yet incompatible with one another. In countless

---

*See, e.g., Willard V. O. Quine, 'Two Dogmas of Empiricism,' *Philosophical Review*, 60 (1951).

places they will diverge in giving, as their respective translations of a sentence of the one language, sentences of the other
language which stand to each other in no plausible sort of
equivalence however loose.

(Quine, 1960: 27)

The problems of referentiality and indeterminacy have historically troubled translation theory, making positions calling for a
one-to-one transfer approach and methods revolving around a
decoding and recoding process increasingly difficult to hold.
Richards, who had hoped to discover the laws revealing literary
meaning, found late in life that the quantity of different interpretations and different translations had actually undermined his
project. Decades after *Practical Criticism*, Richards decided that
the reason his initial project did not succeed was that the fields of
comparison within the process of translation were too broad and
permitted unlimited speculation. His solution in "Toward a
Theory of Translating" became one of narrowing the field and of
choosing the right methodology for the relevant purpose. He
believed that if translators were to agree on their purpose (as
practicing literary translators ought to), then the appropriate
methodology would not be difficult to determine:

> In the concrete, in the minute particulars of practice, these
> comparison-fields are familiar enough. . . . All we have to do is
> to arrange, in a schema as parsimonious as adequacy will allow,
> a body of experience so common that if the purposing of our
> arrangement could be agreed on, there might be little we
> would then differ about.

(Richards, 1953: 252–3)

Despite revision, Richards' initial premises remain intact: he still
believed that the field consists of texts containing a primary "body
of experience" that (an elite few) readers could discern; with the
proper training, a consensus could be reached regarding what
that experience might be. He could not rid himself of the urge to
reduce all differences of interpretation to a single response.

Such a premise allowed Richards to sketch an encoder/decoder
communication model similar to those used by communication
theorists. Richards' diagram was slightly more complex, dividing
the original message into seven components, all of which carry
meaning and require decoding. Richards argued that the translator should not only be aware that a sign (I) indicates some thing;

but that it also (II) characterizes (says the same thing or something new about things); (III) realizes (presents with varying degrees of vividness); (IV) values; (V) influences (desires change); (VI) connects; and (VII) purposes (attempts to persuade) (Richards, 1953: 252–3). Swearing, as an example of his component IV, places value on something in addition to indicating something. Thus "meaning" for Richards had grown to be something very complex, having both implicit and explicit aspects. For example, under "realizing" he allowed that "what is highly realized may be distinct, explicitly structured, detailed, definite in most of the senses of this strategic word. But it may equally well be very indefinite." In addition, the converse may be true: "On the other hand, many devices – from headlines to the routines of the dispatch editor and commentator – reduce the reality of what is presented" (Richards, 1953: 257). Richards was fully aware that signs are never devoid of attempts to persuade.

Yet, despite Richards' revisions and his understanding of complex categories of meaning inherent in every message, his theoretical premises remained largely the same. Richards' 1953 model was specifically tailored for the translator who aimed to arrive at the "proper" translation. Richards was aware that the idea of achieving a unified reading was becoming increasingly difficult to maintain, given the fact that theories of relativity had been introduced into the theoretical framework of twentieth-century literary investigation. While the question motivated this particular essay on translation, in the end it remains unresolved. On the one hand, Richards admitted in the essay that the translation process "may very probably be the most complex type of event yet produced in the evolution of the cosmos" (Richards, 1953: 250). On the other hand, he argued that translators, with proper education and practice, can come to know the proper methodology to achieve the correct understanding of the primary text. Despite allowances made for complexity, the model was still one that suggested that the original message could be properly decoded and then recoded into another language. Richards still maintained that the literary scholar could develop rules as a means of solving a communication problem, arrive at perfect understanding, and correctly reformulate that particular message.

Had Richards presented such a complex model in the thirties, it would have been a *tour de force* in the field; presented when it was, the essay read as a desperate play to retain power within the institution in light of new theoretical developments, and indicates that the time was ripe for new insights. The closing argument was most revealing:

> We are guardians, IV [valuers], and subject therefore to the paradox of government: that we must derive our powers, in one way or another, from the very forces which we have to do our best to control. Translation theory has not only to work for better mutual comprehension between users of diverse tongues; more central still in its purposing is a more complete viewing of itself and of the Comprehending which it should serve.
>
> (Richards, 1953: 261)

Aware that he derived his power from controlling the criticism of literature, Richards attempted to make translation theory subservient to the larger goal of "Comprehending" in the New Critical sense. And he was successful at accomplishing this goal. With the dissemination of the Harvard project students throughout the American university system, New Criticism became the most prevalent approach for decades.

Language, however, did not yield to such controlling forces, a fact especially apparent in the field of translation. Instead of establishing a set of rules which subjugated the text to a limited and unified interpretation and "complete viewing," the actual translations tended to open up new ways of seeing and subverted fixed ways of seeing. Despite all the education and proper training in the right methodologies, research has shown that if one gives two workshop translators the same text, what evolves are two different translations. New texts are constantly emerging that are neither identical to the original nor to other translations. Although Richards derived his power from language, he seems not to have understood the very entity from which his power came. If the American translation workshop has shown anything, it is that the translated text seems to have a life of its own, responding not to the interpreter's set of rules, but to laws which are unique to the mode of translation itself.

EZRA POUND'S THEORY OF LUMINOUS DETAILS

Unlike Richards' theory of proper translation, Ezra Pound's theory of translation focused upon the precise rendering of details, of individual words, and of single or even fragmented images. Rather than assuming the single, unified meaning of the whole work, Pound's "theory" was based upon a concept of energy in language; the words on the page, the specific details, were seen not simply as black and white typed marks on a page representing something else, but as sculpted images – words engraved in stone. Such an approach allowed for more latitude for an individual translator's response; the translator was seen as an artist, an engraver, or a calligrapher, one who molds words. While still one of the most influential, Pound is perhaps also the least understood translator and critic read by the current generation of translators in America. Pound's theoretical writings fall into two periods: an early imagist phase that, while departing from traditional forms of logic, still occasionally contained abstract concepts and impressions; and a second late imagist or vorticist phase that was based entirely on words in action and "luminous" details, in which the importance of the thing being represented recedes and the energy or the form language takes in the process of representing becomes more important.

The distinction between the two periods of Pound's theory was not created by Pound himself, who saw no such division, but by the critical reception of his work. Because Pound's earlier writings appeared romantic, his initial work on an imagist theory seemed metaphysical. However, as Amy Lowell and others began to appropriate his ideas and to turn imagism into something metaphysical – as a form of poetry symbolizing ideas – Pound felt the need to distance himself from the imagist movement. During this period, post-symbolism took on many forms; Pound felt that even Eliot, for example, never quite escaped symbolism. In his own poetry, Pound moved on to more and more direct speech, to capturing exact, even if miniature, details. His words referred to real objects – a painting, the pigment, a stone, a cut in the stone – and not to abstract concepts. To more precisely express his theory, he moved on to "vorticism" and more radical articulations, many of which remain uncollected, still located in unanthologized articles in *New Age*, *BLAST*, and other now defunct magazines.

In his evolution from imagism to vorticism, Pound's thoughts about translation played a central role. Hugh Kenner in *The*

Pound Era (1971) notes that in 1911 Pound began to think "of translation as a model for the poetic art: blood brought to ghosts" (Kenner, 1971: 150). Pound's theory of translation first appeared in a book on Arnaut Daniel, which unfortunately was never published and survives only in a series of twelve articles published in A. R. Orage's weekly *New Age* under the title of "I Gather the Limbs of Osiris." Osiris, when his scattered limbs are regathered, becomes not only the God of the Dead, but also the source of renewed life, the limbs' reunited energies reasserting themselves. A subheading to the articles told how Pound would use translations to illustrate the "New Method in Scholarship," which, according to Kenner, turns out to be a method of recapturing patterned energy and of articulating the "luminous detail," capable of giving sudden insight (Kenner, 1971: 150–2). The first article of the "Osiris" series was called "A Translation from the Early Anglo-Saxon Text," Pound's translation of *The Seafarer*, and implicitly marked the beginning of vorticism (Pound, 1911–12: 107). Pound's emphasis was less on the "meaning" of the translated text or even on the meaning of specific words. Instead, he emphasized the rhythm, diction, and movement of words. Unconscious associations, reverberations of sounds within words, and patterns of energies were used to re-energize in twentieth-century English the "original," or at least the earliest English poem. (The same technique would be used in the first Canto, Pound's translation of the beginning of Homer's *Odyssey*.) The ninth installment of the "Osiris" series was titled "On Technique" and contained the first reference to vortex. In it Pound talked about *words* as "electrified cones," words charged with "the power of tradition, of centuries of race consciousness, of agreement, of association" (Pound, 1911–12: 297; qtd. by Kenner, 1971: 238).

BLAST, an art magazine with reproductions of drawings, paintings, and sculpture, founded in the spring of 1914 by Wyndham Lewis, continued this line of thinking, and the vortex, a cone, and a wire, became the emblem for the journal. Vortex was understood as a form – or as an evolving system of forms or a system of energies – which revolved around a center (a person or a place) and which drew in whatever came near. Vortex was understood as a cluster of words, a network of words, brought together in a radiant node. In the first issue of *BLAST*, Pound defined the new approach by contrasting it with impressionism:

The vortex is the point of maximum energy. . . . All experience rushes into this vortex. All the energized past, all the past
that is living. . . . Impressionism, Futurism, which is only an
accelerated sort of impressionism, DENY the vortex. . . . The
vorticist relies not upon similarity or analogy, not upon likeness
or mimicry. . . . An Image is that which presents an intellectual
and emotional complex in an instant of time. . . . Picasso,
Kandinski, father and mother, classicism and romanticism of
the movement.

(Pound: 1914: 153–4)

In Pound's *Gaudier-Brzeska: A Memoir*, he tried to clarify the
problems of the interpretation of what he meant by imagism. By
"image" he meant "not an equation of mathematics, not some-
thing about *a* , *b*, and *c*, having to do with form, but about *sea*, *cliffs*,
night, having something to do with mood." He continued, "The
image is not an idea. It is a radiant node or cluster; it is what I can,
and must perforce, call a VORTEX, from which, and through
which, and into which, ideas are constantly rushing" (Pound,
1970a: 92).

The movement from early imagism to a theory about the
energy of language is also much influenced by Pound's "reading"
of Chinese ideograms. Pound received the Fenollosa manuscripts
in 1913 and began his first translations of Li Po a year later. While
it is true that at this time Pound could not read Chinese – Pound
did not begin seriously studying Chinese characters until 1936
(Kenner, 1971: 447) – he was well immersed in theoretical questions at the time and in the *culture* of the language he would
translate. He had already read Giles' *History of Chinese Literature*
and had rewritten some of Giles' translations (Kenner, 1971: 194–
5). His wife had found and purchased a set of Morrison's seven
volume *Chinese-English Dictionary* (Kenner, 1971: 250). During
this same 1913–14 period, Henri Gaudier-Brzeska was sculpting
a bust of Pound, and the two were meeting regularly, not only
discussing sculpture and theories of art, but also interpreting
individual Chinese characters. After reading, for example, the
187th radical from Morrison's dictionary, which he read at
Pound's apartment in London, Gaudier-Brzeska is quoted as
saying, "Can't they see it's a horse?" (Kenner, 1971: 250). The
connection between Pound's articles in the vociferous, now defunct journals on sculpture and the plastic arts and the
development of an ideogrammic method of translation was very

close. Given his interest in sculpting as a means for releasing contours and energy in the raw material and his interest in poetry as a means of focusing on the energy of individual, concrete details, it should come as no surprise that he embraced the Chinese ideogram.

Theoretically for Pound, Chinese characters represented not meanings, not structures, but things, or more importantly, *things in action*, in process, things with energy, their form. Words, according to Pound, were always seen in a network of relations; Anglo-American words were signs similar to Chinese characters – always capable of being compounded and capable of being meta-morphosized. Just as Fenollosa was reacting to the tyranny of medieval logic (Kenner, 1971: 225), arguing that there is no verb "to be" in Chinese, so too was Pound *using* the Chinese in a cultural struggle to assail subject/object relations and static metaphysical distinctions that had paralyzed literary and academic discourse in the West. Compounding Pound's alienation was the fact that, at this time, all of Europe was at war and artists were serving on front lines, enough to shake anyone's belief in the rationality of West-ern modes of thinking. By 1915, Pound was writing his memoir of Gaudier-Brzeska, killed in the trenches in France.

Impressionism was a static, mimetic theory of art; imagism, while not intended as such, was being used similarly, much against Pound's conception. The essays on painting and sculpture, the essays on the ideogrammic methods, no less revealing of Pound's literary theory, were deliberately excluded from T. S. Eliot's anthology of Pound's *Literary Essays*. The wealth of criticism generated on Pound's literary theory is invariably based upon the early and easily accessible work, is influenced by Lowell's and Eliot's reception, and fits in better with prevailing aesthetic norms within the literary centers (*Poetry* magazine being just one) of the culture. Perhaps influenced by current trends in literary criticism, more recent scholarship has begun to recognize the breadth of Pound's work and is making connections to post-structuralist theories of language (Korn, 1983; Rabate, 1986).

For Pound, the precision and accuracy of the reference to material reality in art remained fundamental in both periods, but in the later theory the object being presented was substantially different. Pound's writing on translation and the translations themselves, often self-reflexive, best reveal his later theory on the energy of language. During the writing of *The Cantos*, Pound's languages ceased to be clearly distinguishable; English for him was merely part of an evolving Greek-Roman-Latin-Italian-French-Spanish-English language in which all meanings were interrelated. In *The Cantos*, Pound's theory of translation is as visible as his theory of art. He thinks not in terms of separable languages, but of a mesh or interweaving of words that bind people regardless of nationalities. The threads of language run back in time, and as one traces them back, variable connections can be made. Peoples are joined by varying continuities of speech. What was stable, in Pound's mind, was not any unified meaning of any given word or theme across history, but the form (*forma*) in which language and object combine. Pound's ideas were not aimed at fixed things, but at things which can change. Material objects, accordingly, became viewed as charged with energies or strengths and existing in relation to or in opposition to other objects. Donald Davie in *Pound* (1975) cites images of wrestlers who tremble when they lock, of the rose pattern formed by the magnet from dead-iron filings, or of the waterspout or whirlpool swirling downwards as key "images" that express Pound's view of the beat or energy inherent in all material things (Davie, 1975: 66–7).

Given such a dynamic conception of ideas, the "meaning" of a work of art can also never be fixed; it changes as language changes. The range of associations of the words within an older work of art differ with its new reinscription in a different age or culture. Something happens to the entire repertoire preceding a translation in the process of its genesis. Language, according to such a view, seems to have a life of its own; a power to adapt, mutate, and survive that extends beyond theories such as Richards', which attempt to capture it and explain its intricacies. In the section titled "language" of his essay "HOW TO READ" collected in *Polite Essays* (1937), Pound laid out the various ways in which "language is charged or energized." These were *melopoeia*, or the musical property, *phanopoeia*, or the visual property, and *logopoeia*, by far the most complex property, one which includes both the "direct meaning" and the "play" of the word in its context. Pound wrote:

> LOGOPOEIA, "the dance of the intellect among words", that is to say, it employs words not only for their direct meaning, but it takes count in a special way of habits of usage, of the context we *expect* to find with the word, its usual concomitants, of its known

acceptances, and of ironical play. It holds the aesthetic content which is peculiarly the domain of verbal manifestation, and cannot possibly be contained in plastic or in music. It is the latest come, and perhaps most tricky and undependable mode.

(Pound, 1937: 170)

This remarkable post-structuralist statement – foregrounding ironical play and the domain of verbal manifestation – not only gives rise to associations with Nietzsche's dancing star (Nietzsche, 1954: 129) but also to resonances a word calls into play by its intertextual associations with a paradigm of meanings, habitual and otherwise. Pound further explicated this difficult concept by talking about translation: *melopoeia* is difficult to translate except a "half a line at a time"; *phanopoeia* can be translated "almost, or wholly, intact"; and *logopoeia* "does not translate." Pound elaborated:

Logopoeia does not translate; though the attitude of mind it expresses may pass through a paraphrase. Or one might say, you can *not* translate it "locally", but having determined the original author's state of mind, you may or may not be able to find a derivative or an equivalent.

(Pound, 1937: 170–1)

The trouble in interpreting Pound's aesthetic begins here: was he talking about intuition, guessing the author's original intention, or something else? Pound may have been trying to determine and translate how a given word was used in a given historical situation, especially if the word was being used in a new or unconventional way. This quality of "making it new," of constructing new relations to other words at any particular place *and* time lends language its energy. Pound did not say intuit, but "determine" by studying the language, the time, the biography of the author, other texts by the same author and others during the period, the logic of categories of thought in another time and context, and by giving yourself over to that state of "mind." Then, he suggested, one needs to return to the present and try to create new relations, derived from the old, which reveal the logic of the other.

Thus Pound's theory of translation involves being both inside a tradition and outside any institutionalized logic. In order to understand the *logopoeia* of a text, the translator must understand the time, place, and ideological restrictions of the text being translated. Pound asks translators to allow themselves to be subjected by the mood, atmosphere, and thought processes of the text in time. Simultaneously, the mood and sensibility in time and place is to be be transported to the present culture for the translation to become a contemporary text. The only way for this to happen without falling into "translatorese" is to create new connections in the present, to draw attention to the translator as a living and creating subject.

An example of a translation that creates new relations in contemporary culture is Pound's "Homage to Sextus Propertius," which has provoked strong emotional responses among Western scholars. Its reception has been dominated by those who favor "faithful" translation, who argue that Pound was incompetent and who document their position by the number of errors in the translation (Peachy and Lattimore, 1919; Graves, 1955), and by those who advocate "free" translation, arguing that Pound planted "howlers" on purpose and that he was translating something other than the literal sense (Sullivan, 1964). In the case of "Homage to Sextus Propertius," however, what becomes clear is that neither position is remotely close to what Pound himself tried to articulate. Pound's text actually parodied the kind of flat, boring, awkward English which had become characteristic of the scholar's literal translation; according to Donald Davie, one of the meanings of the poem is how *not* to translate (Davie, 1975: 58). At the same time, Pound was not arguing for poetic license or freedom of interpretation; in fact, he vehemently opposed freedom from the form and meter of the source text. Pound *used* the classical text for his own purposes, i.e., to create new relations in the present. Certainly in "Homage" he accomplished that, ridiculing reigning translation theories of the educational and literary establishment and opening new avenues for appropriation of the classics.

While Pound's personal voice as found in "Homage" was interjected into other translations such as "The River Merchant's Wife," "The Seafarer," or the beginning of *The Odyssey* as it appears in Canto I, he was not necessarily being "unfaithful" to the original. Pound's indignation with Western scholars" cloudy conceptual notions, and his emphasis on concrete historical particulars within his theory of translation, can best be illustrated by his letters to W.H.D. Rouse, who was translating *The Odyssey* at the time of the correspondence. The letters reveal Pound's belief that not intuition, but knowledge of the language, history, and economics enables one to understand the classics: "Along with direct teaching of the language, is there any attempt to teach real history? 'Roman mortgages 6%, in Bithinya 12%'" (Pound, 1950: 262). He continues, "Until Latin teaching faces the economic fact in Latin history, it may as well leave out history." Pound believed that the real history had been covered up by the Western scholar. The "parroting" by the teachers, the "tushery" provided by "adorned" translations, obscured the classics and made them inaccessible by creating an elite class which had access to the ideas and whose job it became to pass on that knowledge. Pound was very aware of the socio-economic motives of the creation of this class of interpreters: "Granted the bulk of the sabotage and obstruction is economic and nothing else" (Pound, 1950: 263). Rouse told the story that when he read his translations to small boys they understood every word, but when he adorned them, the children were bored. The adventure, the narration of Homer, was sacrificed at the expense of higher truths and beautified language. Rouse, with Pound's support, aimed at plain language, personal modesty, and narrative drive. Pound realized the difficulty Rouse had holding to his principles, given the mythical status of Homer's story and the political implications for literary institutions if the classics were accessible to the entire population.

When Rouse deviated from his stated aims, Pound continually advised him to return to basics:

> Let's list the aims:
> 1. Real speech *in* the English version.
> 2. Fidelity to the original
>   a. meaning
>   b. atmosphere.
>
> (Pound, 1950: 263)

Although Pound used the term "fidelity" in a humanist/idealistic fashion, he broadened the concept to include "atmosphere" as well as original meaning. His term "atmosphere" referred to both contextual and intertextual associations. Pound clarified the importance of contextual relations in his vehement criticism of Rouse whenever he ceased to locate the words in history: "This first page of book two is *bad*. I mean it is just translation of words, without your imagining the scene and event *enough*" (Pound, 1950: 271). Because words never exist out of context, the translator must at all times keep present in the imagination the context ("scene") and the expression in that context ("event"). According to Pound's translation theory, meaning is not something abstract and part of a universal language, but something that is always already located in historical flux – the "atmosphere" in which that meaning occurs. To unpack that meaning, one has to know the history and reconstruct the atmosphere/milieu in which that meaning occurred.

In the same letter, Pound underscored the importance he gives to intertextual relations, the *logopoeia*, the play of the word in time: "Tain't what a man sez, but wot he *means* that the traducer has got to bring over. The *implication* of the word" (Pound, 1950: 271). The implication of the word entangles the translator in the web of intertextual relations and interrelated meanings. Pound's theory of translation requires the translator to keep the historical atmosphere in which the words occur in view at all times so that the translation process reveals not just what the words mean but the various implications of the word in its "verbal manifestation." All words invoke both a paradigm of expected and habitual associations and play against that very paradigm. Pound's theory suggests that the free play of the word and its distancing itself from what it means may be just as important as its one-to-one correspondence. *Logopoeia* provides a theoretical construct more interested in preserving the irony, the implicit, over literal meaning. For the energy of language – the object in the medium, always changing and newly creating – can be seen only within the irony and play of the word in historical context.

In *The Pound Era*, Hugh Kenner underscores Pound's emphasis upon seizing the "real," citing Pound's sensitivity to detailed sculpted forms as a primary reason (Kenner, 1971: 67). Pound was not interested in abstract concepts at all; instead, he preferred to focus on form, fragments, and specific details, for only in moments, in glimpses, can one "seize the real." Kenner cites the example of Pound's outrage over J. L. Edmonds' translation of Sappho, wherein over 50 percent of the words of the final text were additions by Edmonds. Only fragments remain of much of Sappho's work, and Edmonds felt sufficiently qualified to fill in the gaps and fill out the ideas. Instead, Pound much preferred Richard Aldington's translations, although Aldington was nineteen at the time and had no classical training. Although his interpretation raises questions, Aldington at least did not engage in "tushery" or pure guesswork, nor did he add lines when the original lines were lost. Pound advocated concision, clarity, and the presentation of images of concrete *things*, the very reason he prized Sappho's own poems (Pound, 1915: 55; 1975: 17–18).

For Pound, avoiding abstract concepts did not mean strict adherence to linguistic aspects of the text, either. Pound did not focus on syntactical connections, and, according to Kenner, Pound even suggested that "a preoccupation with syntax may get in the translator's way" (Kenner, 1971: 68). Pound's writing on translation emphasized focusing on specific images, individual words, fragments, and luminous details. His method was modern [not post-modern] insofar as it emphasized juxtaposition and combination, hoping that the new configurations would react chemically, combining into a new compound, and thereby give off energy. Rhythms, diction were more important than syntax. The translator and/or poet was viewed as the catalyst working with specific, individual words. Each word with its etymology, its way of combining, gave insight into new possibilities. Lost in this day and age is Pound's graphic style – the drafts of the poems he sent to publishers contained double spaces between words. In "In a Station of the Metro," for example, he wanted the images set off, but subsequent editors have merged the images and closed up the spaces so the text "reads" more syntactically correct (Kenner, 1971: 197). Words, for Pound, can cut other directions than linear; they can cut backward, historically, and sideways, jux-tapositionally, as well as forward. "Syn'-tax gets merged with "syn'-thesize, or some sort of putting information into a logical order or a coherent whole, one which by its very definition obscures the precision, the details, and the specific images Pound so desperately wished to preserve.

This tendency to generalize, categorize, and draw abstractions was prevalent in the academic and literary institutions in the West, and in part explains Pound's rebellion and his turning to the Chinese ideograms with their single, distinct monosyllables and their own semantic boundaries. Pound, thus, successfully used translation to challenge and change the prevailing literary norms. Working from within the tradition, as with "Homage," and im-porting texts foreign to the tradition, as with Li Po, Pound relentlessly attacked the prevailing Victorian/Edwardian literary tastes. As Pound used translations as a tool in his cultural struggle, so too have Euro-American translators of the sixties and seventies used translation to challenge prevailing tastes and cultural conceptions in Western (American) society as well as to lend energy to the counter-culture movement.

FREDERIC WILL: THE PARADOX OF TRANSLATION

While Richards' work in translation might be characterized as an extension of his literary criticism, Frederic Will's literary theory – initially not unlike Richards' – has changed much because of his involvement in translation. Will's work in translation theory is symptomatic of that of many adherents of the American workshop approach. Will first taught Classics at the University of Texas, where he founded the journal *Arion* with William Arrowsmith. He then moved to the forefront in translation by accepting the directorship of the translation workshop at the University of Iowa in 1964. In 1965 he founded *Micromegas*, a journal devoted to literary translation, each issue focused on the poetry of a different country. His first theoretical text *Literature Inside Out*, published in 1966, raised questions about naming and meaning and indirectly suggests that translation can be viewed as a form of naming, fiction-making, and knowing (Will, 1966: 15). His next book, *The Knife in the Stone*, published in 1973, dealt directly with the practice of translation; and parts of it rearticulated his workshop experience at Iowa.

Although Will's early text did not specifically address translation problems, certain relevant theoretical assumptions are visible. Will's project picks up where Richards' left off: he uses New Critical beliefs to try to reconcile recent critical theories. Will's first essay "From Naming to Fiction Making" in *Literature Inside Out* appears to agree with a theory of cultural relativism. Holding that different languages construct separate realities and that what any particular word refers to cannot be determined precisely, Will calls into question translation theories based on reference to a universal objective reality. Reality can only be learned, he argues, through the names we give it, and so, to a certain degree, language is the creator of reality. Will also distances himself from theories which posit a notion of universal themes or motifs, theories which do not view symbol-making as part of a human activity. At the same time, however, Will argues that knowledge of essence is possible: "The core of the self, the theme of its efforts, is love," which is a power unto itself and can bring the outer reality "into the focus of consciousness" (Will, 1966: 9). Naming, for Will, is the fundamental activity of man – without the power to name we would have remained savages. Language, thus, he argues, takes on our character, our rhythm, our desires, and reveals our true inner selves. Will continues to say that

> the self's effort, in naming, is not mere verbal play but is part of its overall effort to translate the outer into the human. This situation follows from the unity of the self. In such unity the expressions of a core-movement, the self, all bear the character of that movement. Each expression bears the core's character.
> (Will, 1966: 13)

As opposed to an objective outer reality which can be translated across cultures, Will posits a central common core of human experience and emotions which can overcome the indeterminate nature of language and bring that "outer reality" into focus. We translate our selves into language; naming does not necessarily give us any insight regarding outside reality (that to which language refers), but it does help us to better know our inner selves.

The power of this inner understanding and knowledge is further elaborated in the second essay, "Literature and Knowledge," in which the influence of Richards is everywhere to be seen. Literature, according to Will, also "embodies truth and knowledge" (1966: 17). The New Critical tenet of the unity of the original text is also adopted; Will argues that a work of literature "is a deeply unified verbal event occurring in a self." The words which compose a work of literature, so important to Pound, are merged with the whole for Will, and "are, in some sense, literally one." In the literary work, "most or all" of the levels of meaning of words, and Will lists five – dictionary, contextual, symbolic, interpretative, and inner aural and visual overtones – "are made one" (Will, 1966: 18). Will's agenda, like Richards', is fundamentally didactic, not just in terms of developing competent literary critics, but also in terms of a larger, humanistic goal. Literature, according to Will not only "gives us the power to understand," but also serves as a means to understand a higher metaphysical power. Will clearly believes that "the power to understand something is 'knowledge' of something." Yet we have seen that Will is skeptical about our ability to know objective reality. He concludes with the rhetorical question, "What else can knowledge be, even about the natural world or about God, except the power to understand them?" (Will, 1966: 24). Literary works present us with models by which we can "clarify" the real, irrational world which we experience as a "confusion of intermingled space, action, and character." Literature thus deepens and enriches our lives as well as gives us a better understanding of our own true selves.

Will then reexamines his own theory after his experience in the translation workshop at the University of Iowa and after having read Pound. Although his next theoretical text, *The Knife in the Stone*, retains metaphysical concepts, many of his romantic notions of love and humanistic beliefs in the power of the heart dissipate. His concept of text becomes less of a unified and coherent whole; instead it is seen as being interwoven with reality, subject to use, change, and variable interpretations. In *The Knife in the Stone*, Will uses translation as the "testing ground" for his theory, and clearly the goal is to substantiate the metaphysical beliefs he brings to the project:

> The inter-translatibility of languages is the firmest testing ground, and demonstration ground, for the existence of a single ideal body of literature. If there is any meaning, to the idea of such a body, it will show itself through as effort to equate literature in one language with literature in another.
>
> (Will, 1973: 42)

Again, the opposition includes those who are skeptical about the possibility of translation, those who question concepts of literariness, and those who find the concept of referentiality problematic. Will names Sartre and Mead, whose theories posit inner "selves" who are not aware of the universal core of human experience, but are, in Will's terminology, "groundless" and "socially constructed" respectively. Through the test of translation, Will intends to disprove the "relativity" thesis and to show that one universal common ground – that of the single ideal body of literature – does, in fact, enjoy "inter-translatibility." However, Will's argument, when put to the test, does not confirm his initial presuppositions, but causes him to alter his conception of translation in a manner that may be of interest to contemporary theory.

His first test, reported in the essay "The Oneness of Literature," involves a personal experience that occurred during a trip to Hungary where he worked with another poet on the translation of a group of poems by Gyula Illyes. Although Will admits in the article that his knowledge of Hungarian literature is virtually non-existent, he already knows that the text in hand, translations of Gyula Illyes' poems by another writer, are "poor translations." How? Because there is little that "feels" like English poetry (Will, 1973: 42–3). We see that Will's approach is very subjective and ultimately determined by his transcendental view of the power of poetry. He is able to "feel behind" the translation and the original to some ideal form of the poem as part of that ideal body of literature. Because he belongs to that privileged class of poet and translator, because he enjoys the power of "love," he believes he can overcome his specific ignorance of the language in question as well as its indeterminate normal use, and gain access to that "essence" behind the poem. Robert Frost has argued that poetry is what gets lost in translation (Frost, 1973: 159). Will believes exactly the opposite; in fact, given his lack of knowledge of the Hungarian language, the essence may be the only thing he could possibly translate. Will believes that poetry can be made "intelligible," by which he means it can achieve "a kind of 'transcendence' and a kind of becoming-salient" (Will, 1973: 50). Symptomatic of a tendency in American literary translation, Will's methodology actually avoids all theory and returns to the practical "common sense" approach which trusts his intuition ("love" or "ecstasy") of the meaning of these poems. Far from offering new theoretical insights, Will's theory at this stage merely reflects traditional metaphysical theories of the power of poetry. He may think that his translation "success" reconfirms his theory, but for those not yet converted it "proves" little.

A shift in Will's theory of translation first occurs in "Translation and the Limits of Inter-cultural Understanding," from *The Knife in the Stone*. In contrast to many Anglo-American translators, Will focuses on the key period in Pound's development – the 1912–14 period in which Pound began thinking in terms of vorticism, the period in which he became more interested in the plastic and visual arts. Will quotes Pound from "How I began" (1913):

> I resolved . . . that I would know the dynamic content from the shell . . . what part of poetry was "indestructible," what part could *not be lost* by translation, and – scarcely less important – what effects were obtainable in *one* language only and utterly incapable of being translated.

> (Pound, 1913; qtd. by Will, 1973: 59)

Will's presuppositions continue to affect his reading of Pound. For example, citing Pound's Chinese translations, Will argues that Pound is able to leap beyond the words on the page for the "feeling-sense of the original." When Pound literally says that "words" are like cones of steel, Will instead says that Pound is referring to the "core" or the "dynamic content."

Aesthetic presuppositions notwithstanding, Will also uses Pound in the same essay to raise an important epistemological question – the translator's paradox – of how is it possible to know anything we do not already know, and what follows marks a change in Will's theoretical approach. To resolve this epistemological problem, Will first looks at the linguists Noam Chomsky and Norbert Weiner, who argue that the deep structure they posit across languages is only obliquely related to surface structure, and that there exists a "considerable chance for error" if one reaches through the surface structure for the "real argument" (Will, 1973: 69–72). Will then refers to the communication theorist Donald MacKay, who posits the notion that "each individual is a goal-directed system" and that communication acquires meaning when one person sees how others try to influence behavior from within their own system of beliefs. The social unit formed by such interaction of individual systems becomes a goal-seeking system in its own right (Will, 1973: 74–5). Will then reinterprets his early assessment of Pound. If Li Po's poem is seen as one activity taking place within Po's own entire goal-complex, i.e., that Li Po oriented himself to his surrounding culture and tried to change or influence that same society, then Pound, by extension, is both trying to stand inside Li Po's world and trying to influence contemporary events himself. Because he is working on a translation, Pound must account for Li Po's goals; and by placing himself and his own notion of literary relations in this differing historical situation, he thereby must form a new social unit – a new set of relations in MacKay's sense. Will concludes, "the notions of 'oneself' and 'other' are not that unitary or solid. They are intermeshing notions, concerning intermeshing entities (or abstraction-entities). The paradox remains, but itself translated; self, meaning among other things what one becomes through others, returns from the other which it partly is" (Will, 1973: 76).

The change in the logic of Will's argument is most apparent in the final essay of *The Knife in the Stone*, called paradoxically "Faithful Traitors," a play on the Italian aphorism *tradutore*, *traditore*. Briefly, the article reviews his experience teaching at Iowa. In the course of the activity of actual translation, it became clear to Will that what he was translating had less to do with the meaning of the text and more with the energy of the expression, how meaning was expressed in language. He found himself using a kind of Poundian theory. The cultural relativity thesis that once was so problematical is adopted by turning it back in on itself, not to oppose his practice, but to contribute as an equally always present part. Since language is indeterminate, since we never have access to the meaning behind specific language, all the more reason to be free and trust not what language says but what the language does. The traditional notion of translation as "carrying over" is too restrictive, and has caused translation to fall into categories of "faulty equivalences" and of "versions" of the original. What Will advocates instead is an approach that translates not what a work means, but the energy or "thrust" of a work, for which there is no "correct" way of translating. He writes:

> Translation is *par excellence* the process by which the thrust behind the verbal works of man . . . can be directly transferred, carried on, allowed to continue. . . . Works of literature are highly organized instances of such thrust . . . these blocks force themselves on, through time, from culture to culture.
>
> (Will, 1973: 155)

This "thrust" is a new concept in the argument, and is not something represented by language *per se* , but a term coined by Will and derived directly from Pound's Osiris essays. In addition to being Dionysian, Osiris also refers to the male productive principle in nature. Translation is less seen as a "carrying over" of content, but as a "carrying on" of the content *in* language. In translation, texts are reborn, given new life, stimulated with new energy. The paradox present in the title of the essay is resolved in the idea that the translator can be most faithful to the true meaning of the text by being unfaithful to the specific meaning ("indicative" meaning in Richards' theory) of the language of the text.

Will enters dangerous ground here by allowing the translator a "poetic" license to make the necessary changes in order to retain something originally arrived at intuitively. Such a methodology offends most translation theorists, especially scholars and linguists, because it is antithetical to their very definition of translation as a transfer of a message from one code to another. Whatever else may be said about Will, I should like to note the complexity of this particular thought and consider this redefinition of the process. Meaning is redefined by Will not as something behind the words or text, not as an "essence" in a traditional metaphysical sense, but as something different, as thrust or energy, something which is at the same time indeterminate and groundless (as in Sartre) *and* universal and originary (as in Descartes). Translation is possible both because dynamic universals constantly and continually thrust and because language is impenetrable. In translation Will seems to find a possible/impossible paradox of language which not only defines the translation process, but defines how we come to know ourselves through language.

The contradiction in Will's later position is thus different from that in Richards' argument. Whereas Richards found himself fighting against contradiction and trying to solve the problem by narrowing the focus of what is being investigated and by clari-fying the rules of the investigation, Will expands the parameters to include the contradiction and turn it in on itself. The difficulty in understanding Will's text is due to the fact that he is trying to say something obscured by his own metaphysical conceptions. The end of the essay on the Iowa translation workshop is deter-mined by Will's need for closure and his almost romantic notions about poetry as well as by his new hypothesis about language. He says that at the workshop there was "a communal working toward the single language which lies between, or among – spatial meta-phors collapse here – all the national languages" (1973: 158). But then he continues in the different vein:

> Of course we were not, literally, considering a middle or pure or perfect language, but always languages x and y, from one of which we were trying to translate into the other. However the theoretical horizon, which made possible this notion of cross-ing linguistic areas, was the conviction of a single repository of meaning, a *tertium quid*, from which both x and y drew, from which they were both equally nourished, which somehow guaranteed them both in their relationship to each other.
>
> (Will, 1973: 158)

The activity of translation, according to Will, somehow reveals to the translator that language is simultaneously unstable and stable, that texts are interwoven in reality and in a tradition of fiction, and that man, as a complex system, is both subjected by language or systems of discourse and is capable of creating language or new relations in the present. Language always refers to something (other), be that reality or some metaphysical concept. At the same time, human language is necessarily always innovative, additive, and continually being relocated in different contexts, with different referents. That which makes translation possible for Will (universals/deep structures) also makes it impossible (the specific moment/surface structures). Thus language always refers backward and forward, trapped in an intertextual network. Will's multiple conservative ideological preconceptions merely serve to obscure a provocative (and perhaps progressive) hypothesis on the subject of translation theory, arrived at, to a large degree, through reading Pound and working in the American translation workshop.

THE PROCESS OF LITERARY TRANSLATION

Although workshop practitioners invoke Pound as someone who has freed translation from the restraints of literalism, they rarely confront Pound's or any other aesthetic theory directly. Such an atheoretical position allows them to appropriate Pound's theory – freeing them from methodologies that privilege literal correspondence – and grants them license to promote whatever aspect of the original text they please. For example, the interpretation of Pound's theory by poet and translator Ronnie Apter, author of a book called *Digging for the Treasure: Translation After Pound* (1984), illustrates the point. Apter still thinks in terms of "faithful" (called "Victorian") and "free" (called "modern"). Apter then uses Pound to support a defense of the free approach, concluding:

> Pound's innovations have freed modern translators from slavish adherence to sense for sense, rhyme for rhyme, and meter for meter. Instead, they turn to a battery of *ad hoc* strategies (often strategies suggested by Pound) on the original poem in an attempt to give critical insight into why the original poem has importance for them.
>
> (Apter, 1984: 75)

Certainly Pound's strategies were not *ad hoc*; whenever Rouse strayed from the primary strategy, Pound harshly admonished him. True, he was not advocating sense for sense, but this does not imply opening up the field for any intuited or divinely inspired "insight" either. The problem with Apter's and others' appropriation of Pound's theory of translation is that they derive it from Pound's early Provençal translations, his early literary essays, and his imagist writings, which were in fact based on aesthetic intuition and leaps of poetic imagination. Apter, however, does not consult Pound's essays on vorticism, any of his criticism on painting and the plastic arts, nor *The Cantos*, referred to only in an occasional footnote. As a result, Apter's conclusion seems more influenced by the vague and *ad hoc* strategies supported by contemporary taste in America regarding poetry and translation than the specific and well defined strategy demanded by Pound.

If Pound's translation theory is not taken seriously by creative writers and translators today, what are the theoretical premises of the workshop methodology? First, what has been adopted from Pound's theory primarily is his taste – lack of adornments, plain speech, and poetry which is as well written as prose. While I, too, may prefer this tendency, little theoretical basis exists for such a preference, and the prevailing taste could just as well be something different. Although the "plain speech" phenomenon seems intrinsically American and more overtly "democratic," the danger of elevating a nationalistic position is that it reinforces literary institutions. In terms of taste, what was revolutionary and innovative in Pound's era has now become mainstream. License has been given to allow translators to intuit good poems from another language without knowledge of the original language or the culture, and, as long as they have some poetic sensibility and good taste, now governed by plain speech and lack of adornment, their translations are accepted. The journal *Micromegas* was just one journal which reflected this tendency; while many of the issues contained selections and translations by very knowledgeable translators, others contained translations by writers with limited language skills. Foreign language facility does not seem to be a requirement for entrance to a workshop; poetic sensibility and an ability to write well in English are the most important criteria.

Because of the breadth of Pound's language skills, it appears perhaps that he was intuiting some universal language, and the assumption that such a universal language exists is widespread among American literary translators. In fact, Pound had learned the languages of the Greco-Roman Western tradition. He knew some Greek, more Latin, was fluent in Provençal and Italian, his

French and Spanish were excellent, and his English/American legendary. His mind ranged freely over the history of the development of Western culture, and he could think in different languages and thought systems of specific historical periods. Much of his life was spent trying to demythologize a tradition elevated and reified by Western scholars, and to rewrite literary history to make it more widely accessible. Unfortunately, many translators seem to feel they can intuit a particular language and tradition and have access to the mythology without knowledge of the language, let alone the historical/cultural context Pound had. In an article in the *New York Times Book Review*, Milan Kundera writes about this phenomenon in the West:

> In 1968 and 1969, "The Joke" was translated into all the Western languages. But what surprises! In France, the translator rewrote the novel by ornamenting my style. In England, the publisher cut out all the reflective passages, eliminated the musicological chapters, changed the order of the parts, recomposed the novel. Another country: I meet my translator, a man who knows not a word of Czech. "Then how did you translate it?" "With my heart." And he pulls a photo of me from his wallet.
>
> (Kundera, 1988: 1)

The theoretical premise that such translation is possible is clearly Platonic, not Poundian; it allows translators without the facility in a given language to translate, using literal versions as cribs, from which they intuit the "essence," all the while invoking Pound to lend a modernist authority to their approach.

With the workshop method of using only a crib and a creative writer – in most cases the translator is or purports to be the creative writer – almost anything is possible. One example of the American translation workshop practice of translating from languages one does not know has been published by Angela Elston in her 1980 article "The Golden Crane Anthology of Translation." A crib containing information similar to that Pound had available when he translated T'sui Hao's "Yellow Crane Pavilion" was sent to over twenty creative writers, most of whom are well established as poet/translators in America or England, who were then asked to "translate" the poem. The crib contained the original poem, a word-for-word translation, a line translation, and notes on the form, the language, and the legend. The results varied enormously – semantic differences, syntax changes, linear changes, images altered, multiple formal innovations, metaphoric discrepancies, even the typeface and word pattern on the page varied. The diversity of the individual versions certainly calls into question any model of translation prescribing how one should translate a literary text, be it Richards' or any other. Although the exercise used a crib similar to the one Pound had from Fenollosa, Pound would have shuddered at the results. While some of the poems are very creative in their own right, they have little to do with the "theory" Pound called for.

In an essay accompanying the translations, Elston argues that meaning may be expressed in a number of different ways; the crib, she argues, gives us the content through which we may see the meaning. She goes so far as to suggest that it may be easier to work from a crib because it has already done some of the work of separating some of what is translatable from that which is not. If one knew the original, one would surely imitate some of its formal features – style, tone, music, repetition of sound; but if one worked from a crib, since that person would not know the formal features, the translator would not thereby be constrained (Elston, 1980: 16). Elston thus inadvertently reverses Pound's theory of translation; the style, the tone, the music, the repetition of sound were in fact precisely those features Pound valued most. Writing about the process behind her own translation of "The Brown Crane Blues," Elston states that she did consult an Asian languages scholar, but found that most of the information he gave her was not the sort that could survive in translation, again contradicting Pound's theory, which stressed the importance of cultural information in determining implication, the play of the word, in context.

Occasionally glimpses of a more accurate understanding of Pound's theory of translation can be discerned from the prefaces and introductions to translated texts published in America. Generally such essays focus on the problems of translating from one language into another, but W.S. Merwin, for example, who more often than not has immersed himself in the source language and culture, gives us such an insight in the introduction to *Selected Translations, 1968–1978*:

> But if we take a single word of any language and try to find an exact equivalent in another . . . we have to admit it cannot be done. A single primary denotation may be shared; but the

constellation of secondary meanings, the movement of rings of associations, the etymological echoes, the sound and its own levels of association, do not have an equivalent because they cannot. . . . Yet if we continue, we reach a point where some sequence of the first language conveys a dynamic unit, a rudiment of form. Some energy of the first language begins to be manifest, not only in single words but in the charge of their relationship.

(Merwin, 1979: viii)

Traces of a theory drawn from Richards, Pound, and Will can be seen. Merwin is not so naive to even suggest a unified reading is possible; he is too acutely aware of the differences which defy translation, nuances which escape, and connotations lost. Yet at the same time, he is also aware that in the process of translation, that which manifests itself is less what the language says and more what it does, i.e., words take on an energy in their contextual, intertextual life.

What emerges, thus, from the American contribution to contemporary literary translation theory is less an articulated, coherent, rational theory and more a whole new set of questions. The contribution views translations less in terms of identities and equivalents, and more in terms of language associations, etymologies and resonances that would not be normally seen or heard if it were not for their translation. The process generally advocated involves giving in to some kind of "other" voice, hearing the energy of the language, and allowing secondary, marginalized, and forgotten associations to resurface, which are then used to lend depth and resonance to the translated versions. Documenting a concept of energy in language, of words in action, is difficult if not impossible. Yet a genre is emerging in the United States, beginning perhaps with John Felsteiner's *Translating Neruda: The Way to Macchu Picchu* (1980), continuing through Robert Bly's "Eight Stages of Translation" (1984) and Edwin Honig's *The Poet's Other Voice: Conversations on Literary Translation* (1985), which attempt to give us insight into the process of translating. Daniel Weissbort, who co-directs the translation workshop at Iowa, continues this line of investigation in *Translating Poetry: The Double Labyrinth* (1989), a collection of essays by translators, some closely associated with the American translation workshop approach, in which they reveal certain insights as well as dead ends encountered during the process of translation. The text includes several drafts of the translated text as the translators play with various forms of language possibilities before the final version, as well as commentary on some of the more difficult choices.

It is too early to draw conclusions from such documents, and many more are needed. In America, however, the beginning of a unique contribution by the American workshop approach is visible: a first look into the black box of the human mind as it works and reworks during the activity of translating. As many decisions are clearly subjective and often unconscious, the analysis of this process of translation has been the most neglected branch of translation theory. Translation in this country historically seems to subvert itself, disappearing in the process as the translated text emerges as a literary work in its own right in the receiving language. In fact, in American circles, because of the emphasis placed on the finished work functioning as a literary work in the receiving culture, translations more often than not appear self-referential, drawing attention to themselves or to the translator, not because of their accuracy or cohesion, but because of their differences and deviations. There is a kind of cannibalistic activity involved, and those who do not cannibalize are the minority.

With such texts as are collected in the Weissbort edition, a slight opening into a new avenue of thought is emerging, and we are left with more questions than answers. The most obvious question has to do with the very definition of the term translation. The Jakobson term "creative transposition," with the emphasis on creative, seems more operative (Jakobson, 1959: 238). The second question still involves the epistemological problem. When one assumes a Poundian approach to literary translation, what are the referents? Meaning? Things? Energy in language seems too vague of a concept for any sort of rational investigation. Are the criteria totally subjective? Can we call Pound's theory a material theory? To what is the translator bound, the original written text or something heard or intuited? Has translation anything to do with identity? More questions arise when one tries to generalize about methodology. Are there any rules for governing the generation of the translated text? What are the minimum requirements for a translator in terms of knowledge of the source culture and language? Finally, the American translation workshop approach raises many questions regarding the nature of the evaluative standards. Are they totally dependent upon the prevailing taste of the receiving culture? Many books, anthologies, articles exist which address one or more of the above questions, often with a great deal of insight. Yet these texts tend toward the prescriptive rather than the analytical, and focus more on techniques of problem solving and the craft of translation rather than the theory.

Ironically, perhaps because of their lack of an already articulated institutionalized theory, because of their focus on the process of translation, and because of their questions emerging from such a perspective, the American translation workshop proponents may actually find themselves in an advantageous position to contribute to discussions regarding recent developments in translation theory. While an aesthetic of New Criticism still loosely forms the foundation of the American contribution, one must also recognize that many traditional forms of genre and representation seem to be subverted in some fashion or other by these American translator/poets. The very limits and constraints of the activity of translating seem to help in making possible new verbal constructions, and thus the attraction of translation as a mode in itself for this generation of American poets. Will points out that in such a situation, spatial metaphors collapse and new theoretical horizons emerge. A comprehensive theory of translation need also address this double movement – one which perpetuates given aesthetic beliefs and simultaneously subverts those very conceptions.

Chapter 3

The "science" of translation

THE NEED FOR A MORE OBJECTIVE APPROACH

While opening up new perspectives, the general approach as practiced in American translation workshops might best be characterized by a theoretical *naïveté* and subjective methodologies that tend to reinforce whatever theoretical values individual translators hold. Joseph Graham summarizes the theoretical contributions of the workshop approach as follows:

> Much that has been written on the subject of translation yields very little when sifted for theoretical substance because it has always been written as if spoken in the workshop. The personal anecdotes and pieces of advice may well provide some help, but certainly not the coherent and consistent theory required for translation.
>
> (Graham, 1981: 23)

The problem is not just a contemporary phenomenon in America, but one that has troubled translation theory historically. People *practiced* translation, but they were never quite sure what they were practicing. During the sixties and seventies in America, the translation workshop perpetuated the same practice. Clearly, a more systematic approach to translation was needed, and the discipline that appeared to have the theoretical and linguistic tools necessary to address the problem was linguistics.

Up until the early sixties linguistics had been characterized by largely descriptive research in which individual grammars were detailed but not compared, and thus of little theoretical value to translators. The simultaneous development of two theories of grammar significantly altered the course of translation theory, and these theories remain very influential today. The culmination of the evolving theories may be represented by Noam Chomsky's *Syntactic Structures* (1957), Eugene Nida's *Message and Mission* (1960), Nida's *Toward a Science of Translating* (1964), and Chomsky's *Aspects of the Theory of Syntax* (1965). Generative transformational grammar, along with its legitimacy within the field of linguistics, lent credence and influence to Nida's "science" of translation. Nida's theory was based on his experience translating the Bible; his early theoretical assumptions were visible in articles written in the fifties and in his book *Message and Mission* (1960). Although Chomsky published a tentative version of his theory called *Syntactic Structures* in the Netherlands in 1957, Nida claims that his theory of translation was already well developed before Chomsky's formulation. In an article called "A Framework for the Analysis and Evaluation of Theories of Translation," Nida argues:

> Before the formulation of generative-transformation grammar by Chomsky Nida had already adopted an essentially deep-structure approach to certain problems of exegesis. In an article entitled "A New Methodology in Biblical Exegesis" (1952) he advocated the back-transformation of complex surface structures onto an underlying level, in which the fundamental elements are objects, events, abstracts, and relations.
>
> (Nida, 1976: 71)

Despite claims to the contrary, Nida's theory crystallized with the addition of Chomsky's transformational component – Nida read Chomsky's *Syntactic Structures* in mimeograph form two years before it was published. With the adoption of Chomsky's theoretical premise, his transformational rules, and his terminology, Nida's theory solidified, and the result – *Toward a Science of Translating* – has become the "Bible" not just for Bible translation, but for translation theory in general.

Nida's work in the field of Bible translating was initially practice-oriented rather than theoretical. The historical paradigm which he drew on for his strategies was fairly narrow, dominated by translations of the Bible. Nida's development of a translation science was motivated by a personal dislike for what he saw as a classical revival in the nineteenth century, an emphasis on technical accuracy, an adherence to form, and a literal rendering of meaning. The principal exponent in English of this movement, according to Nida, was Matthew Arnold, whose approach was clearly too scholarly and pedantic for Nida's taste, placing too many demands upon the reader to become informed about the original culture. Arnold's literalism, according to Nida, negatively affected Bible translation in the early twentieth century. He cites as one example the American Standard Version, which, although popular with theology students, never caught on with the general public. Nida writes that, "the words [of the American Standard Version of the Bible] may be English, but the grammar is not; and the sense is quite lacking" (Nida, 1964: 20–1). I argue that Nida's arguments against Arnold's approach are governed by his taste, general public opinion, and the economics of his project (converting people to Christianity). Implicit in his approach is a populist evangelical Christian belief (and an anti-intellectual stance) that the word should be accessible to all.

Despite being relegated to a "practical handbook" status within the branch of the field of theology called "missiology," because of its vast number of examples, *Toward a Science of Translating* has enjoyed a particularly influential status in another field, that of translation. Bible translating has generated more data in more languages than any other translation practice: it enjoys a longer history, has reached more people in more diverse cultures, and has involved more translators from different backgrounds than any other translation practice. In generic terms as well, Bible translating has touched all fields, for within the text one finds passages of poetry and prose, narrative and dialogue, parables and laws. The sheer quantity of examples and breadth of scope have made Bible translation a necessary part of any study on the theory of translation. However, in terms of its theoretical contribution, it too can be viewed in terms similar to the practical, anecdotal approach characteristic of American literary translation theory.

Nida, aware of the unsystematic nature of a practice-oriented approach, attempted to scientifically validate his methodology and apply it to translation as a whole. Nevertheless, his religious beliefs and missionary goals – attempts to unite people around a common belief in the inviolable word of God – although not explicitly stated, remain embedded within the scientific framework. Because of the magnitude of theoretical importance the original message receives in any translation of the Bible, the

fundamental governing principle of Nida's theory was correspondingly predetermined: the communication across cultures of
the spirit of the original message is primary throughout. The
particular form in which that message appears is superficial as
long as the meaning of that message is clear. Chomsky was literally
a Godsend for Nida, for with the incorporation of Chomsky's
theoretical framework, Nida's project ceased to be directed
merely at fellow missionaries, but attempted to lay the groundwork for a larger audience. His work became the basis upon which
a new field of investigation in the twentieth century – the "science"
of translation – was founded.

Noam Chomsky's theory of syntax and generative grammar
was not, nor was it intended to be, a theory of translation. In fact,
Chomsky cautioned against its appropriation in such a fashion.
The universal forms that fascinated Chomsky have more to do
with the rules that structure grammars, rules that precede any
concept of specific deep structure to any given sentence of any
specific language. Chomsky's theory involves three levels of con-
ceptualization: (1) a base component made up of "phrase
structure rules" that generate (2) a deep structure, which in turn is
changed, via transformational rules into (3) a surface structure.
Nida simplifies Chomsky's model and adopts only the latter two
parts of the model in order to validate his science. At the same
time, Chomsky's model lends itself to such a misappropriation by
translation theorists; had Nida not formalized it, someone else
would have. It is interesting to note that Frederic Will also
embraced Chomsky's work as one more instance that promised
the possibility of the "mutual interpenetrability of all languages"
and rendered the limits of translatability "transcendable" (Will,
1984: 86). Transformational grammarians work in various languages and continually point out structural similarities across
languages. Such similarities fascinated Chomsky, too, although
again he has cautioned against drawing conclusions, knowing that
the number of languages is vast compared to the similarities
found, and that deep structures need not be like any existing
surface structure.

Although the two theories evolved for different reasons, they
both assume that there exists a deep, coherent, and unified entity
behind whatever manifestation language takes: the "core," the
"kernel," the "deep structure," the "essence," the "spirit" are all
terms used by Nida, many of which derive from Chomsky. While

Chomsky later distanced himself from terms such as "kernel" (it is still present in *Aspects*, but plays an increasingly diminishing role), he still used concepts such as "base component" and "formal universals" which are "innate" in humans and cut across cultures. Both Chomsky and Nida made metaphysical claims about the object of investigation for their respective theories. Chomsky's linguistics probed structures of the mind and changed the focus of linguistics in the modern age; Nida's translation theory probed deep structures common to all languages and found ways to transform those entities in differing languages. The two approaches attempt to demonstrate different kinds of objects at the center – one arguing the existence of universal rules of grammar and universal lexical forms; the other making metaphysical claims about an original divine message. Both linguistics and translation theory are revitalized by their respective theories. Chomsky's deep-structure/surface-structure model, his transformational rules, although monolinguistically derived, lend themselves to justifying a theory of translation. Whether one accepts Chomsky's beliefs on how the human mind is structured or not, his deep structures, postulated to contain all the necessary syntactic as well as semantic information for a correct transformation into surface structure and interpretation, lend themselves well to the translation practitioner trying to represent an "underlying" message in a second language.

I wish to call into question the very object translation science claims to be investigating. Has it been identified? Nida makes theoretical claims, but is there a *non-dit* operative which affects his theory? What are the underlying assumptions? Can there be a "science" of translation? In terms of its importance in the field, Nida's science cannot be underestimated, for his approach is being disseminated in the classrooms of both Germany and the United States. In Germany, the science of translation (*Übersetzungswissenschaft*) has become the approach that governs the teaching of translation, both conceptually and in practice. In the United States, the emergence of Nida's science has engendered textbooks, linguistic institutes, and journals which now dominate the academy. The wealth of linguistic data, numerous examples, machines, computers, and mathematical formulas employed seems deliberately to obscure something very fragile about the science: its theoretical premise. I hope to show how the science of translation is itself a dual activity: in the process of discovering new information and solving translation problems, it simultaneously covers up other aspects inherent in the nature of the subject being studied. If translation necessarily subverts its own institutionalization, then attempts to make a science of the field actually reinforce a different theoretical agenda than originally intended.

NOAM CHOMSKY: "UNDERLYING" STRUCTURES

Chomsky's grammar is more complex than a two-level deep-structure/surface-structure argument. His model has several levels, the bottom of which is a very vague "initial element" (abandoned after his 1957 book *Syntactic Structures*, but conspicuous by its very absence), followed by the "base component," which is composed of two kinds of rewriting rules: "phrase structure rules," which are common to all languages, and "lexical rules," which also derive from universal categories. The phrase structure rules generate the deep structure of a sentence, which, according to Chomsky at the time of the writing of *Aspects of the Theory of Syntax*, contained all the syntactic and semantic information that determine its meaning. Finally, transformational rules modify the deep structure, resulting in the surface structures – all the sentences in a given language. Thus there is a double movement embedded in Chomsky's theory – from the base to the deep structure via phrase structure rules, and then from the deep structure to the surface via transformational rules. According to Chomsky, the phrase structure rules represent the internalized and unconscious workings of the human mind; deep structure determines meaning underlying sentences; and surface structure determines sound (Chomsky, 1965: 22).

Many have raised philosophic objections regarding Chomsky's assumptions about the human mind and how it "knows" language. Yet in addition to questioning such concepts as "innateness," "intuition," and "tacit" knowledge, some critics did not find Chomsky's evidence all that convincing. Ironically, Chomsky's "empirical" evidence of language structure is not based upon living language – how humans actually use language in a social situation – but on sentences found only in an ideal state:

> Linguistic theory is concerned primarily with an ideal speaker-listener, in a completely homogeneous speech-community, who knows its language perfectly and is unaffected by such

grammatically irrelevant conditions as memory limitations, distractions, shifts of attention and interest, and errors. . . . This seems to me to have been the position of the founders of modern general linguistics, and no cogent reason for modifying it has been offered.

(Chomsky, 1965: 3–4)

To those reading such a statement now, the terminology is loaded with suppositions – "ideal speaker-listener," "homogeneous speech-community," "know language perfectly," "grammatically irrelevant conditions" – that have all been called into question during the past two decades. Michel Foucault suggests that not only are there philosophical differences regarding assumptions about "human nature" involved, but also a generation gap regarding how the "subject," specifically, the "creative speaking subject" is perceived (Chomsky and Foucault, 1974: 164). Chomsky has idealized the speaking subject and has empowered it with unique abilities with regard to its creative ability to use language. Through the process of idealization, however, certain usages involving accidents, errors, and slips of the tongue are not incorporated into Chomsky's model, instances which are just as important as "correct" formulations to Foucault's understanding of the speaking subject and its underlying "nature."

Despite such criticism, largely because of Chomsky's humanistic and Cartesian agenda and because of his deep-structure/surface-structure model, Chomsky has been "used" by translation scientists to substantiate their claims. While Chomsky himself has argued *against* the appropriation of his work in such a fashion, one cannot ignore this body of material. George Steiner, whose comprehensive 1975 book on translation theory *After Babel* serves as one example, felt it important enough to deal extensively with Chomsky's theory and its relevance to understanding translation. Two translation scientists have adopted a Chomskian model for their theories. Eugene Nida, who argues that his science of translation is based upon a model similar to Chomsky's deep-structure/surface-structure, has perhaps simplified Chomsky's work and misappropriated it for his purposes. Wolfram Wilss, a leading German translation scientist, who argues that his model is *not* based upon Chomsky's work, has perhaps unwittingly adopted more from Chomsky than he is willing to admit.

The main problem revolves around the "depth" of the formal properties and whether the base structure or phrase structure is common property. While arguing in favor of formal universals common to all languages, Chomsky holds that these formal properties go much deeper than the particular deep structure of a sentence in any given language and that they are not specific to any particular language (Chomsky, 1965: 117). Though Nida perhaps thought that the same deep structure could underlie a sentence in two particular languages, Chomsky does not claim that deep structures are universal. The form of a particular language, according to Chomsky, does not necessarily equal the form of another. Chomsky realized the implications of his thesis for translation theory and advised caution:

> The existence of deep-seated formal universals . . . implies that all languages are cut to the same pattern, but does not imply that there is any point by point correspondence between particular languages. It does not, for example, imply that there must be some reasonable procedure for translating between languages.
>
> (Chomsky, 1965: 30)

While Chomsky assumed that generative rules lie at the heart of man's language facility, and postulated that a formal device may exist behind all languages, he would not jump to conclusions based upon correlations between just two languages, nor assume that a grammar particular to one language would work systematically for another. Surface structures need not be like their underlying deep structures. Nida ignored this caution and derived a translation procedure based upon a very simplified notion of Chomsky's theory, one which focuses primarily upon the deep structure, transformational rules, and surface structures that are similar across languages rather than on the deeper phrase structure rules that actually allow for real structural diversity as well as surface differences in human languages.

From the perspective of translation practitioners, the problem with the generative transformational model is that it is overly idealistic, divorced from all the *problems* of translation – from contemporary neologisms to archaisms, from proper nouns to metaphors, from high registers to dialects and "mistakes" and all those knotty problems that make translation both impossible and fascinating. Quine's calling into question the very notion of synonymity strikes a resonant chord and is perhaps more relevant to practitioners than a theory of language which posits universal structures. A linguistic methodology which isolates its model from spoken language is both overly idealistic and perhaps too "theoretical" for many a translator's taste. Mathematically, it may be possible to develop a system in which a finite number of rules can generate an infinite number of manifestations, yet language, they would argue, operates differently from mathematics, and no matter how precisely a generative transformational linguist describes the generative rules which produce surface structures, other aspects of language will fall through cracks between generative lines of production. The fact that spoken language contains errors, shifts, ellipses, and gaps begs to tell us something about meaning and something about the structural nature of language. One could hypothetically argue that no sentence is ever divorced entirely from error, that this itself is a condition of language, and that language derives its very energy from this inherent instability. The tendency of generative transformational grammar to ignore all errors or to term them grammatically irrelevant probably obscures as much as it reveals about the structure of language.

Although Chomsky's theory revolutionized the field of linguistics, and many consider his theoretical work one of the major contributions to twentieth-century thought, many creative writers, literary theorists, and translation practicioners have remained strangely aloof. They quibble with his examples, doubt his assumptions, question his claim to be scientific, are troubled by his empirical procedures, and, especially, question whether a generative transformational model is useful to the study of literature. A series of questions raised by Barbara Herrnstein Smith is indicative that Chomsky's arguments have not persuaded everyone:

Is linguistics a monolithic discipline? Specifically, is it equivalent to transformational-generative grammar? If not, is Chomsky's theory of language and the transformational-generative grammarians' pursuit of its study the only and/or the most suitable model for the theory of literature and the pursuit of its study? And, in any case, are the assumptions, procedures, concepts, and conclusions of linguistics themselves so well established, so free from internal problems or external criticism that the literary theorists are well advised to adopt and apply them unreflectingly?

(Smith, 1978: 178)

Despite reservations from creative writers, literary theorists, and literary translators, and despite caution from Chomsky himself, one translation specialist found Chomsky's assumptions and methods very attractive and proceeded to construct a translation science around the model provided by Chomsky. As it turned out, the theory became the most influential approach in the field for subsequent decades.

EUGENE NIDA: APPLYING GENERATIVE GRAMMAR TO TRANSLATION

If Chomsky's theoretical base is Platonic, Nida's is Protestant. The religious presuppositions on which Nida's work rests can be amply demonstrated by an analysis of his 1960 text *Message and Mission*, a pre-Chomsky version of *Toward a Science of Translation*. At that time Nida was still writing for missionaries, not translators; thus, while Nida was moving in the direction of a scientific analysis, "breaking new ground with new tools" (Nida, 1960: xvii) in the communication of the Christian faith, the discussion of theological motivations remained overt. The book's general thesis was that biblical translators should not take communication for granted, but should bring it about, employing all the resources of linguistics and communication theory to aid in their task. Nida drew on extensive field work that showed that the religious message often failed to be communicated because of different cultural contexts and world views. Thus Nida came to understand that meaning cannot be divorced from the personal experience and the conceptual framework of the person receiving the message. He concluded that ideas "must be modified" to fit with the conceptual map of experience of the different context (Nida, 1960: 87).

The first difference between Nida's and Chomsky's philosophy is thus readily apparent: Nida's practical experience in introducing new ideas to a culture remote from his own has underscored the importance of including with his theoretical framework the cultural context in which the communication occurs, an aspect lacking in Chomsky's model. Although Nida supports his arguments for such a model by referring to communication theory and cybernetics, the inclusion of this particular component is more than pragmatically motivated: it is also rooted in Nida's religious presuppositions. For both pragmatic and theological reasons Nida shows a strong interest in the response of the person receiving the communication. According to Nida, the Christian faith has behavioral rather than epistemological objectives, and thus Nida's goal is to effect the appropriate response, one which will *start a dialogue* not between the receiver and a text or symbols, but between the receiver and God. For the Protestant, communication is equated with power, and the focus of biblical communication has less to do with the epistemological problem of the relation of the word to the reality behind it and more to do with the *event* of the transfer of the power of the word (Nida, 1960: 224).

Theoretically, then, Nida does not privilege the sign as do Chomsky and many structural linguists, but the response to the sign. If his translation can solicit the response God intends, then the translation is successful. Words and symbols are mere labels, and the form of the message is thus relegated to secondary status. Theological considerations were edited out of Nida's next publication, *Toward a Science of Translating* (1964), but I argue that they are implicit throughout. Whereas Chomsky discounted the Sapir/Whorf approach to linguistics, which he felt was too culture-specific, Nida incorporates it within a larger model. Chomsky investigates the meaning inherent in the sign cut off from cultural context; Nida's primary concern is not with the meaning any sign carries with it, but with how the sign functions in any given society. Nida claims that this "functional definition of meaning" marks an advance over traditional mentalistic and imagistic definitions of meaning which have been characteristic of traditional philosophic investigations. If one accepts Chomsky's own characterization of his science as mentalistic, by extension, Nida's pragmatic interests appear to be at least a deviation from more traditional notions of deep structure.

Although it may appear that Nida's concept of meaning is substantially different from Chomsky's, Nida's pragmatics are not differentiated from Chomsky's concept of deep structure; they merely add to it. The pragmatic aspect of meaning is factored into the structure not at the surface level, but at the base, with the result that Nida's base has a dual nature – a core of syntactic structures *and* of universal human experience. In order to accomplish this difficult maneuver, Nida must necessarily expand the nature of the core of his theory in order to include a "universal" experience of receiving the message. To include a reception component in the base component, Nida redefines the original message now as the "function of the message." Nida argues that the deep structure of the language – composed of the sign in context – can be inferred through study of the language and culture and through exegesis of these signs over the years. Only then can the appropriate response to that structure be determined and universalized. Nida builds his theory on the premise that the message of the original text not only can be determined, but also that it can be translated so that its reception will be the *same as that perceived by the original receptors* . In addition, since the source is clearly unitary – being God – the intention of the communication can also be counted upon as being stable. Nida's theory emphasizes not formal correspondence, but functional equivalence; not literal meaning but dynamic equivalence; not "what" language communicates, but "how" it communicates.

Nida's theory has been perceived as being progressive because it factors in the context of the message, but we see here that it is no less abstract than Chomsky's. "The message in context" or the "message and its reception" is pulled out of history, understood as unified and an essence of itself, and made into a timeless concept. The translated text, according to Nida, should produce a response in a reader in today's culture that is "essentially like" the response of the "original" receptors; if it does not, he suggests *making changes in the text* in order to solicit that initial response (Nida and Taber, 1969: 202). Such a theory of "dynamic equivalence" is less derived from scientific principles and is more an outgrowth of the nature of his religious inclinations. The implicit assumption present but elided from his science is strikingly similar to the Protestant credence regarding communication in general, and translation thus, for Nida, becomes the rearticulation of the power of the word (over people). Contemporary translations are always compared to a timeless *a priori* model in which meaning and response have been completely identified by the translator or, to be more precise, by the theologian. They are then pulled out of history, translated into a new context, and made to work in the *same manner*. The surface manifestation does not really matter to Nida; changes in the text, the words, the metaphors are allowed as long as the target language text functions in the same manner as the source text.

Once Nida has redefined meaning in terms of its function and abstracted the concept to the point where it can assume universal structural status, the appropriation of Chomsky's model with its concept of innate structures of the mind, its "generative" rules of transformation, and its reduction of surface signs to superficial status, follow quite naturally. With the added authority Chomsky's linguistic model lends to his project, Nida can now suggest that his missionary work has yielded to an objective "scientific" analysis of the problem of translation. He goes on to list some of the universals he has been able to determine by "back-transforming," including subject–predicate constructions, formal distinctions between nouns and verbs, and basic structures by which objects tend to be expressed by nouns and events by verb (Nida, 1964: 66–8). After cataloguing these similarities, Nida concludes:

> It may be said, therefore, that in comparison with the theoretical possibilities for diversities of structures languages show certain amazing similarities, including especially (1) remarkably similar kernel structures from which all other structures are developed by permutations, replacements, additions, and deletions, and (2) on their simplest structural levels a high degree of parallelism between formal classes of words (e.g. nouns, verbs, adjectives, etc.) and the basic function classes in transforms: objects, events, abstracts, and relationals.
>
> (Nida, 1964: 68)

Although Nida's interest and goals differ widely from Chomsky, the two reach similar conclusions about the nature of language, positing the existence of deep structures which underlie all surface structures. The terminology is much the same with the use of "kernels" and "transforms." Although Nida is not quite ready to make Chomsky's claim that these kernel structures are universal, given the terminology he uses at their discovery, i.e., "remarkable" and "amazing," Nida seems to accord them supernatural status within his "scientific" approach.

There are significant differences between Chomsky's and Nida's theories, however, which tend to illustrate that Nida's model is a simplified version of Chomsky's, to a large degree misappropriated in order to apply it to translation. At the heart of Nida's theory is a system of "kernel constructions" from which everything else is derived (Nida, 1964: 68). The concept of kernel sentences is one advocated by Harris and adopted by Chomsky in early models of his generative transformational grammar. Chomsky, however, felt the concept was slightly misleading, and it was rapidly disappearing by the time *Aspects* appeared. While the notion of kernel sentences has, according to Chomsky, an "important intuitive significance," it is not one that plays "a distinctive role in the generation or interpretation of sentences" (Chomsky, 1965: 18). Nida seems to conflate the concept of kernel sentences with the base component composed of phrase structures, and one is never clear exactly what he means by such references. Chomsky's base component allowed for an infinite diversity of surface manifestations, a concept he held fundamental to the creativity revealed by the speaking subject.

Methodologically, differences between the two theories are also apparent. Nida prefers to work backwards from the surface of the original text to its deep structure, transfer that deep structure to the deep structure of the new language, and then generate a surface structure in the second language. In other words, he posits a decoding and recoding process in which the original message never changes. Nida summarizes his translation methodology as follows:

> It is both scientifically and practically more efficient (1) to reduce the source text to its structurally simplest and most semantically evident kernels, (2) to transfer the meaning from source language to receptor language on a structurally simple level, and (3) to generate the stylistically and semantically equivalent expression in the receptor language.
>
> (Nida, 1964: 68)

Working backwards and reducing texts to simple structural sentences and most evident kernels are not Chomskian procedures, and again suggest a misappropriation of Chomsky's model. Chomsky's structures are hardly simple or evident. Using a concept such as "back-transforming" to reveal universals of syntax and semantics also raises questions about Nida's concept of transformational rules in general. Although Chomsky does suggest that transformational rules are non-linear, to extrapolate a decoding–recoding process misrepresents his theory. Nida, like other practicing translators, decodes and recodes, and often "proves" his work by translating into a target language and then back into the source language (Nida, 1964: 66–9), but to argue that such a methodology derives from Chomsky, or rephrasing such a practice with Chomskian terminology, distorts a theory of transformational grammar.

How, according to Nida, then is meaning to be determined, if not by accepted linguistic methods? In a section called "Basic Requirements of the Translator" Nida writes:

> He must understand not only the obvious content of the message, but also the subtleties of meaning, the significant emotive values of words and the stylistic features which determine the "flavor and feel" of the message. . . . In other words, in addition to a knowledge of the two or more languages involved in the translational process, the translator must have a thorough acquaintance with the subject matter concerned.
>
> (Nida, 1964: 150–1)

Again, Nida's religious beliefs tend to be very instrumental in the formulation of his scientific approach. Indeed, he seems to be conflating the translator's role with that of the missionary. In fact, the difference between exegesis and translation is beginning to disappear in Nida's theory, since how the message is rendered and what remains of the original formulation seem to be less important than the explanation itself.

In addition to enjoying complete knowledge of the source, Nida requires that the translator have the same "empathetic" spirit of the author and the ability to impersonate the author's demeanor, speech, and ways, with the "utmost verisimilitude" (Nida, 1964: 151). Nida goes on to argue that the translator should admire the author, have the same cultural background, the same talent (not more or less) and present the same joy to the reader that is given by the original. Nida's "empathetic spirit" approaches total devotion to and dependence upon the original author's intent. Unless these requirements are fulfilled, the translator will miss the original message as well as how that message functions. The problem with such a requirement is one literary critics refer to as the intentional fallacy: what a work says and what the author intended it to say are two different things. Such empathy as Nida seems to favor in fact may serve to obscure that which is being translated. Nida's theory of translation seems less scientifically motivated and more a positive reaffirmation of the work. Translation is equated with revelation, making visible that original message which now takes on archetypal status.

I suggest that the relationship between author and text is complex and potentially deceptive, the reduction of a work to "simple structures" invariably distorting, and the transfer of those simple structures from one deep structure to another – across languages and across time – probably impossible. Even in his simplified theory, Nida does not tell us how the deep structure transfer occurs. Given the emphasis "empathy of spirit" receives in the model, intuition must somewhere enter the equation. Certainly faith, devotion, absolute trust become the major theoretical vehicles. In fact, Nida does not give us a general theory of translation; instead he suggests that we trust the theologian and pray that God will provide the answer. I suggest that the center, the deep structure, the text's meaning, may always be absent. The text, as dense as it may be, and the exegesis, as lucid as it may be, are never complete. There will always be gaps, room for differing interpretation, and variable reception. Therein lies the energy of the text. Nida would deny this as a matter of faith, positing instead the opposite viewpoint, i.e., that the original message can be determined and does not change. However, because he is working with words, even in this case the Word of God, and because of the very fact that he is working with language, there will always be present metaphoric indeterminacy and historical change. No text ever explicates its own reception. Nida's translation theory wants to decipher the text and prepare it for consumption. He wants to explain the text as well as describe it, just as Chomsky's theory wants to explain linguistic structures in addition to describing them. Nida does not trust readers to decode texts for themselves, thus he posits an omnipotent reader, preferably the ideal missionary/translator, who will do the work for the reader. His goal, even with the Bible, is to dispel the mystery, solve the ambiguities, and reduce the complexities for simple consumption.

One of the goals in *Toward a Science of Translating* is to redefine the principles which have been used to govern and judge the accuracy of translation. Traditionally, "faithful" has been reserved for literal translations, those which privileged form, and "free" has been used to designate those translations that privileged content. Nida prefers the latter, and has ironically reversed the historical use of the term "faithful," which he now applies to his dynamic approach. He argues that formal translators, who are primarily concerned with correspondences such as poetry to poetry, sentence to sentence, and concept to concept, are more apt to make mistakes misinterpreting the "intent of the author," more likely to select a "less than appropriate interpretation out of several possible renderings," and more apt to "distort the meaning" (Nida, 1964: 191–2). In the course of the argument outlining his preference for dynamic equivalence, a reversal in terminology has taken place. Nida feels that the dynamic translator is able to be more faithful than the literal translator by somehow perceiving "more fully and satisfactorily the meaning of the original text" (Nida, 1964: 192) and then is more likely to leave that meaning intact while surreptitiously providing explanations through additions, elisions, and transformations. Frederic Will at least saw the paradox involved in translation and confronted the "faithful traitor" problem with new insight. Nida does not see the paradox, and wishes to claim one methodology is better than the other, perpetuating the same old faithful/free problem Steiner feels is characteristic of all pre-structuralist translation theory. Nida's prescriptive translation theory, while intended to elucidate the original message and response, invariably results in a distortion of the very sense he claims to wish to preserve, as his translation as exegesis obscures the original text to such a degree that it becomes unavailable to the contemporary reader.

Nida's attempt to redefine the terminology and offer a prescription for proper translation also serves to reveal his theoretical priorities. We see that he presumes some underlying "meaning of the original text" which is accessible. Because of the importance of retaining this meaning, the form the message takes becomes expendable, reducing the surface manifestation of the message to secondary status. Because it focuses on the underlying structures of the surface structure, Chomsky's theory is similarly constructed, making the "logic" of the two models similar. Both Nida's and Chomsky's theories are self-reflective, the major difference being that Chomsky's universal forms exist at a much deeper, more abstract (and less understood) level than Nida's kernels. Yet there end the similarities. At the time Chomsky was writing, the rules of transformation were so tentative that no real translation procedure other than a point by point comparison of limited fields existed, an approach which Nida's science rejects.

In sum, while Nida's *Toward a Science of Translating* appears to be grounded in modern linguistics, the *non-dit* always present is a Protestant subtext. Nida believes, as he argued in *Message and Mission*, that words are essentially labels (Nida, 1960); if they need to be changed or replaced in order to effect communication, then they should be adjusted accordingly. Verbal symbols are only labels of human origin, and the "message" is from a higher source. Texts are equally pliable, adapting themselves to multiple forms without altering the original intention. "Lamb" has been translated into "seal" and "pig" and many other "forms" or "labels" in order to spread the word of God. Missionary work depends upon establishing a point of contact, any point of contact, and building from there. The assumption that this higher, originary message not only exists, but that it is eternal and *precedes* language is always already presupposed by Nida, and it affects his science. He "knows" the message from this higher source, and knows how people are supposed to respond. He does not trust the readers to make up their own minds; in order to achieve the intended response, he has license to change, streamline, and simplify. All potential differences – ambiguities, mysteries, Freudian slips – are elided in order to solicit a unified response that transcends history. This methodology may be very useful for those translating propaganda or advertising, and it seems to work well with certain kinds of religion, but its limitations within the framework of a science of translating are obvious. Nida provides an excellent model for translation which involves a manipulation of a text to serve the interests of a religious belief, but he fails to provide the groundwork for what the West in general conceives of as a "science."

THE SCIENCE OF TRANSLATION IN GERMANY

Although most influential in terms of Bible translating, Nida's work in translation also enjoys surprising academic influence in the fields of linguistics and translation outside a biblical context. The most detailed application of Nida's theory has not occurred in England or America, but in Germany, where the science of translation (*Übersetzungswissenschaft*) predominates in the teaching of translation at the University of the Saarland in Saarbrücken, where Germany trains future translators and interpreters. I can best illustrate Nida's influence by analyzing the work of Wolfram Wilss, who teaches at Saarbrücken, and whose text, *Übersetzungswissenschaft. Probleme und Methoden* (1977) (*The Science of Translation: Problems and Methods* (1982)) , perhaps best articulates his theory and practice. Wilss' science is still in very tentative form – documenting its research with very few examples, and those drawn from only two languages (English and

German). The studies still contain many unresolved contradictions, and the system as a whole still lacks evaluative standards. Yet enough work has been accomplished in terms of linguistic analysis of specific pair-bound examples – both sentence and text oriented – for Wilss to make fairly large generalizations about appropriate methodological and philosophical approaches for a science of translation. I will focus on his theoretical presuppositions, both explicit and implicit, and show how these largely reflect premises similar to those of Chomsky and Nida, and then examine his understanding of translation equivalence, which despite claims of being descriptive, also reflects a tendency to universalize.

Wilss' science of translation is divided into three related but separate branches of research: (1) a description of a "general science" of translation which involves translation theory; (2) "descriptive studies" of translation relating empirical phenomena of translation equivalence; and (3) "applied research" in translation pointing out particular translation difficulties and ways of solving specific problems. The "general science" (1) is heavily weighted toward text-linguistic premises which categorize texts both thematically and functionally. Translators must have what Wilss terms text-analytical competence; text types themselves are classified as "more translation oriented" or "less translation oriented." "Descriptive studies" (2) tend to focus on "text-pragmatic equivalence" or examples which evoke the same set of ideas and concepts. Wilss' method involves both intralingual translation – paraphrasing the meaning of an original – and interlingual translation – transferring that meaning into a target language – and places a great deal of emphasis on the psychological response. "Applied research" (3) offers practical insights on particular translation difficulties and attempts to resolve them by a sort of means-to-an-end approach. In addition, this branch of the program tries to develop a frame of reference for analyzing errors, and attempts to provide an explanative and evaluative structure for assessing quality, or at least acceptable variants. Of the three branches of Wilss' project, applied research is the least defined and raises the most questions; he admits that his "science" has yet to recognize many translation difficulties, and it also has problems in terms of finding an objective evaluative framework.

More developed are the theoretical and methodological branches, which I will now proceed to examine more closely. *The*

Science of Translation opens, "Modern linguistics is regarded as a primarily communicative discipline; this development can be traced to the time it began to break the stranglehold of the generativists" (Wilss, 1982: 11). Wilss' project thus reacts against two dominating linguistic theories, that of descriptive linguistics and that of generative grammar, despite the fact that the two have very different theoretical foundations. The rejection of linguistic approaches such as taxonomic structuralisms that merely describe the surface structure of specific languages and show little interest in translation is easy to understand. Wilss' reasons for opposing generative grammar, however, are slightly less clear. Wilss argues that a similar problem is true for generative transformational grammar as for structural linguistics. He argues that the generativists use the same methodological tools available to a "scientistic science" and seek to produce "a mathematically explicit depiction of the mental processes which allows for empirical verification and confirmation" (Wilss, 1982: 67). In addition, Wilss objects to generative transformational grammar because it is syntax dominated; it does not include psycholinguistics; it studies only individual language systems; it provides no interlingual language model; it ignores reception problems; and it ignores the function of the message in its original context (Wilss, 1982: 68–70). Wilss sees Chomsky in the same camp as the structuralists and empiricists because he does not see the very idealist, Platonic roots of Chomsky's theory. Wilss at one point argues that Chomsky's linguistic theory is governed by a "quasi-cybernetic automatic control system" and that "the generative component in Noam Chomsky's linguistic theory . . . is ultimately mechanistic, not mentalistic" (Wilss, 1982: 15). Chomsky has been attacked by so many linguists for his lack of semantic and pragmatic components in the theory, that Wilss, because he analyzes textual units in addition to sentence structures, does not seem to realize that he is adopting a similar deep-structure/surface-structure framework with an equally similar theoretical rationale.

Wilss chooses, ironically, to invoke the "mentalistic" paradigm for his own "science." He writes that the science of translation is not a sealed, "nomological" science, but a "cognitive/hermeneutic/associative" one. Thus it need satisfy only "to a limited degree" the demands for objectivity and "value-free procedural methods" that characterize the research methodology of the natural sciences. This frees Wilss to find historical precedence for his approach in those pre-structuralist language theories that are based upon a humanist/idealist concept of understanding, to adopt the competence/performance distinctions as outlined by Chomsky, and to accept Nida's modification of competence to include a contextual component. Translation for Wilss is guaranteed by the deep-structure existence of universals – syntactic and semantic, universal forms as well as a core of common experience – and his science becomes a simple matter of creating syntactic, semantic, and reception equivalents. Wilss' "science" is much closer to Chomsky's than even he might care to admit:

> The translatability of a text is thus guaranteed by the existence of universal categories in syntax, semantics, and the (natural) logic of experience. Should a translation nevertheless fail to measure up to the original in terms of quality, the reason will (normally) be not an insufficiency of syntactic and lexical inventories in that particular TL [target language], but rather the limited ability of the translator in regard to text analysis.
>
> (Wilss, 1982: 49)

Thus, with the proper training at his institute, students can learn to expand their inventories of proper equivalents, sharpen their hermeneutic intuition, and produce quality translations. Wilss' didactic position reminds us of I.A. Richards' workshop project since both involve teaching students the proper interpretation of texts.

An examination of Wilss' history of translation theory provides a framework in which to understand his presuppositions better. Wilss moves very quickly through the Romans and Greeks, Cicero, Jerome, and Luther, summarizing each theory in less than a paragraph. He then provides a detailed analysis of two German theorists: Friedrich Schleiermacher and Wilhelm von Humboldt. Schleiermacher becomes important for Wilss' science because he makes a qualitative distinction between "true" and "mechanical" translation, legitimating the need for a science which can translate art, and necessitating a translator who is capable of the hermeneutic leap to the primary message and the "proper" (Schleiermacher's term) translation of the meaning. Wilss' didactic project reinforces the linguistic distinction in German which English does not make: the difference between translation (*Übersetzen*) and interpretation (*Dolmetschen*). Only recently, at the instigation of the Leipzig school, has the term "translation" been introduced to cover *both* the act of translating and of interpreting.

Wilss next emphasizes Humboldt's contribution to translation theory. He is aware of contradictions in Humboldt's arguments regarding translation. Humboldt did not believe in the *a priori* existence of universal conceptual systems that transgress the boundaries of individual languages. Wilss is also aware that such thinking would deny the possibility of ever finding a functional equivalent, the cornerstone of both Nida's science and his own. Yet despite Humboldt's view that languages are essentially dissimilar and translation impossible, Wilss finds him also making claims: "that the natural predisposition to language is a universal one and that *all* [languages] must hold within them *the key* to understanding all languages" (qtd. by Klöpfler, 1967: 55; qtd. by Wilss, 1982: 36). Wilss concludes that translation is possible because the hermeneutic process gives us access to these universals and the generative potential of the universals enables language to transcend specific social and cultural boundaries. He excitedly concludes that "the 'generative' reserves of this potential are so great as to enable a speech community to adequately cover any and all extralinguistic states of affairs, including those beyond the scope of their own sociocultural experience" (Wilss, 1982: 36). Wilss sees a simultaneous, dual argument rather than a contradiction, concluding that both positions are true, i.e., that universals exist at a deeper level, while surface structures are mutually exclusive. He argues that a relationship exists – core structures have the capacity to generate surface structures – between the two. Instead of breaking the chains of Chomsky's generative grammar, Wilss actually adopts Chomsky's distinction between competence and performance and between deep structure and surface structure.

Wilss' translation theory is thus rooted in German idealism and based upon the following: (1) the concept of a universal language, consisting of universal forms and a core of shared experience; (2) a belief that deep-structure transfer is possible via a hermeneutic process; (3) a generative component, which translates intralingually from the base to the surface of a given language; and (4) a qualitative ranking of texts, from a high level incorporating art and science texts to a low level including business and pragmatic texts. Wilss' research methodology is based upon reducing the original text to its thematic content and its text type via an "intralingual" back transformation. By paraphrasing meanings, Wilss eliminates differences, specific word plays, and implications of texts as they occur in history; rather, texts are classified archetypically and ahistorically. The research branch of his science clearly reveals such a methodology:

> Translation research must develop a frame of reference which views a text as a communicatively-oriented configuration with a thematic, a functional, a text-pragmatic dimension; these three text dimensions can be derived from the respective text surface structure.
>
> (Wilss, 1982: 116)

Texts are categorized according to idealized types and complex relations reduced to "empirically" derived formulas classifying texts according to universal genres and themes. These themes are repackaged in a different language and context, but they are designed to produce the same effect as the original. Wilss' theory falls prey to what literary critics refer to as the empirical fallacy: the "empirically" derived categories are never seen: they exist only as some ideal construct in someone's imagination, just as Chomsky's competence is never revealed, only derived. The system is designed to identify and describe finished products, and to prepare those products for consumption in a different time and place. Such universalizing approaches tend to omit the things that do not fit into categories, to omit contradictions, and to erase ironies and distancing devices, which are almost always part of every text. Multiple thematic or generic references tend to get streamlined or eliminated altogether. In addition, not surprisingly, Wilss ends his history with the optimistic pronouncement that "everything can be expressed in every language" and that this view is "widespread in modern linguistics" (Wilss, 1982: 48). Unfortunately, that which has been reduced and repressed in order to accomplish this total success may inform the text as much as its thematized content.

An examination of some of those "modern" linguists who Wilss argues hold the above widespread view reveals that they are not post-Chomsky at all. Wilss reacts against the Sapir/Whorf school of thought which denies the *a priori* existence of universal categories of thought and thus has a skeptical view of the possibility that two languages would share a common core of experience. To dismiss this line of reasoning, Wilss cites first Chomsky and then

Eric H. Lenneberg, whose T*he Biological Foundations of Language* (1967) posited biological universals in language. Wilss suggests that the Chomsky/Lenneberg view of language universals "proceeds from the hypothesis, undisputed to date, that there are semantic and syntactic universals, including universal pragmatics; this holds true in many if not all natural languages" (Wilss, 1982: 39). Wilss next cites Erwin Koschmieder, who argued in 1965 in *Beiträge zur allgemeinen Syntax* that what is signified does not necessarily equal the meaning of a text (1982: 43). Wilss finally concludes that the Sapir/Whorf relativity thesis is now largely "overdrawn and unsupported (if not unsupportable)" (Wilss, 1982: 43). At one point in his argument, Wilss even implies that the Sapir/Whorf thesis is implicitly "racist" by referring to an Otto Kade article "Ist alles übersetzbar" from 1964 to support this politically provocative argument:

> If I assert that a complete translation is not possible, I am asserting that one language (namely, the language that I am translating into) cannot express what was already expressed in another language . . . this implies attaching a rating to those who speak it, and we find ourselves on the surest road to a reactionary racist ideology.
>
> (Kade, 1964: 88; qtd. by Wilss, 1982: 47–8)

The move from an examination of theoretical foundations prevalent in the field to political accusations indicates not only Wilss' investment in his "science," but also his fear that the Sapir/Whorf view may be more widespread than he is willing to admit.

On such foundations Wilss builds his theory; and he asserts that anyone who has dealt with the "realities of translations" will intuitively grasp the veracity of his claims. Wilss argues that the deep structure of language (in which he includes the sign in context) can be determined (via hermeneutic trust) and transformed into "all" languages in any contemporary context. Wilss' deep structure is thus no less abstract than Chomsky's or Nida's. Wilss adopts universals of form from Chomsky's theory and then adds the experiential component found in Nida. Wilss ends his section on modern linguistics by quoting Nida's 1969 article "Science of Translation" in which Nida argued that the impression that interlingual communication is always possible is based upon two "fundamental" factors: (1) that semantic similarities in language are due to "the common core of human experience" and

(2) that fundamental similarities exist in the "syntactic structures of languages, especially at the so-called kernel, or core, level" (Nida, 1969: 483; qtd. by Wilss, 1982: 49).

The "sciences" of translation described so far in this chapter thus tend to be theoretically founded on an assumption about the nature of language that cannot be empirically verified. Methodologically, they tend to proceed by universalizing and generalizing to such a degree that that which is unique, different, and new about ideas as expressed in language becomes obliterated. In terms of positing standards for evaluation, they necessitate that the translator be the authority, and cease to trust the readers to interpret the text on their own. Finally, by investing heavily in the notion of deep structure, they tend to trivialize their own products, the works in translation, and the contributions that acts of translation may make to the development and evolution of the original text.

TRENDS IN TRANSLATION THEORIES IN GERMANY

Wilss' work has evolved over the course of the past two decades, especially his descriptive studies, which works with pair-bound cases and explores the various possibilities for their translation. Given the theoretical foundations of his science, it should come as no surprise that he has begun to explore the mental factors which account for first perception and then efficient translation, for intuiting and the subsequent decision-making process, creative factors not incompatible with what has always been a humanistic approach. He has become interested in cognitive psychology and theories of human behavior largely because the results from descriptive studies have forced modification of the general science branch. What has become clear is the large degree of variability in translated texts, which is viewed by Wilss less as a fault of the well-trained translator, and more as a result of the differing cultural contexts in which translators find themselves and their very subjective, creative decisions. The cultural component was always present in Nida's work, but Wilss expands extraliterary considerations to incorporate cultural factors that not only influence the final product, but also weigh upon the decision-making process. The "subjective" factor was also always part of the Chomskian model, which emphasized the creative potential of the human language. But the subjective factor had been largely absent during the first decade of the Wilss group's "applied research" branch, whose work was directed at the best possible "objective" solution to a pair-bound problem.

Nowhere is Wilss' proximity to Nida's theory more apparent than in his argument against encroaching translation models based upon the Sapir/Whorf hypothesis he objected to years earlier. Although the data accumulated over the past decades indicate that the translation theorist must take into account the variable cultural contexts in which individual translators perform, Wilss calls the Sapir/Whorf hypothesis a radical version of linguo-cultural relativism. He still argues that "nobody in translation research endorses this radical version" (Wilss, 1989: 134). He continues, "Personally, I do not believe that everything is linguoculturally determined. I do believe that there are many aspects of translation . . . that transcend cultural boundaries and that are, in fact, universal." To substantiate this position, Wilss again cites Nida, this time from *Translating Meaning* (1982), in which Nida argues that one reason for the possibility of interlingual communication is that "what people of various cultures have in common is far greater than what separates them" and that "even within an individual culture there are usually more radical extremes of behavior and attitude than one finds in a comparison of so-called normal or standard behavior" (Nida, 1982: 9; qtd. by Wilss, 1989: 135).

Drawing upon modern linguistics and psycholinguistics, Wilss' work in researching and defining human intuition and creativity in translation has perhaps been the theoretically more interesting aspect of his recent work. Half of Wilss' book *Kognition und Übersetzen* (1988) is devoted to the subject, and there is clearly a dissolving of certain rigid notions within the science of translation. He writes that intuition is the opposite of prototypical concepts and that, while translators must systematically orient themselves to a conceptual plan, they must also stand outside the accepted methods and norms of translation and intuit aspects of the text, a behavior he finds "risky" but always part of the process. Wilss concludes that both systematic analysis and intuition need to complement one another. The primary procedure is systematic: that of determining the dominant structure of the text from the myriad of details via a mechanism of abstraction. But Wilss allows that such a procedure is not the only imaginable one and that it is often not practiced (Wilss, 1989:142–3). He also argues that even in a rational, systematic approach to translation, intuition plays a role in how one thinks and formulates solutions. Thus, while holding dear to principles well established in *Übersetzungswissenschaft*, Wilss' recent work is very open-ended, analyzing both cultural components and creative factors in a way that complicates scientific investigation.

Among other "schools" in Germany following a similar "scientific" approach to the study and teaching of translation, the Leipzig school, which began in the mid-sixties, has also evolved considerably. The early work of Otto Kade, such as *Zufall und Gesetzmassigkeit in der Übersetzung* (1968), a text which may deserve reconsideration today, differs greatly from the current approach. Kade allowed for a rather broad scale of *Textgattungen* (not necessarily types, but categorized generically), which are integrated according to the form and content, perhaps more along the lines of a New Critical concept of the unity of the original text. But Kade's main interest at the time was more focused upon the unit or word level, where he proposed four "types" of correspondence: one-to-one (*totale Äquivalenz*); one-to-many (*fakultative Äquivalenz*); one-to-a part of one (*approximative Äquivalenz*); and one-to-none (*Null-Äquivalenz*). After dividing the text up into frames or units, the translator was to pick the "optimal equivalent" from a varying field of equivalents or options; the building of the units then proceeds to the creation of an integrated whole. With its attention to detail and focus on smaller frames of reference, the approach seems to be not all that unlike one Pound may have been suggesting.

As "modern" linguistics became more widespread internationally, the Leipzig school evolved, and the focus shifted from a word-for-word approach to a more transformational model. In the article "Invarianz und Pragmatik," published in 1973, Albrecht Neubert discusses the "central problem" of the science of translation. He posits an "invariant" of comparison for translation, which is based upon the original and called the text type. He writes that the codes which govern the use of language indicate that in any communication situation one can expect a characteristic text type and that this text type is a source language invariant (Neubert, 1973: 16). He adds that text type invariance, whose parameters are set by pragmatics and semantics, also allows for variables of the specific product, and the translation problem then becomes one of optimal comparison (Neubert, 1973: 19). This sounds much like transformational grammar, and when asked how translations are possible, Neubert answers that they are made possible precisely by the unity of their deep structures and that the interpretation process on the surface structure in its grammatical-lexical segments and its pragmatic function are derived from that same deep structure (Neubert, 1973: 20).

This turn to modern linguistics leads Neubert to develop what has come to be known as the "top-down model" for translation. In "Translatorische Relativität" he writes that the essential translation unit is the entire text, from which one calculates backwards to arrive at the global proposition, which is then divided up into smaller, single, transportable sematic units (Neubert, 1986: 101; see also Neubert, 1985: 135). The terminology has shifted slightly: the unified text is now understood as having a kind of "mosaic" quality, an elasticity that allows it to be translated into a variety of "relative" target texts. Neubert introduces the term "translatorial relativity" in the reconstruction process, allowing for a "creative" process of transfer from the source text to the target text. Yet this "relativity" is deceptive, for it has nothing to do with the Sapir/Whorf hypothesis. Instead, Neubert argues that relativity derives from an inherent multiplicity of structural possibilities in the original (Neubert, 1986: 97). Once the translator makes a choice for one given word, i.e., one given structure, the rest of the text follows a clearly set pattern, a network of units – words, sentences, and excerpts from the text – that build coherently. The language in which Neubert presents his model varies from linguistic discourse to often transcendental, visionary notions. On the one hand, he talks about text equivalence in terms of a macroproposition, which corresponds to the semantic content of the source text and which is then broken down into a fabric of words mapped on to syntactic structures (Neubert, 1986: 95). At other times, his argument takes on a less than scientific quality. He conceives of the source text as an "island of invariance" and talks in terms of a spring or a leap coming from the source text. He argues that "true coherence" (as differentiated from surface structure cohesion) is actually the norm for larger sections of the text, and that the choices presented to the translator are "predestined" (Neubert, 1986: 92; see also Neubert, 1985: 81ff.).

Closely related to both the Saarbrücken school and the Leipzig school is what might be called the Reiss/Vermeer approach, which also reacts against Kade's vague notion of *Textgattungen*. In

Möglichkeiten und Grenzen der Übersetzungskritik, Katharina Reiss argued that this kind of linear approach hindered rather than helped the development of a "relevant text typology for the translation process" (Reiss, 1971: 28). Reiss' work draws more on developments in the pragmatic branch of linguistics, and she makes up her types based upon the function of the language in the text. Using work done by Karl Bühler in *Sprachtheorie* (1965), she divides the language in question into its representational, expressive, and appelative functions. While she allows that a single text seldom represents just one of these functions, but rather various mixed forms, she suggests that even in mixed forms one of the functions predominates (Reiss, 1971: 32). She then typecasts texts respectively into *inhaltsbetonte* texts (emphasizing content or information), *formbetonte* texts (emphasizing the form of the language), and *appellbetonte* texts (emphasizing appeal to the reader).

Reiss' work culminates in the co-authored *Grundlegung einer allgemeinen Translationstheorie*, written together with Hans J. Vermeer in 1984, in which they argue that translation should be governed primarily by the one functional aspect which predominates, or, in the new terminology, by the original's "Skopos" (Greek for the intent, the goal, the function) (Reiss and Vermeer, 1984: 96). Without insisting upon one perfect translation as a goal, Reiss suggests that the translators need to strive towards optimal solutions within the existing actual conditions, arguing that the received text must be coherent, and that its coherence is dependent upon the translator's concept of the "Skopos" of the text in question (Reiss and Vermeer, 1984: 114). For this to occur, there must also be coherence between the source text and the target text, or what she calls intertextual coherence. "Right" and "wrong" choices are then judged according to their consistency with the concept of the unified whole. A traditional concept of fidelity upon which to base the analysis is finally invoked; if the derivation is consistent with the original Skopos, it is called faithful, and accepted as a good translation. Much of Reiss' work is aimed less at theory and more at developing standards of evaluation from which she can judge the quality of the translated text.

It is true that these models are being continually revised and expanded to better deal with advances in linguistics and other sciences. The most recent foray into the discussion is Mary Snell-Hornby's *Translation Studies: An Integrated Approach* (1988), widely discussed in Europe. Snell-Hornby finds Reiss' text-typology approach too rigid and too prescriptive, and instead suggests a "prototypology," a more flexible, *Gestalt*-like system with blurred edges. She offers a very complicated stratification model with multiple vertical and horizontal planes, proceeding from a general level (macrolevel) to more particular levels (microlevels) (Snell-Hornby, 1988). Recalling Wilss' citation of Lenneberg/Chomsky, Snell-Hornby bases her claims on what might be called the Rorsch/Berlin foundation. Rorsch's theory, which has influenced American semantics, basically 'disproves' classical theories of categorization and has led to a theory of 'natural' categorization, i.e., in the form of prototypes which have a "hard core" and blurred edges (Rorsch, 1973, qtd. by Snell-Hornby, 1988: 27). Ethnobiologist Brent Berlin argues that such prototypes, or in his words, "folk-generic levels," can be psychologically determined (Berlin, 1974; qtd. by Snell-Hornby, 1988: 28).

Whether the Snell-Hornby model achieves an integrated approach for Translation Studies remains to be seen. Ironically, the problem with all these "sciences" of translation is that they are directed primarily at teaching translators or evaluating translations, and thus are prescriptive in nature. They tend to rely too heavily upon very traditional dichotomies of good/bad and faithful/free, distinctions which Steiner suggests have been superseded by modern structuralist approaches to language. If all modern linguistics can be traced back to Chomsky, we are left basically with a Cartesian theory. The existing "sciences of translation" tend to be largely based upon concepts rooted in religion, German idealism, archetypes, or universal language. The deep-structure/surface-structure approach seems to always posit some sort of hypothetical invariant, which is a consistent and unified whole, and to which competent translators and astute critics have access. The "scientific" approaches all tend to be source-oriented in nature, arguing that the original embodies some sort of deep structure, which contains the information necessary for its subsequent encoding in another language, to which the translator must remain faithful. Far from being scientific, these approaches tend to hold a transcendental, utopian conception of the translation as reproducing the original. Such an approach reaffirms antiquated notions of translation, notions which view translations as second-hand, merely serving as handmaiden of a higher, more creative art. The biggest problem is that the focus of these sciences is too

narrow. They look primarily at what is a non-verifiable space –
i.e., the black-box of the human mind – and make large statements not only about translatability but also about how that
process *should* occur. This is precisely what Chomsky cautioned
against, but which came to pass nevertheless.

One group that is skeptical of such normative and prescriptive
approaches is a group of scholars in Belgium and the Netherlands.
They have not yet been convinced by modern linguistics' complex
terminology and diagrams. Instead of further speculating about
mental processes and innate structures, they have decided to look at
"reality," i.e., at real texts in the target culture that are called
translations by specific cultural groups, and begin their analysis
from there. Their aim over the past two decades has been to
establish a new, less prescriptive paradigm for the study of literary
translation. Theoretically, they shift the focus of study from hypothetical ideal translations to actual texts, however inexact, which
function as translations in any given society. Although Translation
Studies and Polysystem theory developed separately in two different
parts of the world, the two have become inextricably connected.
Thus, the following two chapters will trace the evolution of Translation Studies from its early formative years in Chapter 4, through its
union with Polysystem theory in Chapter 5.

Chapter 4

Early Translation Studies

THE CALL FOR A NEW DISCIPLINE

The two dominant modes of research in the field of translation through the seventies were those focused on primarily literary concerns, rejecting theoretical presuppositions, normative rules, and linguistic jargon, and those focused on linguistic matters, claiming a "scientific" approach and rejecting alogical solutions and subjective speculation. Both sides limited the kinds of texts they addressed to show their methodologies to best advantage, viewing each other's work and accomplishments with skepticism: literary translators dismissed any scientific linguistic analysis; linguists dismissed non-scientific literary analysis. Intervening in this confrontational situation were a handful of mostly younger scholars from the Netherlands and Belgium. James Holmes, in "The Name and Nature of Translation Studies" (1972/5), distanced himself from "theories" of translation, which often merely reflect the attitude and approach of the writer, and from "sciences" of translation, which may not be suited for an investigation of literary texts, and coined the term "Translation Studies" for a non-allied and new approach (Holmes, 1972/5: 8).

A few years later, André Lefevere outlined the crux of the theoretical problem. In "Translation: The Focus of the Growth of Literary Knowledge" (1978), he argues that the antagonism between the two opposing factions – which he calls the hermeneutic and the neopositivistic – is based upon "mutual (wilful) misunderstanding" (Lefevere, 1978a: 8). Lefevere claims that the hermeneutic approach to translation, used primarily by individual thinkers who try to arrive single-handedly at universally valid ideas, truths, and grammatical forms, tends to be non-scientific, bases its system of ideas on epistemological assumptions which are

300 years out of date, and is contradicted at every turn by findings of other disciplines (Lefevere, 1978a: 9). Logical positivism, the dominant strategy employed by translation structuralists, text grammarians, and semioticians, reduces the study of literature to a language intended for physical science, bases truths on hard data and correspondence rules, and posits ideals of science which are monistic, reductionistic, and physicalistic (Lefevere, 1978a: 12–13). Lefevere argues that translation theories based on such approaches do not further the growth of literary knowledge, but tend to have vested interests – ideological as well as corporate – which have impeded the description of an adequate theory of translation. He displays sentiments characteristic of the Dutch intervention in the field:

> Here lies the great scandal of literature in general and meta-literature [translation and commentary] in particular. Instead of exposing and demolishing ideologies that stultify and en-slave, those who claim to be professionally interested in literary knowledge are busy constructing their private ideologies within a safely conventional framework and calculating their profits.
>
> (Lefevere, 1978a: 22)

The scholars in the Low Countries were interested in both linguistics (scientific) and literary translation (non-scientific) and did not see why the two need be mutually exclusive. In order to escape the idealistic and static concepts characteristic of previous approaches to all translation, Lefevere suggests that Translation Studies shift the theoretical focus of the investigation, basing their research "on an evolutionary concept of metascience, not on the logical positivist concept, not on the hermeneutic concept" (1978a: 7).

Smaller nations with fewer people speaking "minor" languages have come to depend upon translation for their commercial, political, and cultural livelihood; thus it comes as no surprise that scholars from such countries would not only know more about translation but might adapt themselves more readily to situations of conflict. Given the countries' geographical location at the crossroads of European intellectual life, it is also not surprising that a new idea or at least a new perspective on the problems facing a theory of translation might find nourishment among the young, and grow. Translation may have been a marginal field of

investigation in countries which have large monolingual popula-
tions, but in Belgium and the Netherlands the field of translation
may unite, or at least mediate, diverse literary theories. Detached
from the ideological investment that characterizes the history of
translation theory elsewhere, a fresh approach emerged from the
Lowlands.

Translation Studies began with a call to suspend temporarily
the attempts to define a theory of translation, trying first to learn
more about translation procedures. Instead of trying to solve the
philosophic problem of the nature of meaning, Translation Studies became concerned with how meaning travels. Most
characteristic about the new field was its insistence on openness to
interdisciplinary approaches: having literary scholars work together with logicians, linguists together with philosophers.
Limiting distinctions such as right and wrong, formal and dynamic, literal and free, art and science, theory and practice,
receded in importance. Translation as a field was no longer
viewed as either literary or non-literary, but as both. New questions were posited regarding the subject of investigation, the
nature of the translation process, how mediation occurs, and how
the process affects both the original (redefined as source text) and
received (redefined as target text) works. Even the distinction
between original writer and translator was called into question.
The object of study was neither an absent core of "meaning" nor
deep "linguistic structure," but rather the translated text itself.

Such an approach is not devoid of theory, and one of the goals
of Translation Studies is to formulate a theory of translation.
Initially, however, this new field was characterized by its hesitancy
to impose theoretical presuppositions and its careful testing of all
hypotheses against descriptions of actual translations and historical case studies. Again, André Lefevere summarizes accurately
the theoretical goals of the field:

> The goal of the discipline is to produce a comprehensive
> theory which can be used as a guideline for the production of
> translations. The theory would gain by being developed along
> lines of argument which are neither neopositivistic nor her-
> meneutic in inspiration. The theory would gain by being
> elaborated against a background of, and constantly tested by
> case-histories. The theory would then not be static; it would
> evolve according to the dynamic consensus of qualified
> scholars, who constitute a forum of competition. . . . It is not

inconceivable that a theory elaborated in this way might be of help in the formulation of literary and linguistic theory; just as it is not inconceivable that translations made according to the guidelines tentatively laid down in the theory might influence the development of the receiving culture.

(Lefevere, 1978b: 234)

Instead of taking preexisting theories about literature and linguistics and applying them to translation, Lefevere and his Dutch/Flemish colleagues reverse the order of thought, suggesting that the field first look at what is specific about translation and then apply that knowledge to literary and linguistic theory. As a result, Translation Studies scholars attempt to avoid preordained, fixed, and immutable prescriptives and remain open for constant self-evaluation and evolution. The variable approach acknowledges that the object being investigated is not something fixed in the real world to be scientifically investigated, nor is it the object of higher, transcendental truth to be revealed in a mystical way. Rather, the objects of study are the translations themselves, which are by definition mediations subject to theoretical manipulation and prevailing artistic norms; at the same time, as Lefevere speculates, translations may reciprocally influence those very same norms which determine them. One goal of this chapter is to show how Translation Studies displaces the epistemological problem of representation by viewing the text as both produced and producing. Its mediatory role is more than a synchronic transfer of meaning across cultures; it mediates diachronically as well, in multiple historical traditions.

Ironically, the process of ignoring existing literary theory and focusing the study on the status of historically marginalized texts actually reveals something not merely tangentially related but of central relevance to literary theory. With their new questions and shift in focus, the intervention by the Flemish and Dutch scholars raises multiple problems for literary theory, including the importance of praxis within theory, the cultural interdependence of literary systems, and the intertextual nature not just of translation, but of all texts. The activity of translation may be marginal, but the theoretical problems raised by the practitioners are crucial to any integrated literary theory.

The establishment of a new field within the domain of literary analysis did not occur overnight. As I argue below, the roots of early Translation Studies can be found in Russian Formalism, and the precursors to the present generation of Flemish and Dutch scholars include a group of Czech scholars well schooled in Russian poetics. Two scholars from the Netherlands – James Holmes and Frans de Haan – attended a conference on "Translation as Art" held in Bratislava in May of 1968 and helped edit (with Anton Popovič) and publish the proceedings in a collection called *The Nature of Translation* (1970). I hope to show how Translation Studies, despite claims to avoid prescription and refrain from judging, implicitly reflects certain modernistic prejudices. At the same time, however, the epistemological assumptions of Translation Studies depend on viewing texts as dynamic and productive rather than static and fixed, and thus contribute to the ongoing post-modern re-valuation of the nature of language. In the next two chapters I will trace the evolution of Translation Studies from the early tentative work by Flemish and Dutch scholars through the positing of a comprehensive system – called Polysystem theory – by an Israeli circle. My examination is based on texts by three Czech scholars – Jiří Levý, František Miko, and Anton Popovič – whose work is not only crucial to gaining an understanding of the work by the group of Dutch language scholars, but also effects a transition from Russian Formalism to the present day paradigm of translation investigation.

JIŘÍ LEVÝ AND THE CZECHOSLOVAKIAN CONNECTION

To set the parameters of the following discussion, I will first briefly summarize some of the main tenets of Russian Formalism, basing my analysis primarily on the summary, "The Theory of the Formal Method," by Boris M. Èjxenbaum in *Readings in Russian Poetics* (Èjxenbaum, 1978; see also Bann and Bowlt, 1973; Erlich, 1981; and Jackson and Rudy, 1985), and discuss their relevance for Translation Studies. First, Russian Formalists attempted to isolate and define what they called "literariness" by focusing solely upon what they viewed to be literary facts, separating literary artifacts from other disciplines such as psychology, sociology, and cultural history. The discipline as well as the texts being studied were viewed as having an autonomy of their own. This notion is important for the current generation of translator scholars interested in what literary translation can contribute to translation theory, for it enables them to focus their investigation on specific determining features of literary texts rather than on metaphysical notions about the nature of literature and meaning. The Russian Formalists avoided deep-structure arguments, looking instead at actual texts and specific features of texts. The move to define literariness led the Formalists to try to determine what makes literary texts different from other texts, what makes them new, creative, innovative.

Translation Studies also distances itself from theories like those of Chomsky and Nida which are more focused on deep-structure generative components than on actual surface-structure characteristics. Formalism and Translation Studies privilege specific surface-structural features and analyze them to learn what determines literary status. Indeed, Russian Formalists, while using thematic concepts, relegated them to secondary status, and were more concerned with compositional concepts. They argued that abstract ideas often look much the same over history; what was important to them was *how* the thematic concepts were expressed. Translation Studies uses thematic concepts in a similar fashion, shifting them from a primary and determining position to a concept dependent upon the culture and language in which they are embedded.

Perhaps the most important and least understood aspect of Russian Formalism was its historical dimension. Attacks on the school tend to criticize its "decadent" art-for-art's-sake beliefs and its lack of historical parameters. Russian Formalists, however, did not just analyze texts synchronically, but also diachronically, trying to understand how texts related to a determining literary tradition. Their formal analysis thus incorporated intrinsic and extrinsic factors in order to determine a specific text's contribution to and distance from any evolving literary tradition. Translation Studies scholars actually show the diachronic effect of translated texts on two traditions: that of the source culture and that of the target culture. Borrowing another aspect of Russian Formalism, perhaps its best known and most easily embraced principle – the defamiliarization (*ostranenie*) device – Translation Studies scholars attempt to measure the text's relation to its tradition. Because they did not inflate the value of the content, meaning, or original idea of a work, Russian Formalists could focus on aspects that did not conform and made the text special, different, and especially strange.

Translation Studies scholars similarly refuse the tendency toward focusing on meaning, on determining the original content (seen earlier in theories like Nida's), and on preparing the text for easy consumption by readers in the receiving culture. If anything, early Translation Studies prescribed that a work in translation *retain* defamiliarization devices, and if existing devices could be transposed in the second language, the translator needed to invent new ones. Proper nouns, for example, have always been troublesome for translators, for they always tend to have a special, specific meaning – such as place names that have a special resonance, location, history in the source culture – that invariably gets lost in translation.

Finally, Russian Formalists remained open to new problems; their methodology could be applied to itself; and they insisted that the discipline of literary scholarship need be an evolving one. Èjxenbaum, for example, writes:

> We possess no theory of such a kind as could be deployed as a rigid, ready-made system. Theory and history have merged for us, not only in what we preach, but also in what we practice. We are too well trained by history itself to imagine that we could do without history.
>
> (Èjxenbaum, 1978: 35)

Similarly, such an incorporation of history into their theoretical model has helped Translation Studies scholars apply theory inwardly as well as externally, enabling them to address problems as raised by their own and other fields of investigation. The spirit of discovery, of evolution, and of multiple applications characterizes Translation Studies. Yet they also limit the field of investigation to specific translated texts, which also perhaps explains the hesitancy for members to make the claim that Translation Studies may have wider relevance for literary theory in general. Its scholars tend to be caught in the bind, on the one hand, of trying to define and limit a field of investigation and, on the other, of being secretly aware that valuable insights and discoveries very relevant to contemporary literary theory are happening as one studies actual translated texts.

The Czech group of translation scholars, including Jiří Levý, Anton Popovič, and František Miko, have evolved from Russian Formalism, simultaneously reflecting and distancing themselves from some of the tenets above. Certainly they have distanced themselves from the concept of literature as autonomous literary works isolated from the rest of the world, a move already underway during the later stages of Formalism. One of the reasons Levý's text *Umění překladu* (Literary Translation) (1963), translated into German *Die literarische Übersetzung* (1969), is so instrumental for Translation Studies is precisely because it takes the tenets of Russian Formalism, applies them to the subject of translation, and shows how Formalist structural laws are located in history and interact with at least two literary traditions simultaneously, that of the source culture and that of the receiving culture.

Levý's Formalist roots are revealed by the specific linguistic methodology which characterizes his project. Levý begins with the linguistic distinctions of translation that his colleague Roman Jakobson, who left Moscow to help found the Prague school of linguistics, laid out in "On Linguistic Aspects of Translation" (1959). The Prague structuralists viewed texts as incorporated within semiotic networks and viewed language as a code or complex of language elements that combine according to certain rules. Every word thus stands in relation to other segments of the same text (synchronic) and other words in texts in the literary tradition (diachronic). Levý also incorporates the interpretive aspect into his translation theory, basing such deduction upon Willard Quine's hypothesis that translation meaning can be logically interpreted. Quine's theory did not involve a metaphysical leap to the deep and unified central meaning of a text, but was built slowly and carefully, not necessarily via a word-to-word or sentence-to-sentence correlation – synonyms and analogy always tend to retain a certain indefiniteness – but by the capacity of learning meaning via structural groupings. Beginning with guess and intuition, moving through comparison, deciphering, matching groups of positive and negative stimulus meaning, Quine argued in an essay called "Meaning and Translation" (1959) that the translator can arrive at "analytic hypotheses," which are finally tested against a network of standing sentences as well as against agreed upon synonyms (Quine, 1959; cited by Levý, 1969: 20).

With the establishment of the semiotic horizons which come into play in the course of translation, and with the positing of the interpretive component which enables the translator to grasp the meaning of the text in question, Levý was in a position to present his translation methodology. Of primary importance in Levý's model is that the literary quality of the work of art not be lost. To ensure transfer of "literariness," Levý foregrounds the particular communicative aspect of specific formal features of the original author's style that give the work of art its specific literary character. Levý bases this aspect of his translation theory on another of the founding members of the Prague linguistic circle, Vilém Mathesius, who wrote as early as 1913 that the fundamental goal of literary translation is to achieve, whether by the same or by differing devices, the same artistic effect as in the original. The meaningful translation of poetry proves that the correspondence of artistic effect is more important than the equivalent artistic devices. Mathesius added that often the translation of the same or nearly-the-same artistic devices often leads to the translation having different effects on the reader (Mathesius, 1913: 808). Levý, like other Formalists, first views language as a semiotic system with synchronic and diachronic aspects. He also elevates the art object to the most privileged position, believing that "literariness" can be logically deduced and defined. His translation theory thus emphasizes less the "meaning" or the "object being represented" in the second language, but instead focuses upon the style, the specific literary features of the text that make it literary. In his famous essay, published in Czech in 1933–4, "What is Poetry?" Roman Jakobson spells out the value placed by Formalists upon the specific "poetic" quality of a work:

> The poetic function, *poeticity* , is, as the "formalists" stressed, an element sui generis, one that cannot be mechanically reduced to other elements. . . . It can be separated out and made independent, like the various devices in, say a cubist painting . . . poeticity is only part of a complex structure, but it is a part that necessarily transforms the other elements and determines with them the nature of the whole.
>
> (Jakobson, 1976: 174)

The Formalist belief that poeticity was a formal quality, something that could be separated out of a work, is crucial to understanding Levý's translation theory. Levý believes that he can logically determine those aspects which make a text art, divorce them from the content, the world, the language system, replace them with stylistic elements from a different language, equally divorced from everything else, and arrive at an equally artistic work. He draws the conclusion, based on Mathesius' and Jakobson's comments above, that the theory of substitution of elements of style has been constructed upon an objective foundation (Levý, 1969: 21).

Whereas Chomsky's theory analyzed the deep structure, especially its syntactic elements, Levý's examines surface structure and stylistic elements. Each theory uses linguistics and "scientific" methods of interpretation to help isolate that aspect of language which they feel is primary. In Levý's process of isolating the "poetic" features, an interesting subtheory simultaneously develops. If one privileges structural and stylistic features, the general "content" of the text is thereby demoted, for it is not stable, but temporarily conditioned by the signifying system in which it is expressed. If one is working in a single sign system, however, the formal features and the content can be made to appear to mutually reinforce each other, producing that "unified work" pregnant with "literariness." But by placing a work in multiple signifying systems, at least two in the case of interlingual translation, the instability and ephemeral nature of the thing expressed becomes visible. The translation is not a unified work, but one which is full of tension and contradictions because the content is intertextually constructed, represented as it were by two perspectives simultaneously: from the view of the original signifying system and from the angle of the second language system.

While recognizing in *Die literarische Übersetzung* that such tensions exist, Levý smooths over the problem and argues that the better the translation, the better it overcomes the conflicts and contradictory structures (Levý, 1969: 72). The subtext that has been developing throughout the argument, i.e., what happens to the content, becomes more problematic at this point in his theory. Levý wants to argue that the translated text must be consistent and unified – contradictions can be resolved and the objective substitution of equivalences is possible. He writes, for example, that the translation as a whole is more fully realized the better it overcomes its own inherent contradictions (Levý, 1969: 73). This leads to a conclusion that is very much like the one reached by American literary translators: a true or "faithful" method which favors the "exact recreation" of the "aesthetic beauty" of the original in the second language (Levý, 1969: 68).

Ironically, then, instead of just constructing a theory of translation which smooths over the inherent problem of how this is to be done, given that the translated text is invariably shot full with contradictions, Levý's theory also reinforces a by-product of Formalism: in addition to the awareness of the correspondence of sign to object, there is the necessary opposite function simultaneously in process, namely that the relationship between sign and object is always inadequate. Content is always unstable, always changing, constructed by discourse, in constant flux, merely "appearing" stable temporarily in its fictional aesthetic construction. As translation always has at least two referents, meaning never appears stable. That which is made manifest in the process and product of translation is the very mobility of concepts, the mutability of signs, and the evolution of the relationship between the two. It would seem that Levý's translation theory is asking the impossible, i.e., to develop objective criteria for isolating and cataloguing in multiple languages the particular poetic formal features which transform a normal expression into an artistic one, and then to establish paradigms enabling the substitution of those elements appropriate to translation.

Yet work in precisely that seemingly impossible field has begun, and I turn to the work of František Miko as just one example to illustrate the process. In "La Théorie de l'expression et la traduction" (1970) he reports on his progress, defining what he calls the "expressive categories" (expressive features or qualities) of language which lend it its artistic quality (Miko, 1970; see also Miko, 1969; and Miko and Popovič, 1978). Miko first makes a distinction between expression as a whole, the expressive character, and the expressive features. The distinction is important, not just to clarify potential misinterpretation of his work, but for theoretical reasons. He shares the Formalist distinction between form and content, or between form and theme, and posits the primary importance of the linguistic elements. The subject matter is contingent upon and constituted by the linguistic structure of the language. In order to determine what an expression as a whole means, what determines its poeticity, one has to look at the smallest details that, when structurally built together, determine the work of art's style. The expressive features form together hierarchically, constructing the work's meaning and value. Given the fundamental belief that language thus determines content, Miko asks the question, what happens when one changes the language system? Is all lost? Miko argues against such a conclusion, believing that he can determine and catalogue a system of expressive features independent of any one specific style, features that can be interchanged as necessary in the act of translation. Miko does point out the difficulty and complexity of the problem, especially regarding the translation of literary texts, but argues the necessity of its resolution because the alternative – the substitution of synonyms, of syntactical structures, of similar themes – has historically proven inadequate.

Expressive features of the text, according to Miko, can best be determined by relating those features of style of a specific text to similar characteristics used within the literary tradition. In that place between the text and its tradition, subjective qualities of style – emotional, irrational, expressive – as well as idiosyncrasies of style – irony, abstraction, brevity, joviality – can be determined. Only through such an historical analysis can the function of the original text be understood, and enable eventual adequate translation. For Miko the problem of translation is either purely linguistic or purely stylistic. The problem of achieving correspondence of style is a delicate one because the nuances are fine, but of primary importance: if such elements are omitted from the translation, it loses its "literariness," the very quality Russian Formalism values most. The addition of an historical horizon, albeit a purely literary one, is an important one for the development of Translation Studies, for it provides not only a basis of comparison but also implies a diachronic evolution of language.

How far did Miko progress with his inventory? He progressed far enough to establish certain hierarchies within a system of cataloguing qualities of expression. He also has identified certain categories which he claims do not permit further distinction. He admits the impossibility of the task, yet enough research has been completed to enable him to draw certain conclusions (Miko, 1970: 67–70; see also Miko and Popovič, 1978). He has been able to equate certain expressive characteristics with certain types of speech found in journals, in popular literature, in speeches, and in literary texts. For example, categories of expression characteristic of literary texts include not just aesthetic/emotional ones, but variability, ambiguity, disequilibrium (unrealized resolutions) as well as conventional resolution, and in certain instances even irrationality (e.g., stream of consciousness texts). Miko suggests these elements can be isolated, analyzed, and translated using a methodology that finds functional rather than literal equivalents. All the while, Miko's categories are subject to the flux of history. He is well aware that stylistic features often are open to different interpretations as social conditions change, thus changing the appropriateness of certain expressive characteristics. Detailed research of the specific characteristic in history is necessary, making translation dependent upon the interpretive as well as linguistic and creative ability of the translator. Miko concludes that the conception of style arrived at is a functional one that uses linguistic categories, but not necessarily in the same way as linguistics. It is based upon a "correlative" definition of expressive categories, never losing sight of the importance of paradigmatic and sytagmatic aspects for the analysis of the *system* of expressive features, taking into consideration the evolutionary and social aspect of style (Miko, 1970: 73).

Anton Popovič's project begins where the work of Levý and Miko leaves off: he begins the comparative work of locating the conformities and the differences that occur when a work is translated and explains the relationship of the translated work to the original. Instead of prescribing a technique which eliminates losses and smooths over changes, Popovič accepts the fact that losses, gains, and changes are a necessary part of the process because of inherent differences of intellectual and aesthetic values in the two cultures. In his essay, "The Concept 'Shift of Expression' in Translation Analysis" (1970), he introduces a new term to characterize this process:

> Each individual method of translation is determined by the presence or absence of shifts in the various layers of the translation. All that appears as new with respect to the original, or fails to appear where it might have been expected, may be interpreted as a shift.

> (Popovič, 1970: 78)

Shifts have been noticed before in terms of translation analysis, but have invariably been attributed to deliberate distortions, incompetence on the part of the translator, or linguistic incompatibility between the two languages. Popovič extends the theoretical horizon by analyzing shifts in terms of the differing cultural values and literary norms. Instead of accusing translators of ignorance or unfaithfulness, Popovič argues that they resort to shifts precisely because they are attempting to render faithfully the content of the original despite the differences between the languages. Thus shifts reveal not the inadequacy of the translation, but something about the primary aesthetic quality of the original. Levý's project left off with the prescription that if an expressive feature does not work in the receiving culture, then the translator must replace it or even invent a new feature so that the overall literary quality is not lost. Popovič extrapolates:

> Every conception of translation of any real significance and consistency finds its principal manifestation in the shifts of expression, the choice of aesthetic means, and the semantic aspects of the work. Thus in a translation we can as a rule expect certain changes because the question of identity and difference in relation to the original can never be solved without some residue. Identity cannot be the only feature characterizing the relation. This conclusion is inevitable if we consider the force of historical factors and the impossibility of repeating the act of translation as a creative process.
>
> (Popovič, 1970: 81)

Accepting the fact that certain elements will fall through the cracks as one moves from one system of discourse to another, Popovič looks not for what fits, but what does not, and picks up the "residue" to examine it more closely. The last sentence quoted above reveals Popovič's rejection of the idealistic notion that literal or functional equivalences can be found, yet he retains formal features as part of his system in order to demonstrate translation differences and the force of history.

As Miko believes that the minute and subtle nuances of expression are the key to determining a work's overall artistic quality, so too Popovič believes that the key to understanding a translation's chief aesthetic means lies in the analysis of the shifts of those very nuances. In Popovič's theory, in which differences are just as important as equivalences, the faithful/free theoretical concerns collapse into the same horizon; the two are always relative depending upon the aesthetic assumptions of the translator. Popovič explains:

> It is not the translator's only business to "identify" himself with the original: that would merely result in a transparent translation. The translator also has the right to differ organically, to be independent. . . . Between the basic semantic substance of the original and its shift in another linguistic structure a kind of dialectic tension develops along the axis of faithfulness-freedom.
>
> (Popovič, 1970: 80)

There are various methods of translating, and while Popovič's own preferences mirror Levý's, his theoretical model lends itself to determining the aesthetic presuppositions of the translator that motivate shifts of expression. His theory reads the shifts symptomatically in order to determine the prevailing literary assumptions governing the translation. With Popovič's theory, the critic can trace the tracks left by the shifts in the translated work to the cultural norms of the receiving culture which govern that text. Instead of proposing stylistic unity with the original as a goal of translation, Popovič accepts the impossibility of achieving an equivalent text and posits a theory to explain rather than criticize its non-identity. Through an analysis of shifts of expression and an analysis of the relationship of the language of the original work to that of the translated work, something about the mediatory, heterogeneous nature of the process of translation is revealed.

At this point, several observations with regard to the Czech contribution to Translation Studies can be made. First, an aesthetic prejudice is revealed by the kind of translation preferred, i.e., one which functions as an art object in the receiving culture. The Czech demand to preserve literariness determines the preferred methodology. However comprehensive Miko's catalogue of "objective" stylistic features becomes, it will always remain inadequate and to a large degree subjectively organized. The hypothesis that a work's overall artistic merit is determined strictly by structural characteristics may be appropriate for examining modernistic or futuristic texts characteristic of the period during which the theory developed, but questions remain about its appropriateness for texts written during other historical epochs. How well does the theory work with symbolic or allegorical texts, with narratives, poetic or prose, with agit-prop theatre or folktales that require common understanding of the referent? In addition, such a preference may in fact influence which third world texts get translated into Western languages. Russian Formalism defines what is to be valued in a text – aspects such as form, self-referentiality, and technical juxtaposition – and evaluates translations on the capacity of the target text to transfer those formal characteristics. Yet different aesthetic approaches as well as different historical moments and cultures may value other aspects of a text. In many ways the translation theory deriving from Russian Formalism reflects precisely those devices – "defamiliarization" devices for example – which are characteristic of the prevailing artistic norms and interpretive theories of a particular time and place, i.e., modern European society.

Secondly, although Popovič expands the parameters of a theory of modernism to point Translation Studies in a new direction, Translation Studies scholars avoid theorizing about the relation of form to content, failing to read symptomatically the implications of their theory for their own methodology. Despite claims to the contrary, the literary text quickly gets divorced from other socio-political factors. Words cease to refer to real life, but to other words used in the same literary tradition, thus creating a system built upon its own self-referentiality and thus reinforcing its own values. Art does become autonomous, as perception of a work's literariness is tied directly to an awareness of form. It is this quality of calling attention to itself that the theory values and asks to be translated; the methodology demands that the receiver perceive those specific formal features that set a work apart from a tradition, again necessitating the incorporation of a "competent" reader into their translation model (I.A. Richards' theory, too, prescribed such an ideal reader). There is an hermetic, self-referential quality in "literary" texts which Formalists perceive, value, and recommend be perpetuated. Because Levý and others tend toward the prescriptive, questions remain regarding the evaluative horizon. Who judges the adequacy of the stylistic substitutions? The demands on the translator are enormous; they include competence as literary critic, historical scholar, linguistic technician, and creative artist. It is little wonder that the evaluative horizon presents problems, for the requirements extend beyond the capacity of any single human's ability.

Despite these reservations about the work by the Czech school, the beginnings of a descriptive methodology can be seen. Although the theory might work better with modern and contemporary texts, it is by no means limited to them. The methodology of systematically analyzing shifts can be applied to symbolic, realistic, metrical, literal, and phonetic theories of translation as well, precisely because it begins to include historical and ideological horizons as well as literary ones. Indeed, in order to explain shifts adequately, the methodology cannot restrict itself to the changes of artistic traditions, but must consider evolving social norms and subjective psychological motivations as well. For these reasons the Flemish and the Dutch became very interested in the work by their colleagues in Eastern Europe.

EARLY TRANSLATION STUDIES: JAMES HOLMES, RAYMOND VAN DEN BROECK, AND ANDRÉ LEFEVERE

Despite its relatively short history, "Translation Studies" already can be divided into early and later periods, the early period the subject of the remainder of this chapter, and the latter, after it joined forces with Polysystem theory, to be analyzed in Chapter 5. Unable to look at all the members' contributions to the emerging field, I will instead examine texts by three founding members whose work may be representative: James Holmes, who first introduced a new way of discussing translation to Western Europe; Raymond Van den Broeck, who addressed the problem of equivalence in translation from the perspective of Translation Studies; and André Lefevere, whose grasp of the theoretical position of the group was unique. Van den Broeck and Lefevere co-authored the Dutch text *Uitnodiging tot de vertaalwetenschap* (Invitation to Translation Studies) (1979), which represents the culmination of the early period. I intend to show a double movement of the paradigm: while attempting to avoid prescription and focus on pure description, early Translation Studies favored a translation methodology much determined by its roots in Russian Formalism. In addition, while limiting the field of investigation to concrete, existing translations, early Translation Studies included the seeds for a comprehensive theory, addressing out of necessity data not only outside of one text, beyond one tradition, but phenomena which had no specific textual realization and had escaped traditional analysis.

James Holmes was a American poet/translator who taught Translation Studies at the University of Amsterdam until his recent death. His work describing the translation process, while dismissing traditional notions of equivalence, was perhaps most responsible for the formation of the new field. In "Forms of Verse Translation and the Translation of Verse Form" (1970), we can see the introduction of new terminology and methodology with which to approach the subject. The most visible change in Holmes' approach is his alteration of the nature of the referent: Holmes argues that the translation does not refer to the same object in the real world to which the source text refers, but rather to a linguistic formulation. The language of translation is different from the language of primary literature, and to designate this distinction, Holmes adopts the term "meta-language," borrowed in this case from Roland Barthes, who divides literature into two classes: the class of poetry, fiction, and drama that "speak about objects and phenomena which, whether imaginary or not, are external and anterior to language," and the class of literature that "deals not with 'the world,' but with the linguistic formulations made by others; it is a comment on a comment" (Barthes, 1964: 126; qtd. by Holmes, 1970: 91). Holmes broadens the definition of Barthes' term, originally limited to merely critical commentary about literature, to include a variety of metaliterary forms, verse translation being merely one.

In addition, Holmes argues that verse translation is different from other forms of commentary or metalanguage because it uses the medium of verse to aspire to be a poem in its own right. While verse translation is a kind of metaliterature because it comments upon and interprets another text, it also generates a new corpus of metaliterature about its own literariness. Thus, the thing to which translation refers not only is different from other kinds of creative writing, but the kind of literature written about translation also differs from other kinds of critical writing, placing it in a unique position in terms of the realm of literary criticism. Referring and producing simultaneously, verse translation is critical commentary on a source text, and yet yields critical interpretation as if it were a primary text. About translation's dual nature Holmes writes:

> All translation is an act of critical interpretation, but there are some translations of poetry which differ from all other interpretive forms in that they also have the aim of being acts of poetry . . . it might be helpful if for this specific literary form, with its double purpose as meta-literature and as primary literature, we introduced the designation "metapoem."
>
> (Holmes, 1970: 93)

Given this redefinition of verse translation, the theory about translation must be similarly redefined. Thus, Translation Studies becomes less concerned with identity and the old problem of reference, and more concerned with analyzing (a) the relationship of the translated text (as a secondary text) to the source text within a framework of the signifying practices inherent in that particular literary tradition, and (b) the relationship of the translated text (as a primary text) to the signifying practices within the framework of the tradition of the target culture.

Because Holmes was less interested in identity and more concerned with the relationship of the translation to other signifying
systems, another shift in Holmes' approach becomes visible: he
begins a description of translated texts not by making universal
claims about the validity (or invalidity) of specific proposed translation   solutions,   but   by   describing   various   translation
methodologies and how they have been used historically. The
goal is not to perpetuate some metaphysical claim about the
nature of language or conceptual knowledge, but to understand
better the various kinds of translation, of "metapoems," as a
unique kind of signifying practice. Holmes defines four types of
translations each relating differently to the original text and
belonging to different theoretical traditions. The first type retains
the form of the original; Holmes suggests that identical form is
impossible, but patterns can be made to closely resemble each
other, and fundamental formal verse structures can be matched,
such as Richmond Lattimore's mimetic hexameters of Homer's
Greek. The second type attempts to discern the function of the
text in the receiving culture and seeks a parallel function within
the target language tradition, creating analogous forms which
will create similar effects, such as Robert Fitzgerald's blank verse
translation of Homer. The third type is content-derivative, taking
the original meaning of the primary text and allowing it to
develop into its own unique shape in the target language, such as
Pound's organic free verse translation of Homer in the first
Canto. The fourth type includes what Holmes calls "deviant
forms" not deriving from the original poem at all, but deliberately
retaining minimal similarity for other purposes, for which
Holmes gives no example, but Robert Lowell's "The Killing of
Lykaon" of books one and twenty-one of the *Iliad* may serve as an
example. Holmes refrains from favoring any one of the four types
of translation, saying that each approach, "by its nature opens up
certain possibilities for the translator who chooses it, and at the
same time closes others" (Holmes, 1970: 97). Recognizing the type
of translation and grasping its corresponding theory, whether
conscious or unconscious on the part of the translator, allows the
reader to understand what the translated text comes to mean in
the receiving culture.

Holmes' early work culminates in "The Name and Nature of
Translation Studies" (1972/5), generally accepted as the founding
statement for the field. In the essay he lays out the scope and

structure for the new discipline. Most importantly, Holmes conceives of the approach as an empirical practice, one which looks at actual translated texts as they appear in a given culture. As a field of study, he breaks Translation Studies down into three areas of focus: (1) the descriptive branch: to describe phenomena of translations as they manifest themselves in the world; (2) the theory branch: to establish principles by which these phenomena can be explained; and (3) the applied branch: to "use" information gained from (1) and (2) in the practice of translation and training of translators (Holmes, 1972/5: 9–10). Thus, the theoretical branch was subordinated to the descriptive branch; as case studies were described and empirical data collected, the theory would evolve. The ultimate goal of Translation Studies is to develop a full and all-encompassing translation theory, one which is "above" and can look down upon existing partial theories, which Holmes felt were often specific in scope and dealt with only one or a few aspects of the larger concern. Holmes realized that in reality, the development of theory would not be unidirectional, but more of a "dialectical" one, with each of the three branches supplying information for the other two (Holmes, 1972/5: 20).

It is important to note that, in this founding statement, Holmes called for several levels of focus within each branch. His descriptive branch, for example, was divided to include product-oriented, function-oriented, and process-oriented descriptions (Holmes, 1972/5: 12–14). The product-oriented branch, which became the approach most identified with later Translation Studies, called for a "text-focused" empirical description of translations, and then a survey of larger corpuses of translations in a specific period, language, or discourse type. The function-oriented branch, which introduced a cultural component effecting a translated text's reception, and the process-oriented approach, which looked at the problem of the "black box," or what was going on in the translator's mind, became less important as the field developed.

André Lefevere, in his text *Translating Poetry: Seven Strategies and a Blueprint* (1975), reveals a similar approach. Lefevere, attempting a more empirical, objective approach, takes one source text – that of Catullus' sixty-fourth poem – and describes seven different types of translation based on correspondingly distinct methodologies which tend to govern the translation process. Each opens up certain possibilities and closes others:

(1) phonemic translation works well in recovering etymologically related words and reproducing onomatopoeia, but shatters meaning; (2) literal translation may transfer a sense of the semantic content, but often by smuggling in explanation and sacrificing "literary" value; (3) metrical translation may preserve the meter but distorts sense and syntax; (4) prose versions avoid sense distortions, but the very form robs the text of poetic resonance; (5) rhyming translations are governed by so many restraints that words end up meaning what they do not mean, and the end result often is boring, prudish, and pedantic; (6) blank verse achieves greater accuracy and a high degree of literalness, but imposed meter forces contortions, expansion, and contractions, often making translated versions verbose and clumsy; and (7) interpretation, including versions and imitations, which interpret the theme to make the text easier for reception may do so at the expense of the structure and texture.

While Lefevere is attempting greater objectivity and historical accuracy in his description of Catullus translations, he does not refrain from revealing his preferences. He finds the last category covers up the least in translating a text's content. Lefevere himself prefers Holmes' second version, one that privileges the function of the text on the original readers. The terminology of Lefevere's "new" prescription, however, recalls the earlier work of Nida and Wilss:

> The translator's task is precisely to render the source text, the original author's interpretation of a given theme expressed in a number of variations, accessible to readers not familiar with these variations, by replacing the original author's variation with their equivalents in a different language, time, place and tradition. Particular emphasis must be given to the fact that the translator has to replace *all* the variations contained in the source text by their equivalents.
>
> (Lefevere, 1975: 99)

Like Nida, Lefevere wants to thematize the text, but like Levý, to do so without smoothing over its "literariness." He talks of "preserving distortions," but what he means here is preserving the *ostranenie* devices which seem strange in the original and set it off from the existing tradition of a particular time and place. His recommendation of a particular historical method (his own), undermines a project that is otherwise historically sensitive.

The contradiction characteristic of this early period in Translation Studies is that it attempts to be both objectively descriptive and subjectively prescriptive. If we contrast Holmes' concept of translation equivalence as revealed in his essay "On Matching and Making Maps: From a Translator's Notebook" (1973–4) and that of Raymond Van den Broeck in his essay "The Concept of Equivalence in Translation Theory: Some Critical Reflections" (1978), the problem is most apparent. Traditional translation theory was based upon premises of original meaning, training translators to interpret that meaning correctly in order to reproduce it properly, and resulted in rules and laws about the procedure whereby products could "objectively" be compared and evaluated. Whereas Richards, Nida, and Wilss are intent upon educating translators to produce unified, coherent, single reproductions of the original, or at least to reach a consensus regarding what the ideal single reproduction should be, Holmes argues that to begin with such a premise misses something essential about the nature of translation. Holmes argues that no translation of a poem is ever "the same as" or "equivalent" to its original (Holmes, 1973–4: 67). He suggests that asking for equivalence extends beyond the pragmatic limitations encompassing the situation:

> Put five translators onto rendering even a syntactically straightforward, metrically unbound, imagically simple poem like Carl Sandberg's "Fog" into, say Dutch. The chances that any two of the five translations will be identical are very slight indeed. Then set twenty-five other translators into turning the five Dutch versions back into English, five translators to a version. Again, the result will almost certainly be as many renderings as there are translators. To call this equivalence is perverse.
>
> (Holmes, 1973–4: 68)

Holmes insists that the focus of Translation Studies should be the process of translation, analyzing the choices from a myriad of possibilities that a translator makes. Once initial choices are made, the translation begins to generate rules of its own, determining further choices. Holmes introduces two elements that translation theory has historically avoided: subjective decisions and accidents. Of the latter Holmes writes:

> Two languages can chance to "interlock" at specific points, quite accidentally, in such a fashion that the translation appears

to come through more or less all of a piece. This happens all too rarely, but when it does, the translation seems almost to write itself.

(Holmes, 1973–4: 78)

Holmes notes that, more often than not, the translation process involves initial decisions that determine later decisions. No choice is made without certain costs; changes will have to be made over the course of the translation which will be deliberate departures from the original. Much influenced by Jiří Levý's article, "Translation as a Decision Process" (1967), Holmes argues that translation establishes a hierarchy of correspondences, dependent upon certain initial choices, which in turn predetermine subsequent moves. For example, if the translator favors expressive qualities over original message, rhyme and meter over free verse, or appellative function over semantic content, these choices will ultimately restrict and determine the kind of correspondences available during the course of the translation of the rest of the text. Such decisions are neither right nor wrong, but both, always limiting and opening up, closing off certain avenues and possibilities, but simultaneously creating new relations and possible alternatives.

Van den Broeck begins his essay "The Concept of Equivalence in Translation Theory" in agreement with Holmes; he avoids much of the same theoretical terminology that characterized translation traditionally. He even quotes Holmes' experiment yielding twenty-five renderings of the same text, concluding that "we must by all means reject the idea that the equivalence relation applies to translation" (Broeck, 1978: 33). He realizes that all the speculation on defining equivalence by linguists, translation theorists, scholars, philosophers, and philologists contain many different and contradictory equations, especially when applied to phenomena as complex as poetry in translation. Van den Broeck clearly opposes the terminology – including terms such as similarity, analogy, adequacy, invariance, and congruence – and the theoretical implications they carry. Yet he then goes on to redefine and recuperate "equivalence" for his own concept of "true understanding" of how one should regard literary translation (Broeck, 1978: 29).

Van den Broeck's redefinition of equivalence is based upon the semiotics of Charles Sanders Peirce, the philosophy of Charles Stevenson, and the linguistics of J. C. Catford. Briefly, Van den

Broeck begins with a revaluation of the conception of "correspondence," drawing on Peirce's distinction between "types" and "tokens" whereby multiple tokens can refer to one type, as in several versions ("additional instances") of the original poem ("prime instance"), shifting the focus of translation studies from a "one-to-one" to a "many-to-one" notion of correspondence (Broeck, 1978: 34). Van den Broeck expands upon Peirce's notion of "type" by borrowing the concept of a universal "megatype" from philosophy, reaching the conclusion that two translations, if they have "approximately the same" meaning, can be identified as representing the "same megatype" (1978: 34–5). Like Holmes, Van den Broeck locates translation in a network of various instances of one "megatype" or "prime instance"; meaning is reduced to approximations of something somehow identifiable yet always textualized in "tokens" or "additional instances." Yet he retains a formal concept of meaning, as did the Russian Formalists, in which meaning is seen as a property of language and not as something extrinsic. Megatype thus is determined by a network of tokens and yet also transcends those types, thereby also transcending language. Quoting J. C. Catford, Van den Broeck arrives at a definition of meaning as "the total network of relations entered into by any linguistic form" and adopts Catford's definition of translation equivalence: "translation equivalence occurs when an SL [Source Language] and a TL [Target Language] text or item are relatable to (at least some of) the same relevant features of situation substance" (Broeck, 1978: 38). For Van den Broeck, those relevant features have nothing to do with semantic reference, and everything to do with textual reference. He again refers to Catford, arguing that "both texts must be relatable only to the *functionally relevant* features of the communicative situation" (Broeck, 1978: 38). In contrast to Van den Broeck, however, Catford regards the functionally relevant features as relatively indeterminate and largely a matter of opinion:

> We can distinguish, then, between situational features which are *linguistically relevant*, and those which are *functionally relevant* in that they are relevant to the communicative function of the text in that situation. For translation equivalence to occur, then, both SL and TL text must be relatable to the *functionally* relevant features of the situation. A decision, in any particular case, as to what is functionally relevant in this sense must in our

present state of knowledge remain to some extent a matter of opinion.

(Catford, 1969: 94, emphasis in original)

Van den Broeck, on the other hand, feels that those functionally relevant features can be precisely determined, standardized, and evaluated. Van den Broeck concludes in agreement with Lefevere that the original author's intent and the original text's function can be determined and translated via a method of typologizing and topicalizing so that it will "possess a literary value" equivalent to the source text and function accordingly. Van den Broeck concludes, "It is therefore right to say with Lefevere that a translation can only be complete, 'if and when both the communicative value and the time-place-tradition elements of the source text have been replaced by their nearest possible equivalents in the target text'" (Broeck, 1978: 39, see Lefevere, 1975: 102).

The demand to preserve literariness at all costs, thus, influences not only methodology, but also evaluative standards. The problem with the early Translation Studies approach of Holmes, Lefevere, and Van den Broeck is that they have foregrounded the internal organization of the text and its inherent framework to such a degree that the referent totally vanishes. Much of the problem centers around the inconsistent use of the term "function." When Miko, for example, refers to the word "function" he is talking about a very subtle linguistic feature of the text that gives it its "literariness." He isolates distinct structural elements in language and describes them, hoping to determine a paradigm of universal elements true for all languages. He has in mind specific ahistorical universals of form which are independent from any specific cultures. Translation Studies uses the term "function" to refer to both the way Nida uses the word – in terms of communication theory and reducing the information load so that the message "functions" similarly in the receiving culture – and the way Miko uses the term – very subtle linguistic features that only the most informed linguistic scholars and literary critics may discern. Miko's reference to "function" presumes an absolutely pristine message channel with an ideal reader who knows an author's original intent, is fluent in numerous languages, can distinguish minute and complex linguistic features, and has creative poetic ability. Few such readers exist; Miko's model presumes not merely a competent reader, but an ideal one. His Translation Studies model, thus, is based upon a non-existent receptor as well as a non-existent referent. Not fully tied to thought or communication, it resembles the modernistic/ futuristic texts of the twenties which referred to nothing but themselves, and were totally autonomous and "meaningless."

The reason why Van den Broeck wants to reclaim the terminology of traditional metaphysical philosophy for Translation Studies is that this so-called new approach retained the same form versus content dichotomy that characterizes traditional philosophical dualism. According to Lefevere and Van den Broeck, the problem with translations that privilege formal aspects – rhyme, meter, phonetics, syntax – is not that they cannot transfer the content, but that they do not adequately translate even the formal properties of the original text. They do not focus *enough* on the "total" form, the proper theme in relation to literary tradition, and the specific "literary" features. While Translation Studies scholars deny its validity, the charge that the group concerns itself only with literary translation is to a large degree justifiable. Their emphasis upon the purely formal characteristics presumes the same form/content dualism without theorizing about the relation of the two. If the *effectiveness* of the formal representation of the object gets translated, then presumably the object itself will be translated as well. Early Translation Studies claimed a position that was theoretically new and mediatory as opposed to hermeneutic, yet it found itself embedded in and often perpetuating that very same metaphysical tradition.

OSTRANENIE AS THE EVALUATIVE STANDARD

In order to demonstrate the reception of this early phase of Translation Studies, I turn to the text *Translation Studies* written by Susan Bassnett, whose book grew out of work with post-graduate students at the University of Warwick in England in close consultation with the Leuven/Amsterdam group. The text was one of the first publications abroad about the Flemish/Dutch project, and was intended to serve as an introduction to the field. Because she was trying to appeal to a larger audience, Bassnett was deliberately didactic and provocative in order to stimulate interest, promote discussion, and clarify differences. She subscribed to the two fundamental yet contradictory tenets of early Translation Studies: that there is no right way to translate a literary text, and that the interpretation of the translation be based on the comparison of the text's "function" as original and as translation. In an analysis of a translation history of various versions of Catullus' thirteenth poem, for example, she uses a very broad definition of the term "function" to "objectively" describe the differing versions. In fact, however, she seems to distance herself from a translation by Sir Walter Marris, who "has fallen into the pitfalls awaiting the translator who decides to tie himself to a very formal rhyme scheme," and seems to prefer a version full of hip jargon and rock and roll lyrics by Frank Copley, which she finds "closer to the Latin poem than the more literal version by Marris." Finally, when talking about a version by Ben Jonson, who translated the sonnet into a forty-one line poem, she suggests that it "comes nearer in mood, tone and language to Catullus than either of the other versions" (Bassnett, 1980: 88–91). Clearly Bassnett is rhetorically trying to break down the readers' narrow concept of what literary translation should be and get us to view translational phenomena in a broader sense. Yet she seems to favor adding *ostranenie* effects when none were there before, adding remarks if the translator feels motivated, and adding entire passages to make the text relevant to the contemporary reader. Her use of the term function is so broad, and her concept of shift is so unspecified, that almost any deviation, addition, deletion could be labeled a "functional equivalent."

Thus, despite the radical appearance of her methodology, her poetics did not represent any theoretical advance in the field. She presented the theoretical issues raised by the Flemish and Dutch scholars as part of "translation problems" which have characterized translation theory throughout its history, and are very characteristic of Anglo-American approaches today. In fact, Bassnett was in large measure justified in her application of Translation Studies to her theatrical approach to translation; certainly theoretical support for her priorities can be found in the work of Levý, Popovič, Lefevere, and Van den Broeck. Her "use" of Translation Studies was partially determined by terminological confusion within the field, its inscription in traditional philosophical dualism, and its privileging an aesthetic that lends itself to appropriation by referenceless and subjective stratagems.

Whereas Bassnett used Translation Studies to support her own translation strategy, one which implicitly retains evaluative standards based upon the prevailing norms characteristic of modernism, James Holmes proceeded in a different fashion, one less functionally and more "materially" oriented. He wanted to reveal first the process of translation in order to understand why certain decisions were made, before judging the result as good/bad, true/untrue, understood/misunderstood. Referring again to Levý's "Translation as a Decision Making Process" (1967), Holmes argues that translation involves decision-making, and one decision affects each other decision (Holmes, 1973–4: 79–80; see Levý, 1967: 1171–4). Yet at a certain point, the translation begins to generate its own set of rules, precluding certain choices and opening up insights that perhaps were not visible before. However the translation turns out, other translations are always possible, not better or worse, but different, depending upon the poetics of the translator, the initial choices and the points when the languages interlock and begin to develop not in the source or target language, but in that grey area in between. The difference in Holmes' and Bassnett's approach is that Holmes tries to preserve the sound, the sense, the rhythm, the textual "material" of the thing in language and recreate those specific sensations – sound, sense, and association – despite inherent limitations in the target language, whereas Bassnett leaps to the central theme and meaning, intuits the "original function," and allows the replacement of much of the text, with all its particular resonance and associations, with something new and completely different, but which theoretically affects the reader the same way. In both instances, in keeping with the definition of the theory of Translation Studies, one can see just how the methods for training translators and/or the actual practice of translators inform any discussion of theory.

TRANSLATION STUDIES AS LITERARY HISTORY

Whereas Holmes was trying very hard to avoid making theoretical generalizations about what the object (the translated text) should look like before the source text has been confronted, the language incompatibilities analyzed, and options weighed which will dictate methodology, Van den Broeck, André Lefevere, and Susan Bassnett confronted the descriptive problem with evaluative standards already in place. The theoretical differences between them, however, did not preclude their co-operation in terms of translation scholarship. For example, Translation Studies has come to an agreement that the translation scholar must analyze the system of *both* the correspondences *and* deviations constructed by the translator. In his essay, "Describing Literary Translations and Methods" (1978), Holmes elaborates:

> The task of the scholar who wishes to describe the relationship between the translated text and its original would seem to be obvious. He must attempt to determine the features of the translator's two maps and to discover his system of rules, those of deviation, projection, and above all, correspondence – in other words, the translator's poetic.
>
> (Holmes, 1978: 77)

However obvious the relationship may appear, such a description is not easy, for two reasons. First, almost invariably, no material for analysis exists except the two texts, the original and the translation, and the scholar has no access to what went on in the translator's mind in terms of the decision-making process. Secondly, even if the translator explicitly elaborates in an introduction or preface the main criteria and poetic system governing the translated text, the result may not correspond to the original intention. Thus, the scholar must trace the relationship between translation and original along an imaginary path, for texts documenting the path are virtually non-existent. To date, none of the disciplines of literary criticism has presented a methodology sufficient to explain objectively the translation process; previous attempts have made comparisons on an arbitrary basis, characterized by intuition and the method of influence studies, and have been glaringly incomplete. Translation Studies proposes a more rigorous approach by trying to reach an agreement on a repertory of specific features to be compared (such as the one Miko outlined above), then establishing where the determining shifts occur (as defined by Popovič above), and finally analyzing those shifts systematically, incorporating both synchronic, structural textual analysis as well as diachronic literary intertextual and socio-cultural analysis, in order to determine the meaning and function of any specific translated text. Van den Broeck concurs, suggesting that limited invariance (approximate meaning) goes hand in hand with translation shifts (functional equivalents) (Broeck, 1978: 41). In order to relate the original and the translation in terms of their stable core and their determining shifts, Van den Broeck also points to Miko and his system of expressive properties (Broeck, 1978: 44–5). Lefevere, using slightly different terminology, makes a similar point, arguing that literature evolves both as new and independent units arise from a basic unit and as progressive changes take place over time. The task of the scholar, he argues, is to codify this evolution as well as the institutions through which that evolution takes place. Only then can the "meaning" of a work be established (Lefevere, 1978a: 25). Holmes, aware of the magnitude of such a task, argues that working out such a system of codification and undertaking the process of describing literature in the above fashion is the next necessary step for the field. He concludes his essay "Describing Literary Translations" as follows:

> The task of working out such a repertory would be enormous. But if scholars were to arrive at a consensus regarding it, in the way, for instance, that botanists since Linnaeus have arrived at a consensus regarding systematic methods for the description of plants, it would then become possible, for the first time, to provide descriptions of original and translated texts, of their respective maps, and of correspondence networks, rules, and hierarchies that would be mutually comparable. And only on the basis of mutually comparable descriptions can we go on to produce well-founded studies of a larger scope: comparative studies of the translations of one author or one translator, or – a greater leap – period, genre, one-language (or one-culture), or general translation histories.

> (Holmes, 1978: 81)

Translation Studies, which began with a fairly modest proposal, that of focusing on the translations themselves and better describing the process of translation, has discovered that the task will be much more complex than initially conceived. The job is certainly beyond the scope of any particular scholar, no matter how knowledgeable of linguistic, literary, and socio-cultural theory – hence the proposal that literary scholars from a variety of fields agree upon a working methodology and unite the efforts around this enormous goal.

One of the pioneers leading the effort to develop a model for better describing translations in a comprehensive fashion has been José Lambert, whose approach differs from early Translation Studies. Lambert suggests that Van den Broeck's and Lefevere's 1979 book *Uitnodiging tot de vertaalwetenschap* was symptomatic of the problem. While Lefevere and Van den Broeck stress the need for more descriptive studies, he argues, ῑhey omit to specify how they should be carried out (Lambert and Gorp, 1985: 42) and that the general methods used during the first period, i.e., the early seventies, were largely "intuitive" rather than systematic. Before beginning to assess the contribution of Lambert and others to the development of the field during the eighties, a discussion of the contribution of essentially two Israeli scholars and their "polysystem" approach is necessary, for it more than anything else has become identified as the theory underlying contemporary Translation Studies.

Chapter 5

Polysystem theory and Translation Studies

TRANSCENDING TRADITIONAL LINGUISTIC AND LITERARY BORDERS

In a series of papers written from 1970 to 1977 and collected in 1978 as *Papers in Historical Poetics*, Itamar Even-Zohar first introduced the term "polysystem" for the aggregate of literary systems (including everything from "high" or "canonized" forms (e.g., innovative verse) such as poetry to "low" or "non-canonized" forms (e.g., children's literature and popular fiction) in a given culture. Even-Zohar recognized *both* the "primary" (creating new items and models) as well as "secondary" (reinforcing existing items and models) importance of translated literature in literary history (Even-Zohar, 1978a: 7–8). Gideon Toury, a younger colleague, adopted the polysystem concept, isolated and defined certain translation "norms" that influence translation decisions, and incorporated these factors in the larger framework of a comprehensive theory of translation, published in *In Search of a Theory of Translation* (1980). These ideas were not new, but based upon work done by late Russian Formalists and evolved from a decade of work by scholars at Tel Aviv University who had undertaken the ambitious project of describing the entire "History of Literary Translation into Hebrew."

Early in the 1970s, Even-Zohar developed the polysystem hypothesis while working on a model for Israeli Hebrew literature; he had published his findings in French as "Aperçu de la littérature israélienne" as early as 1972, though the English version of his theory did not appear until his *Papers in Historical Poetics* (1978). Gideon Toury was one of several scholars at Tel Aviv University who participated in various field studies "testing" Even-Zohar's hypotheses during the seventies and had extensive data upon which to base his theoretical conclusions (Yahalom, 1981; Shavit, 1981; Toury, 1980). Even-Zohar first introduced his ideas to the Dutch/Belgian group at what has now become known as the "historic" 1976 Translation Studies Colloquium in Leuven, Belgium, whose proceedings were published in a collection called *Literature and Translation: New Perspectives in Literary Studies* (1976). The papers presented at two Translation Studies conferences following the 1976 colloquium – the first in 1978 in Tel Aviv, whose proceedings appeared in a special issue of *Poetics Today* (Summer–Autumn, 1981), and the second in 1980 in Antwerp, whose proceedings were published in a special translation issue of *Dispositio* (1982) – illustrate the merging of the Polysystem theory with Translation Studies to the point where, at least during the 1980s, the two were almost indistinguishable.

Why did this union of work going on by scholars in the Low Countries and in Israel occur at this moment in time? One reason certainly had to do with the parallel developments in their social and historical situations: the Flemish and Dutch scholars enjoyed intellectual contacts with the German and Czech literary and linguistic circles, while the Israelis interacted with German, Russian, and later Anglo-American scholars. A similar perspective on translation also existed in both regions: their countries might be characterized as having few people speaking in "minor" languages, both "national" literatures are very much influenced by "major" literatures around them, the Dutch by German, French, and Anglo-American, and the Israelis by German, Russian, and Anglo-American. The situation in Israel was more extreme than in the Low Countries, which had their own indigenous literary tradition, for Hebrew lacked a canon of literary works and was totally dependent upon foreign language texts to provide both diversity and depth. More importantly, however, was the dependence of the culture as a whole upon translation for commercial and political purposes. In the case of the Dutch/Flemish situation, economic, intellectual, and social opportunities were certainly enhanced by multilingual interaction; in the case of Israel, the survival of the nation became dependent on translation. If the Dutch and Belgian scholars found themselves at an intellectual crossroads of Europe, the Israeli scholars found themselves at a crossroads not only between the Soviet Union and the West, but between Western and "Third World" cultures.

In Chapter 1 I noted that Paul Engle asserted that the future of the world may depend upon the accurate translation of one word; nowhere is this assertion more apparent than in the fragile diplomatic and political situation in the Middle East. There Russian culture does meet Anglo-American; Moslem meets Jewish; social and historical forces from the past influence the present; multilingualism is more prevalent than monolingualism; exiles are as common as "local" nationals. To understand one's past, one's identity, an understanding of translation in and of itself is crucial; translation ceases to be an elite intellectual "game," a footnote to literary scholarship, but becomes fundamental to the *lives* and livelihood of everyone in the entire region (and maybe the world).

Another reason for combining a consideration of Polysystem theory with Translation Studies is their similarity: a logical connection exists between what was being suggested in the Netherlands and what was being postulated in Israel. The Israeli scholars do not contradict the early Translation Studies work, but expand upon it, incorporating earlier theoretical notions of translation equivalence and literary function into a larger structure which enables them to historicize actual translated texts and see the temporal nature of certain aesthetic presuppositions which influence the process of translation. The important theoretical difference between their work and early Translation Studies scholars is that the direction of thought about translation becomes reversed. Translation Studies disciples, like several translation theorists before them, tended to look at one-to-one relationships and functional notions of equivalence; they believed in the subjective ability of the translator to derive an equivalent text that in turn influenced the literary and cultural conventions in a particular society. Polysystem theorists presume the opposite: that the social norms and literary conventions in the receiving culture ("target" system) govern the aesthetic presuppositions of the translator and thus influence ensuing translation decisions.

Yet in many ways Polysystem theory is a logical extension of the demands made by early Translation Studies theorists; the Israeli scholars have expanded the parameters of what Lefevere, Holmes, and Van den Broeck intended, to the point where translation theory seems to transcend "legitimate" linguistic and literary borders. In the introduction to *Translation Theory and*

Intercultural Relations, the proceedings of the 1978 Tel Aviv conference, the editors Even-Zohar and Toury write:

> Having once adopted a functional(istic) approach, whereby the
> object is theory dependent, modern translation theory cannot
> escape transcending "borders." Just as the linguistic "borders"
> have been transcended, so must the literary ones be tran-
> scended. For there are occurrences of a translational nature
> which call for a semiotics of culture.
>
> (Even-Zohar and Toury, 1981: x)

With the incorporation of the historical horizon, Polysystem
theorists change the perspective which has governed traditional
translation theory and begin to address a whole new series of
questions. Not only are translations and interliterary connections
between cultures more adequately described, but intraliterary
relations within the structure of a given cultural system and actual
literary and linguistic evolution are also made visible by means of
the study of translated texts.

The problem with early Translation Studies, according to
Polysystem theorists, was that it attempted both to theorize about
the process of translation and to evaluate the success of individual
texts synchronically (texts in terms of their pure "literariness"). It
purported to have a diachronic component, for it did consider the
historical context as well as the target culture (in terms of the text's
function in the receiving culture), yet this component tended
toward the ahistorical: the theory hypothesized the possibility of a
direct importation of an isolated function (the author's original
intended function) across centuries. A synchronic evaluation, like
Van den Broeck's attempt to recuperate the concept of "translation equivalence" for Translation Studies, was in direct
contradiction to a comprehensive diachronic description, which
would relativize rather than universalize any concept of equivalence. Any attempt to prescribe one aesthetic over another in
terms of approaches to translation was doomed to be undermined
by the necessary extension of the parameters of the historical
analysis. Because early translation theory was very much bound
up with metaphysical distinctions separating form from content
and dualistic theories of representation, it failed to adequately
describe the historical situation conditioning specific systems of
representation. The Israeli contribution abandons attempts at
prescription, incorporates descriptions of multiple translation

processes, and analyzes the various historical products. Instead of basing itself on deep-structured grammatic/thematic types or linguistic features which have similar functions, "modern" translation theory incorporates the idea of systemic change which undermines such static, mechanistic concepts.

The process translation theorists now wish to describe is not the process of the transfer of a single text, but the process of translation production and change within the entire literary system. To do so, Even-Zohar and Toury borrow heavily from the ideas of some of the later Russian Formalists, especially those of Jurij Tynjanov, whose project in many ways parallels the development of Translation Studies. Locating his concept of Polysystem theory in the tradition of Russian Formalism, Even-Zohar writes:

> The importance for literary history of the correlations between central and peripheral literature as well as between "high" and "low" types was raised by Russian Formalists as soon as they abandoned their partially a-historical attitude, early in their history. The nature of these correlations became one of their major hypotheses in explaining the mechanisms of change in literary history.
>
> (Even-Zohar, 1978a: 11)

As early Translation Studies tended to call for an investigation into the historical process but often failed to elaborate, so too did many Russian Formalists fail to interpret their results in terms of literary history. Such a process began only later with Jurij Tynjanov, Boris Èjxenbaum, and their students.

JURIJ TYNJANOV ON LITERARY EVOLUTION

The Russian Formalists did not form a totally homogeneous group, and the disagreement within the group over the concept of "form," i.e., whether language was primarily directed toward the sign itself or the external world, was perhaps responsible for the internal division. One of the Russian Formalists who argued for the branching out from autonomous literary works and into history was Boris Èjxenbaum, who in "Theory of the Formal Method" described the moment of the break as follows:

> The fact of the matter is that the Formalists' original endeavor to pin down some particular constructional device and trace its

unity through voluminous material had given way to an endeavor to qualify further the generalized idea, to grasp the concrete *function* of the device in each given instance. This concept of functional value gradually moved out to the forefront and overshadowed our original concept of the device.

(Èjxenbaum, 1978: 29)

The split in Russian Formalism was not merely directed against early Formalist tendencies, but also against the reigning literary history and symbolist scholarship in Russia. Such a change in conceptual thinking forced the later Formalists to consider historical factors, and again they came into conflict with the traditions of literary historicism, then dominated by biological accounts and studies of the influence of canonical authors on other authors. According to Èjxenbaum, literary historians at the time relied on "vague generalities" such as concepts of "romanticism" or "realism" when talking historically, and progress was measured on an individual basis – similar, for example, to the way a father passes something on to his son and a mother to her daughter. Literature was seen as playing no role in social evolution. The symbolist literary theorists, against whom Russian Formalists initially reacted, removed literary scholarship even further from cultural conditions, developing a whole series of "impressionistic sketches" and "silhouettes" that modernized writers by turning them into "eternal companions."

This branching out of Russian Formalism was a natural consequence of the Formalist approach: in the analysis of a particular literary issue, the critic would soon find the literary problem not only enmeshed in history, but also influencing the history in which it finds itself, opening up the complex problem of literary evolution. According to Tynjanov, any new literary work must necessarily deconstruct existing unities, or by definition it ceases to be literary. Literary tradition was no longer conceived of as a continuing straight line, but rather as a struggle involving destruction and reconstruction out of elements (Tynjanov, 1921; Èjxenbaum, 1978: 31). In terms of the development of Russian Formalism and its relevance to Translation Studies, this insight by Tynjanov marks the critical break. In his 1927 article "On Literary Evolution" and then a year later, together with Roman Jakobson, in "Problems in the Study of Literature and Language" (both articles collected in Matejka and Pomorska, 1978), Tynjanov officially repudiated his Formalist colleagues. The

Formalist project, he argued, was just one more instance of a traditional "historic" approach, which isolated "literary" elements and equated them with elements from a system of a different time period and place:

> Tradition, the basic concept of the established history of litera-
> ture, has proved to be an unjustifiable abstraction of one or
> more of the literary elements of a given system within which
> they occupy the same plane and play the same role. They are
> equated with the like elements of another system in which they
> are on a different plane, thus they are brought into a seemingly
> unified, fictitiously integrated system.
>
> (Tynjanov, 1978b: 67)

Tynjanov rejected his colleagues' investigations as superficial and mechanical and their results as illusory and abstract. Instead, he argued that synchronic features depend upon past and future structures, which caused him to reformulate the Formalist concept of diachrony and the function of literature in history. Always in a dialectical relationship with other systems, works could no longer be studied in isolation, for that which was innovative was dependent upon that which was normal. Formal elements took on value not when they could be abstracted and correlated to some concept of the similar or identical form, but when they were different, distancing themselves from a standard form. "Literari-ness" became equated with difference, and phrases such as "innovation" within works and "mutation" of systems were used to illustrate his argument: "The main concept for literary evolution is the *mutation* of systems, and thus the problem of 'traditions' is transferred onto another plane" (Tynjanov, 1978b: 67).

Two changes in Tynjanov's thinking became apparent: first, "literariness" could not be defined outside of history – its exis-tence depended upon its interrelatedness; and, second, formal unities receded in importance as the systemic laws which govern literary relations were elevated. Tynjanov might at this point be characterized as a structuralist rather than a formalist, for the goal of his project was to discover the "specific structural laws" which govern all systems, including literary texts. He proposed a study of the relationship of the function of formal literary ele-ments to other intratextual literary elements, to intertextual literary elements, and to extraliterary orders. The formal abstrac-tion of separate elements of a work – such as composition, rhythm, style, syntax, or parody – had been useful but limited, for at a certain point such work was bound to reveal that the role of a given element varied in different systems. The revelation that formal elements were capable of taking on different functions in different cultures (as in translation, for example) suggested to Tynjanov that the parameters governing literary scholarship needed to be expanded to include the extraliterary. He rejected the non-systemic "origin" of new elements, ideas, and/or genres, whether generated from literary texts ("literary influences") or extraliterary institutions. Instead, Tynjanov and Jakobson posited the thesis that structural evolution determines every specific change: "The history of literature (art), being simultaneous with other historical series, is characterized, as is each of these series, by an involved complex of specific structural laws" (Tynjanov and Jakobson, 1978: 79).

To understand better the relationship of the innovative formal element to the specific text and to the existing literary order, Tynjanov introduced the concept of "system." Elements, he argued, do not exist in isolation, but always in an interrelationship with other elements of other systems. For Tynjanov, the entire literary and extraliterary world could be divided into multiple structural systems. Literary traditions composed different systems, literary genres formed systems, a literary work itself was also a unique system, and the entire social order comprised another system, all of which were interrelated, "dialectically" interacting with each other, and conditioning how any specific formal element could function. Without a concept of sameness, of system, of norms, of conforming, it was impossible to determine that which was new, different, "mutant." Formalism posited the thesis that it could distinguish "literariness" through a concept of defamiliarization. Yet that thesis was dependent upon the assumption that it could also define that which was familiar, for the formal element's function could be viewed as defamiliarizing only in that specific intertextual moment when the norm and the new came in contact. Thus Tynjanov's major contribution to literary theory was to extend, in a logical fashion, the parameters of Formalism to include literary and social norms.

The social order in Tynjanov's model was everything that had become normalized, automatized, regularized – ordinary, everyday, banal life: he argued that the verse found in newspapers, for example, used mainly effaced, banal metrical systems that had long since been rejected by poetry. Thus, the extraliterary in Tynjanov's model was not something which influenced literary works; the literary work influenced the extraliterary. Literary texts introduced change in the way people perceived things in the real world. To illuminate this set of relations, Tynjanov introduced the concept "complex of norms":

> The principles involved in relating these two categories (i.e., the existing norm and the individual utterances) as applied to literature must now be elaborated. In the latter case, the individual utterance cannot be considered without reference to the existing complex of norms. (The investigator, in isolating the former from the latter, inescapably deforms the system of artistic values under consideration, thus losing the possibility of establishing its immanent laws.)
>
> (Tynjanov and Jakobson, 1978: 80)

Thus the individual utterance was first related to the preexisting literary norm to measure its "value" and thus determine the immanent laws of its production. At a third level existed the real, material world, the world of "social convention," i.e., that which existed when literary texts were literally "worn out" and transferred on to other forms of "real life." The social norms, thus, were viewed to a large degree as stagnant, static, dead; literary innovation was what moved society. Real life's function in Tynjanov's model was merely to be the receptor for the tired, worn out phrases which have lost their life.

While Tynjanov was very much committed to a theory of systems over Formalism, his Formalist roots remained visible, for the formal structure of a text was still privileged and the content reduced to marginal importance. The hierarchy of his model proceeded from an analysis of the relation of structural elements within a literary text ("constructional function") to the analysis of the relation of the literary text to literary order ("literary function") and finally to the analysis of the relation of literary system to social conventions ("verbal function"). The hierarchy was compartmentalized so that a single literary work could not be related to the social order; only a literary order to the extraliterary (Tynjanov, 1978b: 74). Tynjanov's concept of how literature evolves was based upon the very same defamiliarization device so highly valued by the early Formalists. Despite apparent claims to the contrary, even in late Formalism, literature was still perceived as cut off from the rest of the boring, banal, automatized world; literature was viewed as developing autonomously, adjacent to the real world.

As advanced as Tynjanov's model was, the purported diachronic, evolutionary model still was primarily determined by his synchronic conceptual predispositions. A contradiction within Tynjanov's work characteristic of his project was his attempt to broaden the perspective of Russian Formalism by introducing historical perspective and social realities into his model, yet at the same time retaining synchronic conceptual categories – a text's "constructional" function – which traditionally governed Formalism. What had value was that which defamiliarized (poetic verse); and what had no value was that which conformed (journalism, popular literature). His call for a value-proof "science" of literary evolution privileged signs referring to other signs – the innovation of form was the determining factor – and not to the material world. Literature thus evolved autonomously according to literary laws of evolution, independent of external factors. Literature remained above the normal, humdrum world, evolving on its own. Literature did not mediate, it only influenced, via some sort of "trickle down" effect. The concept that different cultural milieux, economic conditions, or literary institutions (like the press) might have an effect upon the evolution of a literary system was inconceivable within Tynjanov's framework of analysis. In Tynjanov's model, the material world, the content of the work of art, its historical referent, and its meaning were all relegated to a subsidiary status.

ITAMAR EVEN-ZOHAR: EXPLORING INTRASYSTEMIC LITERARY RELATIONS

Itamar Even-Zohar is not specifically a translation theorist, but a cultural theorist: he adopts Tynjanov's concept of a hierarchical literary system and then "uses" the data collected from his observations on how translation functions in various societies to describe the hierarchical cultural system as a whole. He coins the term "polysystem" to refer to the entire network of correlated systems – literary and extraliterary – within society, and develops an approach called Polysystem theory to attempt to explain the function of *all* kinds of writing within a given culture – from the central canonical texts to the most marginal non-canonical texts.

Concepts borrowed from Tynjanov – such as "system," literary "norms," and the notion of "evolution" as an ongoing struggle between various literary systems are used to frame his research: the analysis of the intrasystemic relations between conflicting literary structures. Although the analysis of translated literature is just one aspect of his investigation, it proves more than marginal, for his data show that translated literature functions differently depending upon the age, strength, and stability of the particular literary "polysystem." In fact, his thinking about translation, especially in relation to the unique situation of Hebrew literature, with its general lack of texts and the unique role translated Russian and Yiddish literature play in its literary system, leads Even-Zohar to some of his most provocative hypotheses about literary systems.

Even-Zohar adopts Tynjanov's concept of system, his hierarchical structure of differing literary systems, his concept of defamiliarization as the measuring device for historical literary significance, and finally his concept of literary mutation and evolution. Even-Zohar's definition of polysystem is the same as Tynjanov's concept of system, including the literary, semi-literary and extraliterary structures. The term "polysystem" is thus a global term covering all of the literary systems, both major and minor, existing in a given culture. The substance of Even-Zohar's research involves his exploration of the complex interrelations between the various systems, especially those between the major systems and the minor subsystems. In a more controversial move, aware of the ideological implications of Tynjanov's hierarchically structured system, Even-Zohar nevertheless adopts the same set of structural relations with their correspondingly varying "value" within the structure as a whole:

> According to what is presumed about the nature of systems in general and the nature of literary phenomena in particular, there can obviously be no equality between the various literary systems and types. These systems maintain *hierarchical* relations, which means some maintain a more central position than others, or that some are *primary* while others are *secondary*.
>
> (Even-Zohar, 1978a: 16)

The third concept borrowed from Tynjanov is that of "defamiliarization" or, in the late Formalist terminology, "deautomatization." As the above passage indicates, Even-Zohar's model again presumes the privileged status of the "high" literary elements of "primary" importance to the polysystem, and of "low" automatized elements at the bottom of the cultural hierarchy, of "secondary" importance. At the lower levels, the elements, although "materially" unchanged, lose their "original function" and become "petrified" (Even-Zohar, 1978a: 16). Even-Zohar reverses our notion of canon as an unvarying and generally accepted body of literature which operates as a standard norm in a given culture, and now uses it to help define that which is innovative, new, and different:

> While canonized literature tries to create new models of reality and attempts to illuminate the information it bears in a way which at least brings about *deautomatization*, as the Prague Structuralists put it, non-canonized literature has to keep within the conventionalized models which are highly automatized. Hence the impression of stereotype one gets from the non-canonized works.
>
> (Even-Zohar, 1978a: 16).

The historical horizon is introduced along the lines of Russian Futurism as well: the shock caused by the appearance of new and innovative elements in the existing codified system is what causes a literary system to evolve. Throughout history, competing literary subsystems are thus constantly challenging and infiltrating higher orders, and then resolving, so the entire system evolves in a systematically "unsystematic" fashion: a sort of boiling caldron, manifest within a text as an interplay of intersecting and competing paradigms of formal elements, indicative of the conflicting heterogeneous systems struggling within the "polysystem" as a whole.

Such a theory rearticulates the system theory proposed by the late Formalists; Even-Zohar resurrected them after a period of silence partially imposed by political conditions in the Soviet Union. His work incorporating translation into his model, however, marks a further development within the field of historical poetics:

> It is necessary to include *translated literature* in the polysystem. This is rarely done, but no observer of the history of any literature can avoid recognizing as an important fact the impact of translations and their role in the synchrony and diachrony of a certain literature.
>
> (Even-Zohar, 1978a: 15)

Not all polysystems are the same, and through the analysis of the relationship of translated to original literary works, Even-Zohar arrives at a better understanding of the nature of polysystems. In all previous systems models, translations were invariably classified as secondary systems; Even-Zohar's data show that such classification may be inaccurate. The polysystems of larger, older cultures, such as Anglo-American or French, for example, differ from the polysystems of younger or smaller nations, such as Israel or the Low Countries. The former, because of the length and self-sufficiency of their traditions, according to Even-Zohar, tend to relegate translated literature to the margins of society (except in periods of crisis), whereas within the latter systems, for opposite reasons, translations play a more central role. In his essay "The Position of Translated Literature Within the Literary Polysystem," Even-Zohar suggests that the relationship between translated works and the literary polysystem cannot be categorized as either primary or secondary, but as variable, depending upon the specific circumstance operating within the literary system.

Even-Zohar outlines three social circumstances enabling a situation in which translation would maintain a primary position: when a literature is "young," or in the process of being established; when a literature is "peripheral" or "weak" or both; and when a literature is experiencing a "crisis" or turning point (Even-Zohar, 1978a: 24). In the first case, as is characteristic of the Israeli situation, and as seems to be characteristic of nineteenth-century Czech culture (Macura, 1990), translation fulfils the need of a young literature to use its new language for as many different kinds of writing as possible. Since it cannot create all forms and genres, translated texts may serve as the most important for a certain amount of time (though not limited to just this role in the hierarchy). The same principle holds true, according to Even-Zohar, in the second situation, when a weak literature, often of a smaller nation, like the Low Countries, cannot produce all the kinds of writing a stronger, larger system can – thus its inability to produce innovations and subsequent dependency upon translation to introduce precedent-setting texts. In such circumstances, translated texts serve not only as a medium through which new ideas can be imported, but also as the form of writing most frequently imitated by "creative" writers in the native language. In the third situation, perhaps analogous to the cultural situation in

America in the sixties, established literary models no longer stimulate the new generation of writers, who turn elsewhere for ideas and forms. Under such historical circumstances, or combination of circumstances, both established and avant-garde writers produce translations, and through the translated text new elements are introduced into a literary system that would otherwise fail to appear.

The opposite social conditions, according to Even-Zohar, govern the situations in which translation is of secondary importance to the polysystem. In strong systems such as the French or Anglo-American, with well-developed literary traditions and many different kinds of writing, original writing produces innovations in ideas and forms independent of translation, relegating translations to a marginal position in the overall functioning of the dynamic system. In this historical situation, translation often (but not necessarily always) assumes forms already established as a dominant type within a particular genre, and the translated literature tends to remain fairly conservative, adhering to norms which the "higher" forms have already rejected. Despite playing a secondary role, translations produced under these circumstances may paradoxically introduce new *ideas* into a culture while at the same time preserving traditional forms.

Having observed the position of translation within varying cultural systems, Even-Zohar next explores the relationship between the translated texts and the literary polysystem along two lines: (1) how texts to be translated are selected by the receiving culture and (2) how translated texts adopt certain norms and functions as a result of their relation to other target language systems (Even-Zohar, 1978a: 22). In his early work on Polysystem theory, Even-Zohar's debt to the Tynjanov and the Russian Formalists is very clear, and the conspicuous absence of extraliterary factors can be noted. Selection, according to Even-Zohar's research, appears to be governed by conditions within the receiving polysystem. Texts to be translated are chosen because of their compatibility with the new forms needed by a polysystem to achieve a complete, dynamic, homogeneous identity. Thus, the socio-literary conditions of the receiving culture in part determine those texts which get translated in the first place. If features such as techniques, forms, or even genres are missing – Even-Zohar talks in terms of "vacuums" within a literary culture – in all likelihood texts providing such functional elements will be imported in order for the system to achieve full dynamic diversity. If not, the receiving polysystem remains "defective." If indeed a system begins to stagnate, again translation will tend toward the innovative, move to the canonic center and provide the system with the impetus to move on.

With regard to the way translated literature influences the translation norms of a given culture, Even-Zohar suggests that when translated literature assumes a primary position, the borders between translated texts and original texts "diffuse" and definitions of translation become liberalized, expanding to include versions, imitations, and adaptations as well. Governed by a situation where their function is to introduce new work into the receiving culture and change existing relations, translated texts necessarily tend to more closely reproduce the original text's forms and textual relations (adequate to the source language). If the form of the foreign text is too radical, too estranging, the translated text runs the risk of not being incorporated into the literary system of the receiving culture; however, if the new text is "victorious," it tends to function as primary literature, and the codes of both the receiving culture's original literature and the translated literature become "enriched." If translation tends to be a secondary activity within a given polysystem, the situation is reversed: the translators" attempts to find ready-made models for translation result in translations that conform to preestablished aesthetic norms in the target culture at the expense of the text's "original" form. For example, according to Polysystem theory, nineteenth-century Anglo-American translations (by Rossetti, Longfellow, FitzGerald) based on approaches (such as Matthew Arnold's) that emphasize "faithfulness" to the original form and textual relations, functioned as primary. Certain modern translations (contemporary Bible translation or theatre adaptations) using approaches (such as Bassnett's or Nida's) that prefer finding existing forms which function as equivalents in the target literature, would be secondary systems, reinforcing the current dominant aesthetic (modernism) rather than importing new ideas and techniques.

Even-Zohar revised the polysystem hypothesis in 1977 to better allow for the relationship between a literary system and socio-economic forces within a society. In an essay called "Polysystem Hypothesis Revisited" he writes:

One only need assume the center-and-periphery relation in order to be able to reconciliate heterogeneity with functionality. Thus, the notion of hierarchy, of strate, is not only unavoidable but useful as well. To augment this with the notion of a system of systems, a multiple system, i.e., a system whose intersections are more complex, is but a logical step necessitated by the need to elaborate a model "closer" to "the real world."

(Even-Zohar, 1978a: 29)

The advantage of Polysystem theory is that it allows for its own augmentation and integrates the study of literature with the study of social and economic forces of history. Even-Zohar uses the term "poly" just to allow for such elaboration and complexity without having to limit the number of relations and interconnections. The principles which he uses to describe relations within the literary system are also applicable to its relations with the extraliterary (Even-Zohar, 1978a: 29–30). Even-Zohar's early work is important to translation theory because of the attention and thought given to the role of translation within a literary system, a role traditionally ignored by literary theorists in general. Yet, by his own admission, the hierarchy described, the means by which translations were chosen, and the way they functioned within the literary system are too simplistic, and the theory needs revision. With such a revision, Polysystem theory is entering a new phase in which extraliterary factors such as patronage, social conditions, economics, and institutional manipulation are being correlated to the way translations are chosen and function in a literary system. Despite the fact that his theory allows for expansion, Even-Zohar's own work and hypothesizing tend to focus primarily upon the literary, as demonstrated by his more recent work formulating "universals" based upon his findings.

Since the goal of structural theories is to establish the rules and laws which govern any given system, to find the "deep structure" of the surface manifestation being investigated, Even-Zohar's approach, despite its apparent focus upon heterogeneity and difference, still, because of certain theoretical presuppositions, posits such universals. Even-Zohar reads the text of the cultural fabric and tries to discover those rules which regulate the system of cultural heterogeneity, the "polysystem." In doing so, he raises the Formalist approach to a higher degree: his theory becomes a formalism of forms. Although he assumes that literary systems are composed of multiple differing systems and constantly undergo change, at the core of his theory is a concept of a totally integrated and meaningful "whole." Though the competing subsystems are in a constant state of flux, they also variously (cor)relate with other elements and systems forming a complex but unified structure. Even-Zohar does not analyze single texts and classify them; instead, he analyzes multiple texts and the complex intra- and interrelations they enter into as they form a highly stratified but unified whole. For Even-Zohar, culture is the highest organized human structure.

The tendency to overgeneralize and establish universal laws is one of the more controversial parts of Even-Zohar's theory. In his essay "Universals of Literary Contacts" Even-Zohar lists thirteen such universals derived from his new data, the first of which – *"all literary systems strive to become polysystemic"* (Even-Zohar, 1978a: 43, emphasis in original) – serves to illustrate his approach. Upon first observing the data, translation in particular, it seemed to him that certain polysystems were unstratified or lacked certain elements or subsystems. But further analysis revealed that this was not the case, that indeed stratification was "always" present, and that no literature ever functions as a non-stratified whole, leading him to the formulation of the first "universal" of cultural history. Such conclusions not only veer perilously close to traditional theoretical terminology – which is based on sameness, eternal verities, and homologous systems, but they also tend to reinforce many traditional notions of the definition of "literary" and reify the literary systems of the "strong" systems. Even-Zohar's work is perhaps the most important to date in the field of translation theory; he uses notions of translation equivalence and literary function, yet does not pull them out of history and prescribe a translation model that transcends time. His work is highly innovative, making manifest the temporal nature of aesthetic presuppositions by looking at actual translations within the larger sociological context. His work makes a significant contribution not only to the field of translation theory, but to literary theory as well, as it demonstrates the importance of translation within the larger context of literary studies specifically and in the evolution of culture in general.

Despite the advances Even-Zohar is making, several minor problems with Polysystem theory can be noted. The first problem, which he recognizes, is his tendency to propose universals based on very little evidence. A more extensive analysis of textual and cultural relations must take place before "universals" can be persuasively posited. The contradictions in his own data demonstrate the ephemeral nature of many of his hypotheses and tend to distort the theoretical importance of what he is trying to articulate. For example, Even-Zohar says in his characteristically definitive fashion that "no literary structures on any level were ever adopted by the non-canonized system before they had become common stock of the canonized one" (Even-Zohar, 1978a: 17). Yet, for example, in his analysis of late-nineteenth-century French literature, the data seem to indicate otherwise: pornographic literature was widespread in the non-canonized literature before traces of it were adopted by the canon. Even-Zohar perhaps too uncritically adopts the late Russian Formalist model, positing a hierarchy of relations in which the innovative ideas trickle down to reside eventually in the stagnant forms of popular literature. His own evidence suggests that at least a more dialectical relationship of mutual interaction is often the case, or that in some instances the opposite movement – i.e., that the popular influences the canonical – is to a large degree true.

This leads to the related problem of Even-Zohar's uncritical adoption of the Formalist framework, perpetuating concepts such as "literariness" which underlie, yet seem inappropriate to, Even-Zohar's complex model of cultural systems. Despite his historically based model, Even-Zohar retains a concept of "literary facts," based on a Formalist value system of defamiliarization, perhaps in contradiction to his own thesis of literary texts being culturally dependent. This presupposition influences his concept of hierarchical relations within a society, his definitions of "primary" and "secondary," which still retain ideological residues of an ahistorical system of judging literature, despite defensive claims to the contrary. If translated literature seems to function as both primary and secondary, might not the same be true for children's literature, detective novels, folktales? Within the theoretical framework of Even-Zohar's model, folktales will always be relegated to secondary status, for they do not develop the form or genre. Although the plots and characters may change, the tales do not change structurally, and thus can never occupy a "primary" position within the hierarchy. Yet certainly enough evidence exists documenting literary systems in which oral tales are highly valued.

In addition, the problem of locating the referent applies to Even-Zohar's Polysystem theory as it does to Formalism. Despite allowing for such a possibility, Even-Zohar seldom relates texts to the "real conditions" of their production, only to hypothetical structural models and abstract generalizations. The extraliterary continues to be significantly absent from his analysis. The *thing* signified – the content, the meaning, however arbitrary – shared by the author and the reader is all but absent in Even-Zohar's model; his analysis focuses primarily on the signifier and how it formally interacts with other literary/cultural systems of significance. A theory that addresses only form and systemic function misses something. In terms of translation theory, the problem of reference, of how one translates the signs without further concealing or distorting the thing to which the signs refer, still remains. In a system with different signs having different cultural associations, how can one minimize the losses of reference? Do ideas develop independently of the literature? Even-Zohar seems to share Èjxenbaum's and Tynjanov's belief that literature develops autonomously according to rules of its own, for, despite his allowing for augmentation of his theory, he also holds that the literary system is, to a large degree, autonomous – a "self-regulating system" – and that the stratification is carried out by "interrelations within the system" (Even-Zohar, 1978a: 30). Even-Zohar thus tends to read the multiple texts of the cultural life of a society with similar formalist presuppositions that the Russian Formalists brought to individual texts.

Finally, Even-Zohar's own methodology and discourse limit the scope of his investigation. He purports to observe "objectively" the interplay of systems, to eliminate all bias, and to "rationally" describe and order literary phenomena. He suggests that a "non-elitist" and "non-evaluative" approach can "eliminate *all* sorts of biases" (Even-Zohar, 1978a: 28, emphasis in original). Somehow he locates his theory above other translation theories, giving him an independent perspective on translational phenomena. Such total objectivity is of course impossible, especially given the nature of the subject matter. His methodology of making rules, developing hypotheses, testing them, arriving at a consensus of the "qualified" literary historical scholars (those who agree upon the same scientific method) may, in fact, eventually close down avenues of investigation. While the content of Even-Zohar's theory is "dialectical" and challenging to theories which universalize and homogenize, his methodology also leads him to generally agreed upon and thus "proven" theses which serve as literary "facts."

Although his argument is convincing and well supported, Even-Zohar's formulation of principles occasionally contradicts that which he is trying to prove. He has accumulated new data which tend to disprove old theories and require new interpretation, yet he retains a conceptual framework and scientific approach which forces him to make such universal statements. Such a tendency to generalize, especially with so little data on which to base conclusions, most of which are drawn from a very unique and specific culture, runs the risk that elements for analysis will only enter into his model when they find a place in the structural whole of the polysystem. With unity postulated from the beginning, and a scientific method aimed at eliminating contradictions, the methodology may eventually limit and obscure that which it purports to be opening up. Systems that do not conform to the rules and laws of the structural polysystem are thus viewed as "defective." Non-conforming models have "vacuums" which need to be filled to achieve completeness. The whole system is based on order and regularity, and the ability of the investigator to satisfactorily explain all the phenomena. The implicit subtext to Even-Zohar's theory calls to mind Platonic forms and classical aesthetics, by smoothing out contradictions and eliminating that which does not fit. Just what is that complete, dynamic, homogeneous system against which all other systems are compared? Contradictions in reality and problems of literary creation are "solved" by his methodology; variations are regulated; and texts are viewed as "more" or "less" innovative, and classified accordingly.

Despite these reservations, Even-Zohar's Polysystem theory demonstrates an advance in the development of Translation Studies specifically and translation theory in general. Unlike earlier models, Even-Zohar's system is not text-specific and does not analyze individual texts isolated from their cultural context. According to Even-Zohar, a text does not reach the highest hierarchical level within a given culture because of some inherent eternal beauty or verity, but (1) because of the nature of the polysystem of the receiving culture and its social/literary historical circumstances, and (2) because of the difference between certain elements of the text and cultural norms. A text is never totally autonomous (although the entire literary system is postulated to be); the text is always already involved in a multitude of relationships with other elements of other systems at both the center and margins of a cultural whole. The theoretical advance of Polysystem Theory for Translation Studies should be readily apparent: instead of having a static conception of what a translation should be, Even-Zohar varies his definition of "equivalence" and "adequacy" according to the historical situation, freeing the discipline from the constraint that has traditionally limited its previous theories. By expanding the theoretical boundaries of traditional translation theory, based all too frequently on linguistic models or undeveloped literary theories, and embedding translated literature into a larger cultural context, Even-Zohar has opened the way for translation theory to finally advance beyond prescriptive aesthetics. This opening is seized upon by Even-Zohar's colleague Gideon Toury, who focuses specifically upon the translation component of Even-Zohar's model, and begins the search for a new theory of translation.

GIDEON TOURY: TOWARD A TARGET-ORIENTED APPROACH

Gideon Toury's work may be divided into two periods: the first from 1972–1976 and reported in 1977 in *Normot šel tirgum ve-ha tirgum ha sifruti le-ivrit ba šanim 1930–1945* (Translation Norms and Literary Translation into Hebrew), involved a comprehensive sociological study of the cultural conditions affecting the translation of foreign language novels into Hebrew during the period 1930–45 (later expanded to include children's literature); the second, from 1975 to 1980 and summarized in a series of papers collected in 1980 as *In Search of a Theory of Translation*, involved an attempt to develop a more comprehensive theory of translation based on findings from his field study. The first project was begun with Itamar Even-Zohar and used the Polysystem theory framework; the second study, although still based on Polysystem theory, posits theoretical hypotheses which distinguish Toury's model from that of his predecessor.

Toury's initial field study was set up within the scope of a larger project called "The History of Literary Translation into Hebrew" being undertaken at the University of Tel Aviv at the time (Toury, 1980: 123). His study catalogued the prose fiction translations from English, Russian, German, French, and Yiddish into Hebrew during a fifteen-year span and generated quantitative data on, for example, the number of writers translated, number of books by each writer translated, and the number of translators and publishers involved in the process. One of the goals of the field study was to discover the actual decisions made during the translation process, through which he hoped to discover a system of rules governing translation in this particular polysystem. As Popovič postulated, the aesthetically determined rationale for certain translation decisions were most visible in the "shifts" between the source and target texts. The analysis of the shifts showed that there were very few linguistic changes in operation during the period, and those few omissions and fewer additions tended to be irrelevant to the identity of the text. More changes were noted with regard to word choices and style, resulting in the discovery of "textual" norms such as a tendency to "elevate" the text by choosing words to reflect the "highest" style from the possible alternatives.

Ironically, according to Toury's field study, linguistics and aesthetics played a very small role in the translation process; in fact, Toury found that most texts were selected for ideological reasons. Preferences for social and even "socialist" works, for certain subjects and topics, and of course for Jewish writers and subjects were demonstrated, but few choices based on aesthetic criteria were identified. Toury, in accordance with Even-Zohar, did find that the texts which were selected for literary reasons and for which equivalent literary formal models were found did tend to occupy and shape the center of the system of translation within the Hebrew polysystem. Yet, in addition to the formal innovativeness of the central texts, other elements in common with all central texts were also noted: for example, their "didactic" attitude and their general agreement with (and almost rigid application of) the translation norms. Accidents also played a large role in terms of texts selected and texts published as well as in terms of linguistic equivalents found and not found. Yet despite the changes in the texts and lack of conformity with predetermined linguistic and literary theories of translation, the translated texts, according to Toury, still functioned as translations in the Hebrew polysystem. The texts entering the Hebrew system as translations tended to be only *partially* linguistically and functionally equivalent to the source text; nevertheless, they were accepted in the target culture as translations and occupied all positions from the center to the periphery. Despite this general lack of conformity with hypothetical models of translation equivalence, examples of "mistranslations," translations considered "inadequate" in the target culture were generally rare. On the other hand, examples of complete linguistic equivalence to the source text were even rarer, and the instances of near-adequacy to the source text, when they did occur, were usually "accidental". (Toury, 1980: 137). The reason for this general lack of concern for "faithfulness" to the source text, Toury concluded, was not that the translators were indifferent to the textual relations within the source text, but that their main goal was to achieve acceptable translations in the target culture. The operational decisions were thus a natural outcome of a preference for the translators' initial teleological goal; the changes were dictated by the cultural conditions of the receiving system.

It thus should come as no surprise that when Toury turns his attention to developing a theory of translation he finds fault with existing source-oriented theoretical models of translation. Following Even-Zohar's "use" of translation to discover rules about the literary system in general, Toury attempts to better detect and describe all those laws – linguistic, literary, and sociological – which govern translation. His field study results caused him to be skeptical of abstract theories involving ideal author–original text/translated text–reader models. By avoiding a predefinition of what a translation "should" be, and looking at actual translations in a real cultural context, it becomes clear that aesthetic theories of literary transfer and even pair-bound "objective" descriptions of linguistic possibilities do not account for various factors which clearly influence the translation product.

The theoretical context against which Toury locates his project is one dominated by translation models which posit a definition of equivalence as functional-dynamic. Toury suggests that, despite their advance over linguistic definitions of translation equivalence, such theories are still source-oriented and invariably "directive" and "normative" because they recognize only "correct instances" and "types" (Toury, 1980: 39–40; 1981: 14). The correctness of translation, the adequacy of the equivalent second language text, is, according to these theories, always measured against the degree of correspondence with the source text, by trying to reconstruct all the "relevant" functional features – be

they linguistic or literary elements – of the source text. Requirements for translation traditionally have been conceived as being
determined by the source text, and as a result, have necessarily
been idealized. Toury's theory opposes theories that are based
upon a single unified and abstract identity or a proper interpretation of "equal" performance. His model is based on difference
and assumes structural differences between languages: "every
linguistic system and/or textual tradition *differs* from any other in
terms of structure, repertory, norms of usage, etc." (Toury, 1980:
94, emphasis in original). Positing hypothetical poles of total
acceptability in the target culture at the one extreme and total
adequacy to the source text at the other, Toury locates translation
as always in the middle: no translation is ever entirely "acceptable"
to the target culture because it will always introduce new information and forms defamiliarizing to that system, nor is any
translation entirely "adequate" to the original version, because the
cultural norms cause shifts from the source text structures. Historically, translation criticism has been characterized by its
tendency to find fault with the translator because the actual text
can never meet the ideal standards of the two abstract poles: from
a linguistic point of view, errors can always be pointed out and
better solutions proposed; from a literary point of view, the
functional elements can invariably be judged as less dynamic or
innovative than the source text's features.

By considering translation from the point of view of the target
culture, however, Toury argues that translation equivalence is not
a hypothetical ideal, but becomes an empirical matter. The actual
relationship between a source text and a target text may or may
not reflect the postulated abstract relationship; nevertheless, the
translated text exists as a cultural artifact for the replacement of a
source text by an acceptable version in the receiving culture.
Content to identify the causes for deviation from the standard,
Toury's theoretical project is unified by the acceptance of translated texts without a judgment of their solutions as correct or
incorrect. Only by analyzing translated texts from within their
cultural-linguistic context can one understand the translation
process. Toury argues that translations themselves have no
"fixed" identity; because they are always subject to different socio-
literary contextual factors, they thus must be viewed as having
multiple identities, dependent upon the forces that govern the
decision process at a particular time. Distancing himself from

models which posit single conceptions of translation equivalence, Toury suggests a different theoretical framework in which to conceptualize phenomena regarded as translation. Borrowing from Ludwig Wittgenstein the concept of family of resemblances, Toury now views "original" texts as containing clusters of properties, meanings, possibilities. All translations privilege certain properties/meanings at the expense of others, and the concept of a "correct" translation ceases to be a real possibility (Toury, 1980: 18). Toury successfully pushes the concept of a theory of translation beyond the margins of a model restricted to faithfulness to the original, or of single, unified relationships between the source and target texts. Translation becomes a relative term, dependent upon the forces of history and the semiotic web called culture. The role of translation theory is correspondingly altered, ceasing its search for a system from which to judge the product and now focusing on the development of a model to help explain the process which determines the final version.

Early Translation Studies, which attempted to be objective and to study actual translated texts in the target culture, is no less implicated in the paradigm of static, source-oriented translation theories which Toury rejects. Behind early Translation Studies' definition of translation, argues Toury, is James Holmes' concept of "metatext," and although it has been elaborated by Anton Popovič (and others) and revised by Van den Broeck (and others), translated texts are still viewed by Translation Studies theorists as one kind of metatext, measured and evaluated in comparison with the source text or some idealized interpretation of that initial version (Toury, 1980: 39). Toury wants to expand the boundaries of even that which early Translation Studies has already augmented, getting further away from hypothetical constructs that tend to study translated texts in isolation. As opposed to another Source Text (ST) determined theory, Toury posits a Target Text (TT) theory for translation, focusing not on some notion of equivalence as postulated requirements, but on the "actual relationships" constructed between the source text and its "factual replacement" (Toury, 1980: 39). He does not reject the work of contrastive linguistics or semiotic-functional approaches; linguistic/literary limitations of course operate and condition the nature of the translation product. He does argue, however, that such rules and laws are merely one set of factors operating on the translation process; his project introduces a new set of factors which may be more powerful than other factors. The eventual goal of Toury's theory is to establish a hierarchy of interrelated factors (constraints) which determine (govern) the translation product. In short, Toury demands that translation theory include cultural-historical "facts," a set of laws which he calls "translation norms."

Occupying the center of Toury's theory and operative at every stage of the translation process, these translation norms mediate between systems of potential equivalence. In his paper "The Nature and Role of Norms in Literary Translation," Toury outlines his definition of translation norms and describes his methodology. A given society always has multiple and conflicting norms, all interconnected with other functioning systems, but if situations recur regularly, certain behavioral patterns can be established. Thus, in terms of translation, in order to distinguish regular tendencies, it is necessary to study not just single texts, but rather multiple translations of the same original text as they occur in one receiving culture at different times in history. Toury distinguishes between three kinds of translation norms: preliminary, initial, and operational norms. "Preliminary norms" involve factors such as those which govern the choice of the work and the overall translation strategy within a polysystem. Because the definition of translation varies historically, certain preliminary questions need to be answered in order to establish the cultural context which frames the translation process. What is the translation "policy" of the target culture? What is the difference between translation, imitation, and adaptation for the specific period? What authors, periods, genres, schools are preferred by the target culture? Is intermediate or second-hand translation permitted? What are the permitted mediating languages? The "initial norms" categorize the individual translator's choice to subject oneself either to the original text with its textual relations and norms, or the target culture's linguistic and literary norms, or some combination thereof. The initial norms are placed at the top of the hierarchy of operational norms for, if consistent, they subsequently influence all other translation decisions. "Operational norms" are the actual decisions made during the translation process, some of which were discussed in Toury's field study of translated prose fiction in Hebrew: "matricial" norms determining location, additions, and deletions, and "textual" norms revealing linguistic and stylistic preferences. Polysystem theory informs Toury's model: in terms of initial norms, the translator's attitude toward the source text is affected by the text's position in the source culture's literary polysystem; in terms of operational norms, all decisions are influenced by the position – central or peripheral – held by translated literature in the target culture polysystem.

In the course of discussing translation norms and the methodology for determining them, Toury also posits a new set of theoretical premises which seem to contradict his original intent. Similar to Lefevere's methodology in *Translating Poetry: Seven Strategies and a Blueprint*, Toury arrives at translation norms by *comparatively* examining several translations of one original text carried out in different periods by various translators. The comparison reveals the different definitions of translation, the priorities of the translators, and the often subconscious rules influencing the decision process. Ironically, Toury's comparison technique does not involve actual texts. In order to carry out a series of comparisons and to measure the shifts revealing the norms which determine them, Toury "uses" an ideal invariant third text which is the "adequate translation," not based on a comparison to the original and various historically bound texts, but on abstract linguistic and literary theory (Toury, 1978: 93; 1980: 58). Toury has already posited the hypothesis that no translation is ever entirely acceptable to the target culture because of its estranging structural and verbal elements, nor can it be adequate to the source text because of the new cultural context in which it finds itself. Yet in order to determine the position of the translated text between the poles of source and target text extremes, Toury *also* posits the necessity of an ideal "invariant of comparison" which underlies the text in question and his entire theory in general:

> Thus, the transformed concept of adequacy finds its main use in the methodology of TT–ST comparison. In the methodological framework it is conceived of as a *hypothetical entity* constructable on the basis of a systemic (textemic) analysis of ST, and it is used as *the invariant of the comparison* (i.e, as a *tertium comparationis*).
>
> (Toury, 1980: 49, emphasis in original)

Contradicting everything his theory seemed previously to explicate, this hypothetical invariant is not conceived of as something which is subjectively determined or historically conditioned, but as something which exists in another realm, as a universal literary/linguistic form, which all (bilingual) humans have the ability to intuit. Surprisingly, Toury appeals to Chomsky's concept of competency and of formal universals:

> I would claim that the occurrence of interlanguage forms in translation follows from the very definition of this type of activity/product, thus being a formal "translation universal." [For the difference between the substantive and formal types of universals, cf. Chomsky (*Aspects of the Theory of Syntax*), 1965: 28–9.] Moreover, there are situations where interlanguage as a whole, or at least certain types/degrees of it, is not simply *present* in translation as living evidence of the universal, but even *preferred* to "pure" TL forms.
>
> (Toury, 1980: 72, emphasis in original)

The appeal to formal universals in an otherwise performance-oriented and material theory is an unexpected move. Toury's entire project has been to deconstruct source-oriented, static theoretical models of translation. Yet this hypothetical construct is based on that very same source-text oriented theory, completely static and unconditioned by literary evolution, exactly that which his evolutionary theory opposes. On the one hand, Toury posits the premise that every literary system is *different* from every other in terms of its structure and norms of usage; on the other hand, he suggests that the *same* structural universal form underlies two different language systems. This is the crux of the theoretical debate within current translation theory, and Toury adopts both positions. How is this possible?

Toury's work is based on Polysystem theory, which in turn is based on Russian Formalist conceptual thinking. His use of formal universals, of invariants of comparisons, although surprising, has an implicit foundation in the theory. Despite efforts to include differing socio-historical conditions, there is the underlying tendency throughout this "historically determined" theory toward "pure" formalism. Toury's theory evolves from his formalist and structuralist predecessors, and as such carries certain absolute notions which limit the conceptual framework. Toury's historical model includes numerous other static concepts as well: translated texts are viewed as empirical facts, cultural norms are defined as static, non-contradictory rules influencing the generation of actual texts, and multiple tendencies within historical epochs are reduced to unified behavioral laws. One has the sense, for example, from reading his conclusions of the study of translated prose fiction into Hebrew that his five or six "norms" apply to *all* the texts included in the study. His analysis documents the conformity, not the exceptions; perhaps of more interest, and more revealing about the nature of translation, would be a list of all the exceptions to the rules. In addition, both Even-Zohar and Toury still confine their analyses to entities called "literary" and tend, despite claims to the contrary, to divorce the evolving literary polysystem from other signifying systems in a culture. Toury, as Even-Zohar before him, tends toward structuralism; and although on the surface he accepts the "fact" that all languages are different, he suggests that underlying that difference is a unified and universal structural form. Because of our linguistic differences and cultural norms, we cannot articulate this form, but as "competent" bilingual speakers, we can still "know" it.

Fortunately, Toury's theory does not depend upon the existence of the *tertium comparationis* to function. Recent Translation Studies has found itself effectively using Toury's model in spite of his theoretical contradictions. In a review of Toury's book *In Search of a Theory of Translation*, Ria Vanderauwera finds that even Toury himself ignores his own formalist tendencies when applying his theory:

> Information about these norms can also be derived from extra-textual material (statements of translators, editors, publishers, critics) but first and foremost through a comparative study of source and target texts. Toury insists that this should happen via a *tertium comparationis*, a hypothetical third text and invariant of the comparison. I consider this an unnecessary complication and a relic of the formalisation urge that swept through linguistics and semiotics. Ironically enough, in his own two valuable case studies which conclude the book, Toury makes no use of this *tertium comparationis*.
>
> (Vanderauwera, 1982: 52)

The part of Toury's translation theory Translation Studies has adopted focuses on the socio-literary norms that govern the target culture and directly influence the process of translation. Several aspects of Toury's theory have contributed to development within the field: (1) the abandonment of one-to-one notions of correspondence as well as the possibility of literary/linguistic equivalence (unless by accident); (2) the involvement of literary tendencies within the target cultural system in the production of any translated text; (3) the destabilization of the notion of an original message with a fixed identity; (4) the integration of both the original text and the translated text in the semiotic web of intersecting cultural systems. Theoretically, Translation Studies adopts the performance aspect of Toury's theory, viewing translation as a process by which subjects of a given culture communicate in translated messages primarily determined by local cultural constraints. Inescapable infidelity is presumed as a condition of the process; translators do not work in ideal and abstract situations nor desire to be innocent, but have vested literary and cultural interests of their own, and *want* their work to be accepted within another culture. Thus they manipulate the source text to inform as well as conform with the existing cultural constraints.

TRANSLATION STUDIES IN THE EIGHTIES

Since Toury's 1980 book, the focus of Translation Studies has shifted from theory to descriptive work. A fairly well-defined group with similar interests has been meeting regularly (usually at meetings of the International Comparative Literature Association). Most of the discussions center around improving methods for describing literary translation and determining cultural and translational normative behavior. Only then, they argue, can one return to theory. Unfortunately, many of the discussions have been lost or have gone unpublished, making the 1985 collection edited by Theo Hermans titled *The Manipulation of Literature* a valuable record. In the introduction, Hermans, summarizing the basic assumptions of the group, argues that "the work of Itamar Even-Zohar in particular is directly associated with the new approach," and suggests that participating scholars share "a view of literature as a complex and dynamic system; a conviction that there should be a continual interplay between theoretical models and practical case studies; an approach to literary translation that is descriptive, target-oriented, functional, and systemic; and an interest in the norms and constraints that govern the production and reception of translation" (Hermans, 1985: 10–11).

Such a target-oriented empirical approach depended upon and was derived from case studies, which is why the methodological concerns for describing translations became increasingly important. José Lambert and Hendrik van Gorp offer a report on their efforts, sketching a very complex model in "On Describing Translations" in *The Manipulation of Literature*. Briefly, they suggest that all functionally relevant aspects of translation activity in its historical context need to be carefully observed. Thus, the author, text, reader, and literary norms in one literary system is juxtaposed to an author, text, reader, and literary norms in another literary system. The link or relationship between the two systems is an open one, and Lambert and Van Gorp argue that predictions about the relationships initially should be kept to a minimum. Only after careful study and the analysis of the dominant norms of the target system can the nature of the relation be determined. Lambert and Van Gorp call for not only a study of the relation between authors, texts, readers, and norms in the two differing systems, but also for relations between authors' and the translators' intentions, between pragmatics and reception in source and target systems, between authors and other writers in the source and target systems, between the differing literary systems, and even between differing sociological aspects including publishing and distribution (Lambert and Van Gorp, 1985: 43–5). While admitting that the process is "utopian" – it is impossible to summarize all the relationships generated – Lambert and Van Gorp do suggest that the scholar, by establishing priorities, can find a means of being systematic instead of intuitive.

The advantage of the systemic approach over previous approaches is perhaps best demonstrated by its application. A school has grown up in Leuven, Belgium, centered around such case studies and descriptive work. Lambert, Lieven D'Hulst, Katrin van Bragt, and graduate students at the University of Leuven, for example, have been researching *Littérature et traduction en France, 1800–1850* (D'Hulst, Lambert, Bragt, 1979; see also D'Hulst, 1982; Lambert, 1982; Bragt, 1982). Several other students have written master's theses based upon such descriptive models, and other projects are forming. Lefevere, Hermans, and Van den Broeck have been researching the translations into Dutch during a similar period as the French study. Still others have been dealing with intracultural relationships of the *literatures* within Belgium. Yet virtually nothing has been published, and the silence is itself problematic. Two books on the research at Leuven have been promised: one is a comprehensive summary of the research project on "Literature and Translation in France 1800–1850"; the other by Van Bragt on her case study of *The Vicar of Wakefield* translations.

Indications exist, however, where this research is headed. Lambert begins to talk about insights gained from the research of translations into French during the nineteenth century in a 1986 article entitled "Les Relations littéraires internationales comme problème de réception" and in his 1988 article "Twenty Years of Research on Literary Translation at the Katholieke Universiteit Leuven." In the development of the French literary system, Lambert argues that the motivation behind text selection and translational policy was directly related to the genre system in the target culture (Lambert, 1988: 131). Genre rules and genre policy clearly played a central role in literary policy at the time, in which translated literature played a role as literary imports, and thereby influenced the complex relationships of imports and exports within the literary tradition. Lambert then compares such literary "interferences" with a different situation in Belgian French literature in search of regularities in systemic behavior. He sees the possibility of further checking such hypotheses by studying the situation in other European countries. By focusing on "norms" and "models," he argues, scholars may find the "ground for comparison" they are seeking (Lambert, 1988: 132). Norms determine what kind of translational relations ensue; every instant of the translation process is governed by norms. Only when the researchers/scholars know the preliminary and operational norms can they see the principles that shape the subsequent text. The theoretical contribution during the eighties by the Polysystem theory and Translation Studies scholars may be the discovery of the importance of first establishing what norms govern translation behavior before analyzing specific translations (cf. Hermans, 1991). For Lambert and the Belgian/Dutch group, norms determine the way foreign material is "imported" and "domesticated." Thus, the very definition of translation becomes dependent upon norms and how they work in any given system/society.

Kitty Van Leuven-Zwart, Head of the Translation Studies Department at the University of Amsterdam, also begins with

Toury's argument that the descriptive branch must focus upon investigating norms and strategies, but argues that the systematic comparison of translations and source texts has been neglected by Toury's followers in Leuven. She argues that many researchers lack a system of description, which makes their claims about norms and strategies unverifiable. Instead, she has devised a system for the comparison and description of translations that traces shifts on a microstructural level (words, clauses, and sentences), relates the consequences of the microlevel shifts on the macrostructural level (characters, events, time, and other "meaningful" components), and categorizes them (Van Leuven-Zwart, 1984; 1989: 154–5). In contrast to much of the "top-down" work going on in Germany, Van Leuven-Zwart's approach might be characterized as a "bottom-up" approach. Beginning with Popovič's neutral concept of "shift," and extending Miko's inventory for categorizing devices to include not just stylistic shifts, but syntactic, semantic, and pragmatic shifts as well, she has developed a very complex and difficult model with great numbers of categories and subcategories which her students – some seventy are involved (most working on translations of twentieth-century Spanish prose into Dutch) – use to describe translation. Her method in fact not only shows that every word contains shifts, but that frequently the words or clauses translated show multiple shifts. Shifts come to be seen not as mistranslations or violations of rules of equivalence, but as the rule itself. According to the Amsterdam study, 70 percent of the translations *averaged* a 100 percent number of shifts (Van Leuven-Zwart, 1990: 88). These shifts, she argues, cannot help but impact the text at the macrostructural level. Designed primarily to help practicing translators better understand the process of translation and contribute to descriptive studies, her research is also documenting certain unseen complexities of the cultural transfer process and giving valuable insights not only into the nature of translation, but the nature of language itself.

Thus one can see how the descriptive branch in Translation Studies of the eighties in turn influences the theory. By looking for regularities in translational phenomena in real cultural situations, the very definitions of the phenomena being investigated are changing; traditional concepts are being undermined; and the theory is evolving. Much discussion has taken place revaluating the very definition of what a translated text is. The Dutch/

Flemish group has found that translations sometimes "hide" within the foreign model. In daily use, for example, people occasionally find themselves using a translation without being aware of it. Borderline cases such as pseudo-translations (translations when no original exists; Toury, 1984) and translations via an intervening language (secondary translations; Toury, 1988) are being investigated. Translations not identified as such by a culture, including extreme cases of translational activity such as film adaptations, versions, imitations, or false translations, are being included in research efforts (Lambert, 1989a). Non-translation within a translation (proper names, etc.) seems to be much more prevalent than initially anticipated.

As the research expands to incorporate new phenomena, so too are larger frames of reference needed in order to carry out further investigation. Data seem to indicate that translations are much harder to identify than was initially apparent. As a result, translations cannot be investigated without recourse to an investigation of other kinds of discourse. Definitions of what a society is and the links between society and language are also being questioned. Questions are being raised as to whether one should study translations as texts, as concepts, or as systems (Toury, 1986). The translational relationships between the source and target text are being replaced by networks of relationships and concepts of intertextuality (Toury, 1986; Lambert, 1989a). If anything can be agreed upon regarding the theory of Translation Studies, it is that the field requires an "open" theory, less involved in *a priori* definitions, and more involved in raising questions. If at any given time the theory being used does not prove productive, excludes certain translational phenomena, or limits certain insights, Translation Studies scholars tend to reject or revise it. Questions raised in theory, in turn, influence research projects for the accumulation of more data. Holmes' call in *The Name and Nature of Translation Studies* (1972/5) for a dialectically evolving theory interacting with descriptive research has indeed been realized.

Even-Zohar's and Toury's system theory work has helped Translation Studies break down certain conceptual barriers and find a method for better describing translations. The data from the descriptive research informs further theoretical speculation. Even-Zohar has not only furthered our understanding of the translation process; he also is the only system theorist to recognize the importance of translation within the study of any individual literature. Yet, in many ways, he seems almost dogmatically committed to Polysystem theory, which, as another kind of structuralism, limits that which it can conceptualize. The empirical claim upon which Polysystem theory was founded, i.e., that it looks at actual texts in a target system, seems to be dissolving in light of recent investigations. Even-Zohar's claim for "objective" analysis of "literary" facts seems even less tenable. He remained surprisingly silent during the eighties, and his theoretical contributions have been missed. Despite the usefulness of his method for studying translated texts, Van Bragt, Lambert, Van Leuven-Zwart, and others seem open to other theoretical interpretations of the data and other theoretical possibilities regarding the nature of translation. Toury and Even-Zohar seem to always embed systemic features and norms into ever broadening systems, which seem hierarchically conceived from their initial presuppositions. Lambert, on the other hand, while beginning from a similar position within systems theory, seems more inclined to observe the data and to see how it fits without presuppositions, acknowledging that the observed facts may or may not fit within the hierarchical structure. While retaining a systemic approach and reasoning inductively, Lambert seems to be suggesting that the system as conceived may not function as the investigating scholar initially thought, and is open to the study of "other" patterned behavior which may help explain translational phenomena. While being one of Polysystem theory's strongest advocates during the eighties, Lambert and his Leuven colleagues have simultaneously been revaluating the terminology, hierarchical structures, and fixed notions of what a translation is.

Translation scholars in England and America like Bassnett, Lefevere (who moved to America in the early eighties), David Lloyd, and Maria Tymoczko seem to be distancing themselves even further from Even-Zohar's polysystem model, which they find too formalistic and restrictive. Adopting more of a cultural studies model, they focus both on institutions of prestige and power within any given culture and patterns in literary translation. While the Polysystem theory hypothesis is being "used" by this Anglo-American branch of Translation Studies, they also suggest further considerations need to be included. In a series of articles over the past decade, all written since his move to the United States, Lefevere, for example, seems in the process of dropping the inductive and scientific approach in favor of a more deductive and less formalistic method. While distancing himself from polysystem vocabulary, he introduces a new set of terms to better analyze the influence of the extraliterary upon the literary.

In 1981 in "Beyond the Process: Literary Translation in Literature and Literary Theory," Lefevere argues that literary systems do not occur in a vacuum and to his list of predecessors he adds the name of Pavel Medvedev, who locates the literary system within the "ideological" milieu of an era (Lefevere, 1981a: 56). Medvedev's 1928 book *The Formal Method in Literary Scholarship*, which became a model for the "science" of ideology may actually have been written by Mikhail Bakhtin. Lefevere begins in the article to not just look at lexical shifts and the introduction of literary devices via translation, but to also ask questions about the ideological pressures on the translator and strategies that the translator has for influencing the intellectual milieu. By "ideology" Lefevere understands, "a set of discourses which wrestle over interests which are in some way relevant to the maintenance or interrogation of power structures central to a whole form of social and historical life" (Eagleton, 1985: 116; qtd. by Lefevere, 1988–9: 59). The dominant set of discourses can be overtly manifest, as was the case in Eastern Europe for many years, but more frequently function covertly, as is perhaps true in many Western countries. While various subsystems – the literary included – wrestle over often competing interests, they are all subject to, either consciously or subconsciously, a prevailing ideology characteristic of the society at a given point in history.

In another 1981 article, "Translated Literature: Towards an Integrated Theory," Lefevere talks less in terms of Polysystem theory, and more in terms of studying existing translations and constructing "historical grammars" in order to describe translational phenomena. In order to show how the ideological component limits literary discourse, he introduces the concept of the "refracted text," by which he means "texts that have been processed for a certain audience (children, for example), or adapted to a certain poetics or a certain ideology" (Lefevere, 1981b: 72). Abridged and edited versions of classics for children or for television might be characterized as the most obvious forms of refractions. In Germany, both during the Nazi period and subsequently in what was East Germany, many texts by writers such as Heine and Schiller were often refracted to conform to a specific poetics and ideology. Yet refractions are often less obvious. Lefevere, for example, has written an article called "Mother Courage's Cucumbers: Text, System and Refraction in a Theory of Literature" (1982b) that shows how Brecht's work has been refracted in the West to better conform to prevailing artistic norms and ideology in the Anglo-American world. Another good example of how ideological constraints influence the production of literary texts can be found in David Lloyd's "Translator as Refractor; Towards a Re-reading of James Clarence Mangan as Translator" (1982), in which he applies Lefevere's concept of refraction not only to much of the writing of Mangan, but also to the broader field of Irish literature in general in the nineteenth century. The questions the Anglo-American branch raise at this point do not ignore the fact that translated texts introduce new literary devices into another literary system, but also suggest that refractions are much involved in larger sociological phenomena as well. In 1984, in "That Structure in the Dialect of Man Interpreted," Lefevere defines and adds the concept of "patronage" to his model in order to better investigate such ideological pressures. By "patronage" he means "any kind of force that can be influential in encouraging and propagating, but also in discouraging, censoring and destroying works of literature" (Lefevere, 1984: 92). Patrons, he argues, can be individuals, such as the Medicis or Louis XIV; groups, such as a religious body or a political party; or institutions, such as publishing firms or school systems.

By the time of his article "Why Waste our Time on Rewrites" in Hermans' 1985 collection *The Manipulation of Literature*, Lefevere's tone is very reader friendly, and he avoids the scientific vocabulary characteristic of Polysystem theory discourse. He also stops trying to be purely objective in his investigations, arguing that nobody can escape one's own ideology, suggesting that those disciplines which claim objectivity are "dishonest." He raises questions about distinctions between literary and non-literary, especially when made by those governing literary discourse in a given society. He distances himself from any theory that sees literature as deterministic and that makes predictions about its evolution. Instead, he introduces the term "stochastic," a Greek word that recalls both proceeding by guesswork and, literally, proceeding by "skillful aiming," to describe a system whose evolution involves probability *and* random variables. He also begins to see that the study of literary systems cannot be divorced from studying other systems of power, such as the educational system.

And most importantly, for the first time within the Translation Studies perspective, he acknowledges that the study of literary systems cannot be isolated to its Euro-American development.

The best example of a scholar using Lefevere's methodology and new terminology is Maria Tymoczko's 1986 article "Translation as a Force for Literary Revolution in the Twelfth-Century Shift from Epic to Romance" (Tymoczko, 1986). Tymoczko looks not only at new literary devices introduced into the French culture via translation, but also uses concepts such as patronage and socio-economic forces at play during the era to explain systemic evolution. She uses the polysystem hypothesis to look at shifts in the literary system as introduced by translation, and recognizes changes in genre, meter, and rhyming strategies. But she also sees changes that cannot be explained using a formalist methodology: innovations during the twelfth century included new value structures, changes in the role for women, and the introduction of romantic love. Using Lefevere's terminology, she traces the evolution of the patronage system, showing how, by the end of the twelfth century, the position of epic singers had gone down and the patrons favored instead lettered translators, adaptors, and authors. She explains this shift by contextualizing the literary system within the socio-economic system, including factors such as the increasing power of the clerical class, the emerging universities, and the importance of translation for facilitating communication between French, English, Scandinavian, Irish, Welsh, and other specific regions of French culture (Tymoczko, 1986: 18–19). Translation thus plays a crucial role formally and ideologically in the emerging written system. Upper-class society became more secure during this period, and translations served both to provide employment for underemployed clerks as well as satisfy the aristocratic classes' demand for new ideas. Translators, she argues, were not disinterested parties, but tried to secure advantage within the patronage system, and thus conformed to as well as participated in the changing ideology of the age. By using both inductive and deductive reasoning, Tymoczko shows how the written literature was responsive to and reflective of ideological as well as poetological forces.

Thus, after a decade of research, Translation Studies scholars seem to be diverging, and whether they will continue to constitute a "school" remains open. Yet certain generalizations can be ascertained. Despite explicit claims to the contrary, there is a tendency to view translations less as an empirical fact – a concrete text as defined by the target culture – and more as a complex set of translational relations in any given situation. The translated text is viewed as simultaneously drawing on families of resemblances as well as writing itself into other families of resemblances. Descriptive Translation Studies research during the eighties shows how the translated text is inscribed in the shifting web of intertextuality and how translation "facts" seem to be more constructed than material. Ironically, although Translation Studies defined itself as an institutional science and derived support from the government, the academia, and even private sectors, the research by both the Belgian/Dutch group and the tangential Anglo-American branch seems to be preparing the ground for post-structuralist analysis. As a phenomenon, translation seems to subvert any such systematic approach to its own study, and may indeed subvert itself, disappearing as claims categorizing it are articulated. The next chapter will deal with one such possibility for further thought, that of deconstruction, which offers ways of viewing translational phenomena that Translation Studies scholars have systematically avoided.

Chapter 6

Deconstruction

TURMOIL AND *TEL QUEL*

The translation theories examined thus far all depend upon some notion of equivalence: the same aesthetic experience (Chapter 2), linguistic structural/dynamic equivalence (Chapter 3), corresponding literary function (Chapter 4), or similar formal correlation governed by social acceptability in the target culture (Chapter 5). Despite differing approaches, each theory is unified by a conceptual framework which assumes original presence and a re-presentation of it in the receiving society. Even-Zohar and Toury tried to escape the epistemological strait-jacket that the power of the original text retains over the translation by reviewing the problem of translation in terms of the actual product rather than the ideal of a "faithful" version, but in the end they found it difficult to escape limitations imposed by their Formalist roots, scientific approach, and dualistic epistemological assumptions. The question remains whether it is possible to think about translational phenomena in other than traditional terms. To date, all translation theories have made rigid distinctions between original texts and their translations, distinctions which determine subsequent claims about the nature of translation. Yet a radical redrawing of the questions upon which translation theory is founded is being undertaken by deconstructionists. While certain practitioners distance themselves from the term "deconstruction" in favor of "affirmative productivity" (Vance, 1985: 135–6), for the sake of clarity I will use the term deconstruction.

Questions being posed by deconstructionists include the following: What if one theoretically reversed the direction of thought and posited the hypothesis that the original text is dependent upon the translation? What if one suggested that, without translation, the original text ceased to exist, that the very survival of the original depends not on any particular quality it contains, but upon those qualities that its translation contains? What if the very definition of a text's meaning was determined not by the original, but by the translation? What if the "original" has no fixed identity that can be aesthetically or scientifically determined but rather changes each time it passes into translation? What exists *before* the original? An idea? A form? A thing? Nothing? Can we think in terms of pre-original, pre-ontological conditions? Deconstructionists not only raise questions challenging fundamental notions prevalent in all the theories discussed above but also question the very nature of the act of raising such questions. Foucault, as we shall see later, calls into question the questioner, suggesting that this particular age is characterized less as one in which man poses the questions and more as one in which questions arise from something inherent in language itself. Deconstructionists go so far as to suggest that perhaps the *translated text writes us* and not we the translated text.

Deconstruction challenges limits of language, writing, and reading by pointing out how the definitions of the very terms used to discuss concepts set boundaries for the specific theories they describe. While not offering a specific "translation theory" of its own, deconstruction, however, does "use" translation often both to raise questions regarding the nature of language and "being-in-language" as well as to suggest that in the process of translating texts, one can come as close as is possible to that elusive notion or experience of *différance*, which "underlies" their approach. Such thinking about the nature of translation and the nature of language, thus, becomes important to translation theorists, not because it necessarily defines another approach, but because it deepens and broadens the conceptual framework by which we define the very field itself. I suggest that the shift to a more philosophic stance from which the entire problematic of translation can be better viewed may not only be beneficial for translation theory, but that after such a confrontation, the discourse which has limited the development of translation theory will invariably undergo a transformation, allowing new insights and fresh interdisciplinary approaches, breaking, if you will, a logjam of stagnated terms and notions.

In Anglo-American circles, deconstruction is not an approach normally associated with translation theory, either by literary translators or linguists; in Belgium and the Netherlands, few of the researchers mention its existence, let alone deem it appropriate for their discussions. I would like to suggest, however, that the deconstructionists' entire project is intricately relevant to questions of translation theory, and that their thinking is seminal to any understanding of the theoretical problems of the translation process. Jacques Derrida, for example, suggests that deconstruction and translation are inexorably interconnected, intimating that in the process of translation, that elusive impossible presence he refers to as *différance* may, to the highest degree possible, be visible: "In the limits to which it is possible or at least *appears* possible, translation practices the difference between signified and signifier" (Derrida, 1981: 21). All of Derrida's writing, regardless of the "subject matter" or text in question, continually revolves around problems pertaining to the possibility or impossibility of translation. According to Derrida, *all* of philosophy is centrally concerned with the notion of translation: "the origin of philosophy is translation or the thesis of translatability" (Derrida, 1985b: 120). He challenges the reader (and especially the translator) to think and rethink every moment a translation solution is posed, an item named, an identity fixed, or a sentence inscribed. With each naming gesture, Derrida suggests a footnote, a note in the margin, or a preface also is in order to retrieve those subtle differing supplementary meanings and tangential notions lost in the process of transcription. With the focus of philosophical investigation redirected from identity to difference, from presence to supplement, from text to preface, translation assumes a central rather than secondary place; for it is here that Derrida creates tension, casts doubts, and offers alternatives. The process of translation offers, as near as may be approached, a mode of differing/deferring that subverts modes of traditional metaphysical thinking that have historically dominated assumptions about translation specifically as well as philosophy in general.

In contrast to all the theories discussed in this study, at the foundation of Derrida's thought is the assumption that there is *no* kernel or deep structure, nothing that we may ever discern – let alone represent, translate, or found a theory on. Rather, Derrida "bases" his "theory" of deconstruction on non-identity, on non-presence, on unrepresentability. What does exist, according to Derrida, are different chains of signification – including the "original" and its translations in a symbiotic relationship –

mutually supplementing each other, defining and redefining a phantasm of sameness, which never has existed nor will exist as something fixed, graspable, known, or understood. This phantasm, produced by a desire for some essence or unity, represses the possibility that whatever may be there is always in motion, in flux, "at play," escaping in the very process of trying to define it, talk about it, or make it present. The subject of translation theory has traditionally involved some concept of determinable meaning that can be transferred to another system of signification. Deconstruction questions such a definition of translation and uses the practice of translation to demonstrate the instability of its own theoretical framework. Deconstruction resists systems of categorization which separate "source" text from "target" text or "language" from "meaning," denies the existence of underlying forms independent of language, and questions theoretical assumptions which presume originary beings, in whatever shape or form. In translation, what is visible is language referring not to things, but to language itself. Thus the chain of signification is one of infinite regress – the translated text becomes a translation of another earlier translation and translated words, although viewed by deconstructionists as "material" signifiers, represent nothing but other words representing nothing but still other words representing.

The deconstructionist alternative arose primarily in France in the late 1960s during a time of social and political upheaval. At the same time that the events of May 1968 were threatening to topple de Gaulle's regime, a group of formalists joined a group of leftists and began collectively publishing their work in the Parisian journal *Tel Quel* , the name which became associated with the group (see Sollers and Hayman, 1981; Kristeva, 1983; Bann, 1984). *Tel Quel* in the late sixties was composed of publications by central members Philippe Sollers, Julia Kristeva, Marcelin Pleynet, Jean Pierre Faye, Jacqueline Risset, and Jean Ricardou as well as by more temporary members such as Roland Barthes, Tzvetan Todorov, Pierre Boulez, Jean-Louis Houdebine, Guy Scarpetta, and Derrida. Todorov, who had joined the group from Bulgaria, and Barthes were decidedly Formalist, and Kristeva, also from Bulgaria, was well versed in the study of Russian Formalism. From another direction, Louis Althusser, although not considered a member of the group, practiced a form of deconstruction while retaining a Marxist dialectic and a scientific methodology, and exerted enormous influence. The members of *Tel Quel* read both Jakobson and Marx at the same time, neither rejecting nor identifying with either, deliberately refusing to resolve the contradiction of such a stance in order to open up new avenues of thought.

That its evolution reflected the political and social turmoil in France during the late sixties was more than coincidence. In his book *Readings and Writings: Semiotic Counter-Strategies*, Peter Wollen suggests that May 1968 "brought *Tel Quel* in its wake" (Wollen, 1982: 210), but clearly the alternative mode of thinking by the young radicals served to bring about the events of May as well. In 1965 Tzvetan Todorov published *Théorie de la littérature* , the first translation of a selection of Russian Formalist essays to appear in France, and it had enormous impact on the group. Julia Kristeva, who joined the *Tel Quel* editorial board in 1970, was well-versed in both Chomskian and Czechoslovakian linguistics. She greatly admired the work of Bakhtin, for example, but suggested in her essay "The Ruin of a Poetics" (1973) that although his work was substantially correct, it did not go far enough, especially when it began to introduce sociological and ideological aspects into the structuralist framework (Kristeva, 1973). Derrida, too, admits the necessary stage of structuralism for the activity of deconstruction. In *Of Grammatology* he suggests that Saussure did not see his project through to its ultimate conclusions, that what was "chased off" by its attempt to limit and contain has come back "to haunt language" (Derrida, 1974: 43–4).

Deconstructionists, like Translation Studies scholars, analyze the differences, slips, changes, and elisions that are part of every text. Indeed, it is within such a notion of comparison that social and subjective factors can be seen to operate as constraints. Just as Formalist roots have helped Translation Studies focus on actual texts rather than on hypothetical ones, so too is deconstruction tied to the text which it reads. As both "fields" move toward a position that attempts to avoid independent, preconceived concepts from which to categorize, interpret, and evaluate texts, the value of deconstruction for a post-structuralist theory of translation may now be apparent. Yet Russian Formalism, as Saussurian linguistics, is based upon form/content distinctions, on the signified/signifier distinctions that ground traditional metaphysical philosophy, and still troubles Translation Studies. This dichotomized thinking and the hierarchies generated by such distinctions (privileging literary over non-literary, the metaphysical over the referential, or pure thought over surface structure) are the same distinctions that deconstruction finds limiting and against which it operates. In terms of translation theory, which invariably posits some determinable meaning as that which must be reconstituted in another language, the very separation of language from an identifiable meaning or deep structure becomes the target of deconstruction's questions and thus a fruitful place to begin reexamination of translation theory in general. Derrida frequently refers to "something which is never spoken" – something unthought or, as I will argue, language itself speaking, a notion traditionally viewed as beyond the scope of translation theory. In this chapter I suggest that translation theory can no longer avoid such questions.

FOUCAULT AND DE-STRUCTURING THE CONCEPT OF ORIGINAL

In the epigraph to *Language, Counter-memory, Practice* (1977), Michel Foucault cites Jorge Luis Borges as saying, "The fact is that every writer *creates* his own precursors. His work modifies our conception of the past, as it will modify the future" (Foucault, 1977: 5). The notion that the translator creates the original is one which is introduced by deconstructionists and serves to undermine the notion of authorship and with it the authority on which to base a comparison of subsequent translated versions of a text. Deconstructionists argue that original texts are constantly being rewritten in the present and each reading/translation reconstructs the source text. In his essay "What is an Author?" in *Language, Counter-memory, Practice*, Foucault addresses these problems, noting that traditional notions of original authorship, of original acts of creation, of the unity of an original text, of translation equivalence or similitude, and systems of valorization are at the foundation of our understanding of literature and translation. He suggests that by granting primordial status to writing, we reinscribe in transcendental terms an affirmation of the text's sacred origin. Traditional translation theory holds dear such notions of both the author and the primordial status of an original text. Any translation of an original into a second language involves a violation of the original, thus the impossibility of ever creating "pure" equivalents. Foucault attempts to break down the traditional notion of the author, and instead suggests we think in terms of "author-function" (Foucault, 1977: 130–1). Instead of a fixed originary identity, Foucault recommends focusing on the relationships of texts with other texts and viewing the specific discourse of a particular text within its historical situation. According to Foucault, the author's work is not the result of spontaneous inspiration, but is tied to the institutional systems of the time and place over which the individual author has little control or awareness. Thus the "act of creation" is in reality a series of complex processes which the designation "author" serves to simplify. Foucault prefers not to think of the author as an actual individual, but as a series of subjective positions, determined not by any single harmony of effects, but by gaps, discontinuities, and breakages.

The discourse of the text will show how these discontinuities destructure the notion of a unified, ahistorical, transcendental, original text. With such an historical approach, Foucault argues, critics will learn to laugh at the "solemnities" of truth and instead focus on the interplay of forces, of subjectivities, of positions and possibilities. Gaps, reversals, differences, contradictions, and silences are just as important in determining "meaning" as that which is coherent, unified, and explicitly articulated.

A definition and conception of what Foucault calls the Modern versus the Classical Age is central to his argument in "What is an Author?" Traditional translation theory, based on conceptions of harmony, unified texts, an original idea which can be captured by an analogous text, can be thought of as grounded in what Foucault calls a "classical" conception of representation. During the eighteenth century, according to Foucault, language established relations to identity – language was perceived as a form of knowing and knowing was already discourse. Just as scientists such as Linnaeus researched the natural sciences during this period, so too can the "theory" of the world be seen as interwoven in a theory of words. Natural history, for example, always attempted to reveal the true order, the true foundations behind the scene of everyday life, by using names to give things their true denomination. In the chapter "Classifying" from *The Order of Things* (1973), Foucault suggests that, during the eighteenth century, to "know" nature was to "build" upon the basis of language a "true" language, one which revealed the conditions in which all language was possible (Foucault, 1973: 161–2). Patterns

of reality were discovered, taxonomies begun, abstract characteristics defined, and essences described; orders and genres were
established that continue into today's age, including some of the
translation theories discussed in this book. For this enterprise,
language required the similarity of impressions, and thus the
presupposition of an arrangement of reality to conform to the
discourse of the period – one which posited universals of being,
the primacy of the knowing subject, and a language capable of
describing those universals.

This harmonious view of the world was shattered at the end of
the eighteenth century. In the chapter entitled "Labor, Life and
Language" of *The Order of Things*, Foucault elaborates, suggesting
that in the nineteenth century discourse becomes the subject of
discourse. The author no longer uses language and then stands
outside of it, but the language is conceived as also "inside" the
creating subject and as having its own producing effect. Humboldt, Bopp, Grimm, and others begin their investigations and
comparisons of languages; philology makes its appearance, and
grammatical structures are described. Foucault suggests that a
double break occurred during this period: languages broke with
their ties to the represented thing and broke their link with the
general continuity of the natural order, thus gaining a life of their
own. As the "discontinuity" of subsystems revealed "organic"
structures in all their diversity, so too were languages detached
from a broad, unified system and the heterogeneity of various
grammatical systems emerged (Foucault, 1973: 292–3). According to Foucault, while language becomes divorced from the thing
represented, it also paradoxically remains the only medium
through which the thing can be known. Language thus becomes
simultaneously elevated and demoted during this period, and
grammatic structures are seen as an *a priori* of what can be
expressed. Philosophical truths are thus trapped in the web of
discourse, and analysis must work backwards from the opinions,
truths, and even sciences to the *words* that make them possible.
Production of anything – from commodities to literary texts – is
no longer conceived as structured around individual consciousness, but rather around the age, or, according to Foucault, the
discourse of the age, which actually *creates* the individual. Language, especially "literary" language, therefore, takes on a whole
new mode of existence; it ceases to play the role of the metaphysical revealer/mediator of philosophical truths and becomes more

and more self-referential, merely a manifestation of its own "precipitous" existence. Foucault argues that it breaks with the whole definition of genres and becomes merely a manifestation of language that has "no other law than that of affirming" (Foucault, 1973: 300). During this period, then, forms of authority cease to impose laws; genres and forms cease to be viewed as eternal; and the structure of any notion of originality breaks down.

In the "Modern Age," language has become an authority unto itself. Even the author becomes a "function" of discourse, dissolving into the text writing itself. In "What is an Author?" Foucault quotes Samuel Beckett as posing the Nietzschean question "What matter who's speaking?" Man as well as God has disappeared into the evolution of language writing itself. The fundamental question of the Modern Age, according to Foucault, is no longer how one accumulates knowledge to become an authority and pass judgment on the world, but one of how we can think that which we cannot think. In "Man and his Doubles" from *The Order of Things*, he argues that that which is unthought, that which escapes as language writes itself, but nevertheless forms us, our speech, and thought patterns, has become the object of the deconstructionist inquiry:

> The question is no longer: How can experience of nature give rise to necessary judgments? But rather: How can man think what he does not think, inhabit as though by a mute occupation something that eludes him, animate with a kind of frozen movement that figure of himself that takes the form of a stubborn exteriority? How can man *be* that life whose web, pulsations, and buried energy constantly exceed the experience that he is immediately given of them?
>
> (Foucault, 1973: 323)

Although Foucault makes no predictions as to what the answers to his own questions are, he does point us in a direction: toward a reflection on that which is silent, an illumination of that which is dark, and a restoration to language of that which has been mute. This "Other" has not been, nor can it be, illuminated in the sense of a positive knowledge, but rather as a blind spot or dark region which accompanies conscious thought. He conceives of the "Other" as man's double because it has, "like a shadow," accompanied man "mutely and uninterruptedly" since the nineteenth century (Foucault, 1973: 326–7). Deconstruction thus shifts the nature of the questions being asked about a literary work and its meaning from the audible to the mute. The author's creative role is reduced and new questions are raised about where the discourse of any particular text comes from, if not the author. The originality of the initial text is thus also called into question, and other determining factors emerge with regard to what can and cannot be thought within a particular discourse. Most importantly, the "meaning" of a text is reconsidered, and silent elements are returned to the language of a text, visible in contradictions, gaps, and omissions. In addition (im)possible meanings are returned to words, meanings which always accompanied them, but were covered up by the nature of the evolution of the discourse in Western culture in general, and in the eighteenth century in particular. Thus, in practice, deconstructionists tend to exhibit a great indifference to authors and explicit meanings, and instead tune into the language speaking itself, listening for the unheard, the ungraspable – that which is there and yet is not there, lost in that space between signified and the signifier.

Deconstructionists are attracted to translated texts, in which they claim the affirmative play of words in and of themselves can be seen and repressed meanings can and do return, often implicitly, to the present. By means of their practice of writing – even their most "philosophical" texts, with all their footnotes, prefaces, supplements, *double entendres*, and notes in the margins, can be viewed as a kind of translation – deconstructionists are challenging traditional translation theory to expand its borders, encouraging it to consider its own limitations, psychology, unconscious restraints, and the implications of its rhetoric. In translation, the possibility that *nothing* exists behind language except its own pattern of infinite regression can be confronted, and the mere play of language in and of itself can be revealed. This openness to absolute nothingness, to death, to finitude is characteristic of the thought of Martin Heidegger, who has destructured metaphysical theories of translation and opened the way to thinking about that which language denies.

HEIDEGGER AND THE LIMITS OF NAMING

One of the first attempts to break the stranglehold of metaphysical conceptual approaches to translation was Heidegger's *Sein und Zeit* (1927) (*Being and Time* (1962)), wherein one can locate the beginnings of the practice of deconstruction. Ironically, it was not an allusion to any philosophical truths that enabled Heidegger to escape the metaphysical limitations, but writing about questions of language, about poetry, and about translation, which disclosed new avenues of thought. In a return to the most basic and most concrete question upon which all Western philosophy is based, Heidegger refrained from a discussion of the "meaning" of Being and instead asked about the very *conditions* for the possibility of ontological thought. *Being and Time*, thus, is less a philosophical description and more of a pre-ontological inquiry. The language framing such questions, however, is itself paradoxical in that the (thing) being investigated is defined by those very terms which are being cast into doubt. Yet, because of the provisional nature of Heidegger's text – he was not trying to answer the question, but to "stir" it, to provide a place and context for that question to occur – Heidegger avoided traditional conceptual notions and thus was able temporarily to circumvent the paradox. The text does not offer a proof, outline an argument, or reach a conclusion, but rather elaborates a process of de-centering, of beginning over and over again, of asking the questions of the being (*Seiende*) who is asking the question of Being (*Sein*). The process of really thinking about the question, of experiencing the question existentially (by not escaping into preconceived notions or historical definitions of Being outside of oneself) destructures the history of ontology and of how Being has traditionally been interpreted.

In *Being and Time*, Heidegger suggests that Being does not exist outside anything, certainly not outside of the place where the question occurs. The question happens only in the question, only happens as relations in language, poetry, and thought are formed. Being is not an answer to anything, for it is not an entity, a thing, a concept, an idea which is graspable, but more of a doubt, a lack of presence, an anxiety which signals absolute nothingness, always beyond the grasp. Heidegger avoids philosophic truths that serve merely to obscure this pre-ontological experience and tries to think in the absence of preconceptions, in the absence of timeless verities. His thought thus turns more and more to language as the essay unfolds, and he continually raises the question of Being, only to see any resemblance of an answer simultaneously disappear as he comes closer to coherently structuring the question. The two become intricately linked and intricately exclusive as Heidegger attempts to think through the discourse in which his own question is framed, and the question *without an answer* becomes the one which primarily guides his subsequent thinking.

Through the attempts to structure a question from where one might begin to locate an answer, Heidegger was able to see that language/thought restraints limited his thinking, and he began to destructure or deconstruct those limits. His method involved more and more play with the language, allowing it to speak for itself through its own variations and windings. In a process very similar to that of translation, and one which has become the governing methodology of deconstruction, Heidegger – by letting language speak itself, letting it take on its own energy and etymological resonance – was able to point to one way metaphysical thinking might be overcome. There is a sense in Heidegger's writing that once the philosophical debris is dismantled, a return to a pre-original moment is possible and that pre-ontological thought can be experienced. In the double movement of deconstruction – as a clearing-away of structures that congest *and* as an entering made possible by leaping over generations of traditional thought – translation enters theory (see Bernasconi, 1985: 15–17; Krell, 1986: 80–94). Translation becomes understood in terms of returning to the pre-originary, of allowing the virginal experience of language to occur. In order to speak original speech, to think the "Other" in Foucauldian terms – i.e., pre-metaphysical thought – one must *do* a translation. Translation is viewed as action, an operation of thought, a translation of our selves into the thought of the other language, and not a linguistic, scientific transfer from something into the present.

The movement of Heidegger's thought in *Being and Time*, thus, becomes important for translation theory. In *Being and Time* Heidegger was discussing questions cardinal to Western metaphysics, dealing with the idea of man as the being which raised the question of Being. Distancing himself from his own idea of the importance of the subject as a knowing being, Heidegger's thought soon turned to the importance of language as the force that destructures the subject, and, thus, in Foucauldian terminology, man becomes the subject of language. Being, as Heidegger first began thinking about it, disappears in language: the discourse of *Being and Time* points toward a way to transgress the limits of the literary text itself. Heidegger has progressed to the point Foucault suggests is characteristic of a certain kind of twentieth-century thought: rather than any one person speaking, language is speaking itself, and man is listening. If such a listening is possible, what does one hear? Heidegger argues that we do not hear everything, for there is something essential to the nature of language which cannot be heard or read. Something is withheld as language speaks. Words not only reveal what is there – "language is the house of Being" – but language also holds back. If we let language speak for itself, what is revealed is something about the nature of language: words not only show what is there, but also show what is there and at the same time is not (*was es gibt und gleichwohl nicht ist*) (Heidegger, 1971a: 88).

In "The Anaximander Fragment" in *Early Greek Thinking*, Heidegger gives us a glimpse of his theory of translation in his own translations of the Anaximander Fragment, the oldest fragment of Western thinking, the interpretation of which becomes crucial for Heidegger's philosophical claims. Heidegger rereads early Greek thinking primarily to discover an alternate way of viewing the world, of unearthing pre-Platonic and pre-Aristotelian modes of discourse. Heidegger does a little case study, first viewing two definitive translations into German – one by Nietzsche in 1873 and another by Herman Diels in 1903 – and then offers his own translation (Heidegger, 1975: 13–14). Despite the different intentions and methods by the two translators, Heidegger notes the similarity of the two translations, not just in terms of their literal "faithfulness," but also regarding the "conception" of Anaximander underlying both versions. The standard for judging the pre-Platonic or pre-Aristotelian philosophy is much the same, and is taken from the very philosophers who set the standard. Heidegger argues that this view has become firmly entrenched in Western philosophy (and Christian theology) as "universal conviction" (Heidegger, 1975: 14).

Heidegger raises the question whether the fragment can speak to us after all these years. Can the translator somehow circumvent the weight of history and the domination of historical explanation? To unearth the fragment's meaning, the translator is not helped by classical philology, historical interpretation, or psychology. Instead, by being in tune with the language, a "bond" which is "broader and stronger, but far less apparent" develops, and in this "thoughtful dialogue," the fragment can be translated (Heidegger, 1975: 19). Heidegger then offers his own version, allowing, he argues, the manifestation of the essence of Being in its withdrawal. Disassociating himself from literal connections and pre-conceived associations, he opens his mind for other possible meanings. For example, he does not translate *adikia* literally as "injustice," but instead hears *a-dikia* , suggesting that *dikia* is absent, that all is not right with things, and that something is out of joint, and offers "disjunction" as another possibility. Clearly, Heidegger is using the translation to achieve a kind of double writing: first, to displace and unsettle preconceived notions which Western readers bring to language in order to let something else occur; second, to raise again the question of Being as in *Being and Time*. Whether we accept his translation or not is less a goal of the essay; what matters is the recovery/return of the silent resonance of the saying. If this activity happens, language and thought yield to some other meaning, not some definitive entity outside of language, but something which dwells in, yet is covered up by, the dominant structures of language.

Despite apparent differences, Heidegger's translation theory is not all unlike early Translation Studies. He does assume that translations are conditioned by the conceptual categories govern-ing any given epoch, despite attempts to circumvent them. He also believes that with study and historical recontextualizing, one can come to some sort of conclusion as to what the author's intent was and thus uncover layers of obfuscation in order to arrive at some sort of originary intent or presence *before* its distortion. He then chooses words which defamiliarize, which function dif-ferently in today's society, to try to achieve the same effect or response which the original version evoked, in the process break-ing down the conceptual categories of his reader. In the above essay, he clearly presumes an originary intactness which has been covered over by the Greeks; the poet/translator is able to translate/transport himself to that original culture and recover that original naming which linguistic naming obscures. The intentional fallacy would apply no less to Heidegger's early Greek translations than it would to any purely functionally oriented theory.

Reservations about residues of originary presence notwith-standing, Heidegger's translation theory marks a significant shift, for he is not uncovering any author's original intention, but recovering a property of language itself. Heidegger comes to terms with that which *language* denies and which no theory outlined in this book remotely approaches. What is revealed to Heidegger by letting language speak for itself is that "the word implies the relation between the 'is' which is not, and the work which is in the same case of not being a being" (Heidegger, 1971a: 59). Heidegger points to a new kind of thinking – not thinking about what is there, what is named, but thinking about what is there and simultaneously not yet named, and can never be named, for it *is* not. One could relate this silent non-entity borne by language to what Foucault calls The Other, the twin of man, which is always carried by man and which has come to define the mode of being for modern (post-modern?) man. Thinking about what can never be named is difficult – Heidegger calls it a "simple ungraspable situation" – but for all its difficulty, theoretically it has become "properly worthy of thought" (Heidegger, 1971a: 88) and may force reconsideration by any contemporary theory of translation. The question of how man has disappeared as a speaking subject and how one can illuminate that which is silent in language is not answered, but used by Derrida, as I will attempt to show in the following section, to dismantle previous attempts to arrive at a theory of translation.

DERRIDA: TRANSLATION AND *DIFFÉRANCE*

Derrida's thinking about translation begins with the Heideggerean "concept" of a showing of that which is there and yet "is" not. In his essay "Différance" from *Margins of Philosophy* (1982), Derrida coins the neologism *"différance"* to refer not to what is there (language), but what is not there, and thus calls into question any ontological approach that attempts to determine a notion of Being based on presence. The term *différance* is derived from the Latin verb *differre* – meaning both to defer, to delay (implying a temporal horizon), and to differ (implying a spatial horizon) – yet with one distinct alteration: Derrida deliberately alters a letter, making a mistake, albeit inaudible: instead of writing *différence* – the substantive derived from the verb according to the rules of grammar – he writes *différance*, which sounds the same, yet graphically forces the reader to think in terms of the unheard – thereby invading the reader's subconscious with a non-existent sound. Yet Derrida is doing more than altering a letter to achieve a mere formalistic alienation effect. The term also calls to mind the gerund derived from the present participle *différant*, which does not exist in present-day French. He thus locates a non-term between a verb and a non-existent noun, suggesting a verb/noun between a subject and object, something that has been lost (or repressed) in the development of language. Derrida likens the term to something like the middle voice, an operation neither passive nor active, neither temporal nor spatial (Derrida, 1982: 9; see also Heidegger, 1962: 51; Scott, 1987: 67), a voice for all intents lost in Western metaphysical discourse.

Recalling Foucault's definition of "The Other" as man's mute twin, Derrida's rhetorical strategy in the essay "Différance" not only uses a term which explicitly refers to scission and division, but also, via its violation of the laws of writing with its inaudible mistake, via its subconsciously recalling a forgotten conceptual mode, uses "mute" irony to create a discourse of graphic and theoretical disorder below the surface of audible and rhetorical conformity. The technique works to defer traditional notions of reference and to delay its being subsumed within the discourse in which it occurs – not allowing it to be passed over, subsumed, understood and thus silenced. The method is not unlike certain formalist theories of translation, but Derrida's strategy differs slightly. Whereas formalist approaches are very much bound by the laws of grammar, and are calculated in order to achieve graphic accuracy and precise reference, Derrida's tack is more an empirical wandering, not bound to the responsibility of philosophy, to tradition, to evolution of language or thought systems, foregrounding instead movement along a surface of the written language, *play* without calculation, wandering without an end or *telos*.

As Heidegger talks about an aspect of language holding back, of withholding, so Derrida suggests the thinking in terms of *différance*, of deferring/differing, of an indeterminate play without an end, a referent, or a specific function. Derrida has also hypothesized that such thinking is impossible in this day and age, but he suggests that we may begin thinking at the margins of metaphysical categorical thinking and speculatively follow the detours of language instead of the agreed upon central path. In terms of translation, he suggests not looking at the original message, nor its codification, but the multiple forms and interconnections through which it must pass in order to speak, to refer at all. Derrida thus speculates, "supposing a play of forms without a determined and invariable substance, and also supposing in the practice of this play a retention and protection of differences, a spacing and temporization, a play of traces" (Derrida, 1982: 15)

By extension, one could also project a translation theory aimed at protecting differences, reinvigorating language with lost etymological resonances, thereby opening up new avenues of thought.

This is, of course, precisely the "ungraspable situation" Heidegger referred to as being older than writing, older than the pre-ontological questions even he raised, and certainly older than the "truth" of Being as pursued by Greco-Western philosophic investigation. Such an approach is alien to the psyche of man – the discourse which governs our thought, forces us to make reference to objects, narrows meaning, closes off alternative possibilities. Derrida's project is one of trying to unveil such a play of covered-up but subconsciously discernible traces without referring to some sort of deep underlying meaning. The problem, according to Derrida, is that the trace (of that particular thing which *is* not) can never be presented as a phenomenon might. (It) is always differing and deferring, erasing itself in the act of disclosure. Despite the difficulty of thinking this "inaudible" thought, Derrida does give us some valuable guidelines as to how one might approach the "concept" of understanding an unheard thought:

> Perhaps we must attempt to think this unheard-of thought, this silent tracing: that the history of Being, whose thought engages the Greco-Western *logos* such as it is produced via the ontological difference, is but an epoch of the *diapherein*. . . . Since Being has never had a "meaning," has never been thought or said as such, except by dissimulating itself in beings, then *différance*, in a certain and very strange way, (is) "older" than the ontological difference or than the truth of Being. When it has this age it can be called the play of the trace. The play of the trace which no longer belongs to the horizon of Being, but whose play transports and encloses the meaning of Being: the play of the trace, or the *différance*, which has no meaning and is not. Which does not belong. There is no maintaining, and no depth to, this bottomless chessboard on which Being is put into play.
>
> (Derrida, 1982: 22)

Like Heidegger before him, Derrida is suggesting that the entire "history" of Greco-Western thought – wherever metaphysics "normalizes" as within Western discourse – can be thought of as a single epoch produced by *diapherein* interpreted as ontological difference.

Derrida is also suspicious of how Greek texts have been translated and offers another interpretation. Referring to the
Heraclitean play of *hen diapheron heautoi* as one differing from
itself, on the surface, now, at this moment, *as* it presences, Derrida
suggests that frame of reference for the term "to differ" was lost as
the definition as ontological difference came to the fore (Derrida,
1982: 22). Derrida is interested in both the literal and metaphori-
cal resonance of the Heraclitean expression: the verb *diapherein* is
based on the root *diaphero* , which means "to carry from one to
another, to carry across, to bear through, to transport." In addition, the Greeks used the term metaphorically to convey "to put
the tongue in motion, to speak" and Derrida relates the phrase to
language, especially to oral language (and the inaudible). In
addition, Heraclitus used the term to mean "to toss about, to be
disrupted;" Aristotle used it to mean "to tear asunder, to disjoin;"
and Plutarch used it to convey "to distract" (Liddel and Scott,
1925: 417). It is only much later that the term solidifies into its
literal meaning of "to make a difference." Derrida is trying to
restore to the term a sense of the early Greek usage, revitalizing
the word to convey a sense of movement along the surface,
simultaneously bearing meaning as it also eliminates, distracts,
and defers meaning. The play of the trace thus "transports" and
"encloses," always revealing and concealing. Derrida is listening to
the middle-voice aspect of the verb – resurrecting the sense of
something that is disjoined or disrupted from *within* – in language
itself – as opposed to something set apart and distinct from others
as viewed from the *outside* – with "objective" distance – and trying
to reinscribe that voice or lost mode of discourse within the
current mode.

In terms of informing translation theory, Derrida's "play of the
trace" belongs not to a translation which carries identifiable
meaning across boundaries, but to a movement along an absent
road, one that has disseminated or evaporated, of a voice which
tells but cannot be captured, an echo disappearing as it is heard. It
is a bearing via "a notion of motion" which is more conveyed by the
movement of Heidegger's prose and Derrida's rhetorical inven-
tions rather than that which they are trying to literally express.
Yet, although the techniques are related, they are not the same.
For with Heidegger, especially in his translations, there is always
the sense that he is searching for some sort of pre-ontological
presence, which, if we could break down our closed conceptual

framework, we could conceivably understand as (more) meaningful than culturally agreed upon meaning. Derrida, in contrast,
seems to suggest that the play of trace can never be presented, for
as it is named, as one tries to stop its movement and grasp it, it
disseminates, separates, and continues to move on, crossing over
to another place. Translation can also be correspondingly redefined. Instead of being defined merely as a crossing over in
order to grasp something, translation can also provide a place or
forum for the practice of a crossing over which disseminates and
escapes. Instead of translations fixing the same meaning, translations can also allow further room for play, extend boundaries,
and open up new avenues for further difference. Translation can
be conceived of as an action in which the movement along the
surface of language is made visible, the play without calculation is
made manifest. The focus of such a redefinition shifts away from
the "meaning" of a text, for, according to Derrida, the *play* has no
meaning. There is no *maintaining différance* – it is metaphorically
conceived of as "this bottomless chessboard on which Being is put
into play."

The differences between Heidegger's and Derrida's views
regarding translation can best be seen in Derrida's response to a
question posed by Rodolphe Gasché in a roundtable on translation collected in *The Ear of the Other* (1985b). Gasché asks how
Derrida situates himself in relation to Heidegger, especially with
regard to Heidegger's recognition of a fundamental lack in every
mother tongue (in this case, the Greek language, and by extension, every Western language, including French). Derrida
responds by suggesting that the difference between his translation theory and Heidegger's is that Heidegger presumes some
sort of "archi-originary intactness," an intact "kernel," which
although covered over, forgotten, and mistranslated by the
Greeks, is nevertheless presumed to exist (Derrida, 1985b: 114).
Derrida's response to Gasché's question points out, justifiably, the
quasi-religious tone assumed by Heidegger's writing, one from
which Derrida must distance himself if the deconstructionist
project is to challenge traditional philosophy. Yet his position *vis-
à-vis* Heidegger is not as distant as may first appear. In fact,
Derrida historicizes the discourse of Heidegger within a Greco-
Western paradigm which always has wished for – and theoretically presumed – an intact originary presence, be there one
or not. Whether the unified "kernel" is fiction or fact, Derrida

does acknowledge that the *desire* for such an entity is very real, and it is precisely *that* upon which every saying, every appeal – including that of literature and philosophy – is based (Derrida, 1985b: 116).

By calling into question that upon which language is founded, Derrida actually goes one step further than Heidegger. Derrida calls into question any definition of translation as transporting, reproducing, representing, or communicating the "meaning" of the original. Instead, he suggests translation might better be viewed as one instance in which language can be seen as always in the process of modifying the original text, of deferring and displacing for ever any possibility of grasping that which the original text desired to name. In fact, from the deconstructionist position, translation is viewed as an activity that continually conceals presence and thwarts *all* desire. Reinforcing Derrida's position, ironically, is that the very thwarting of desire is a necessary condition for desire itself to unfold, the always already silent twin accompanying the emotion as we define it, and the accordingly impossible presence uncannily manifests/conceals itself within Derrida's argument. In a similar fashion, translation can be viewed as a lively operator of *différance*, as a necessary process that distorts original meaning while simultaneously revealing a network of texts both enabling and prohibiting interlingual communication.

Elaborating upon this redefinition of translation in his 1985 essay "Des Tours de Babel," Derrida adopts Walter Benjamin's concept of *Überleben*, the "survival" of language, to explain how translation modifies or supplements the original. The title of the essay again illustrates the graphic force of Derrida's writing, the strange ring, the overdetermined ambiguity, the semantic overloading that Derrida sees always present in every word. "Des" for him resonates with "some," with "of the," with "from the," with "about" (see "Translator's Note," Derrida, 1985a: 206). More importantly, it carries the connotation of "on" in the sense of "living-on" or "sur-vival" (Derrida, 1979: 76). "Tours" conjures up notions of towers, twists, tricks, and turns. Together, "Des" and "Tour" form *détour*, which recalls the defer/delay connotations important to the neologism *différance*, as well as the tangential, supplemental writing Derrida sees implicit in part of any set or static text. "Babel" is even more complex, containing a reference to "father" (*Ba* in oriental tongues) and "God" (*Bel* in the same), father in this case of Babylonia. Derrida suggests that even proper nouns always resonate polysemantically, for this proper noun already carries with it notions of "confusion" as in "incoherent babel" or a "confusion of tongues" and as in a "confused state of mind" when a permanent structure is interrupted (Derrida, 1985a: 166–7). For Derrida, God is seen as a deconstructionist, for He interrupts the construction of the Tower of Babel (Derrida: 1985b: 102). In this act, God interrupts himself and thereby produces "disschemination," which a translator's note by Joseph Graham tells us refers to dissemination, deschematization, de-Shemitizing, and detouring from a *chemin* (path). Addressing the tribe of Shems, Derrida argues that God is saying, "You will not impose your meaning or your tongue, and I, God therefore oblige you to submit to the plurality of languages which you will never get out of" (Derrida, 1985b: 103).

Thus, merely by thinking about four words in the title of the essay, we see how Derrida's writing does more than alienate or estrange; it actively intervenes in metaphysical, religious conceptual schemes and offers an alternative. The "task" of the translator, argues Derrida, adopting Benjamin's argument, is no less than to insure the survival of language and, by extension, the survival of life. Derrida argues that Benjamin's preface – for "The Task of the Translator" is a preface to Benjamin's 1923 translations of Baudelaire's *Tableaux parisiens* – is about giving life, transforming the source text so that it "lives on," that it "lives more and better," that it lives "beyond the means of the author" (Derrida, 1985a: 178–9). Derrida quotes and parenthetically explains his reading of Benjamin as follows:

> Just as the manifestations of life are intimately connected with the living, without signifying anything for it, a translation proceeds from the original. Indeed not so much as from its life as from its survival [*Überleben*]. For a translation comes after the original and, for the important works that never find their predestined translator at the time of their birth, it characterizes the stage of their survival [*Fortleben*, this time sur-vival as continuation of life rather than life as post-mortem].
>
> (Derrida, 1985a: 178)

Thus, for Derrida and Benjamin, the "original" always contains another structure or form – a "stage" for future survival – even if the text itself is never translated. That structure is not visible, not something complete and unified; it has more to do with a state of being incomplete in relation to future possibilities, an openness unchanged by any static or definitive version. Psychologically, this unfulfilled entity might be expressed as the text's unending desire for life and a desire for translation. Derrida talks about such a half-completed structure, whose completion one can merely guess at, as related to the "law" governing translation, which Benjamin also sees as a "debt" (*Aufgabe*) constitutive of the translator's "task." The original gives itself (*aufgeben*) in the very modifying of itself; it survives by its mutation, by its transformation. And in its renewal, the original too is thereby modified – it grows, matures. The growth via translation responds to the original, filling in that open structure of the source text (Derrida, 1985a: 188).

In such a process, not only texts but languages are rejuvenated as well. Translation, for Derrida and Benjamin, marks or "re-marks" in the sense of "expresses" a single text's affinity with other languages. Languages, for Derrida, are not unrelated and abstracted from one another, but are always interrelated and mutually derivative. Translation puts the writer in touch with Benjamin's concept of "pure language" (*reine Sprache*). By transgressing the limits of the target language, by transforming original texts in the source language, the translator extends, enlarges, or makes languages grow. The enlargement is not a linear, systematic one, but one which is fragmentary, happening only at "infinitely small points," similar to Pound's concept of fragments of language, of sculpture, having "luminous details." The metaphor used by Benjamin and cited by Derrida is the one of enlargement by adjoining along the broken lines of a fragment. Derrida quotes Benjamin as follows:

> For, just as the fragments of the amphora, if one is able to reconstitute the whole, must be contiguous in the smallest details, but not identical to each other, so instead of rendering itself similar to the meaning of the original, the translation should rather, in a movement of love and in full detail, pass into its own language the mode of intention of the original: thus, just as the debris become recognizable as fragments of the same amphora, original and translations become recognizable as fragments of a larger language.
>
> (W. Benjamin, 1955; qtd. by Derrida, 1985a: 189–90)

For Derrida, there are no Platonic forms which underlie our conceptual notions. We have no sort of *Ur*-knowledge of what "life" or "families" are. There is nothing, no pure meaning behind words, behind language. Instead, for Derrida, life – or "living on" (*Überleben*) – is essentially present in the term "translation" (*Übersetzen*) and becomes for him the starting point from which he begins to understand what life and the family mean. Derrida's writing is never devoid of a sense of love of life, love of language, of play of language. In a life-affirming sense, Derrida's writing is quasi-religious, which might explain his attraction to Benjamin/ Heidegger. Deconstruction is conceived of as a positive force extending the body of language not just in a symbolic sense, but in a physical sense, too. By a process which physically, materially touches and opens rather than one that abstractly grasps and closes, deconstruction, in reconstituting without representing, allows receiving and giving, allows for love and growth. Translation, more than any other mode or form, complements and reaffirms, enacting survival via a birthing, rebirthing process; hence translation's importance in the deconstructive scheme of things. Benjamin writes that, in translation, the original becomes larger; Derrida adds that translation behaves like a "child" which is not just a "product" subject to the law of "reproduction," but has, in addition, "the power of speak on its own" in a new and different fashion, supplementing language, sounding the "Babelian note" (Derrida, 1985a: 191) which causes languages to grow. The translation process ensures the rebirth, the regeneration, the emergence, "the holy growth" of languages in general, and, for Derrida, the means by which we understand ourselves.

Translation, so conceived, puts us in contact not with some sort of original meaning, but with the plurality of languages and meanings. According to Derrida, one never writes in just one language, but is always already writing in multiple languages, composing new meanings while eradicating others. Even "correct" translations conceal, and even exact replication carries different meanings. Originary intactness dissolves as the translator augments and modifies the original. Gray areas between languages – the borderlines – begin to appear. Traces, marks of dissipated meaning once again become visible – neither intact nor objectified – but still somehow living on, surviving.

Derrida's translation "theory" is not a theory in a traditional sense – it is not prescriptive nor does it propose a better model of transporting. Instead, it suggests that one thinks less in terms of copying or reproducing and more in terms of how languages relate to each other. Marks, traces, affinities with other languages are present simultaneously with the presentation of whatever the text purports to be about. For in translation languages do touch, in whatever miniscule or tangential way, before they again separate; possibilities present themselves before the act of naming and identifying stops the interactive play. Fleeting moments of what Heidegger refers to as the ungraspable situation perhaps can be uncannily sensed by the translator during the activity of translation. Derrida's interest in translation is in the process before the naming takes place, while the "thing" still is not. Thus the process of translation deconstructs texts and returns to a point before a thing has been named, thereby making visible a path by which meaning has been rerouted or diverted.

Derrida's main theoretical point seems to be that there is no pure meaning, no thing to be presented behind language, *nothing* (in an absolute sense) to be represented. Therein lies the radicality of the deconstructionist project. Similar to the formalist position, what does exist, according to deconstructionists, is a continuous chain of signification comprised of languages in a constant state of interplay, mutually supplementing each other. Yet in addition to such a continuous chain, the Formalists tend to posit unified works of art as a goal within the system, a very fragile assumption, according to Derrida. Moreover, Formalists impute some sort of underlying structure to the linguistic system and some sort of order to the evolution of language, whereas Derrida implies bottomless chessboards and random, accidental development, without an end. Derrida thus demythologizes the forms underlying Formalism.

Translation, accordingly, ceases to be viewed as merely an operation carried out between two separate languages, but instead is seen as a process constantly in operation in single languages as well. Borderlines between languages disappear. In every linguistic system several languages are always already in operation – all languages contain elements from other languages, as well as an instability, an ambiguity, within their own terms. Translation theories historically – both before and after Jakobson – presume differing and distinct systems. According to Derrida, in translation, the impurities manifest themselves, the accidents occur and the deschematization process becomes visible. There are parallels between "translate" and "differ/defer" of which Derrida and practicing translators are well aware. Etymologically, "translate" is derived from the Latin word *translatus*, "carried over." *Translatus* is the past participle of *transferre*. If divided into *trans* and *ferre*, we can see the proximity of the word to *dia* and *pherein*. The Latin term *ferre* means "to carry" or "to transport" as in carrying a shield, and was often used to mean to bear or convey with the notion of motion (Homer), as in ships borne by the forces of wind. It also meant to endure, to suffer, as in to bear a mental burden, and survives in expressions such as "you're not faring well." Significantly for the deconstructionists translation refers to the sense of roads or ways which lead to a place, as in a door leading to a garden, or a road leading to a city, conveying a sense of stretching or extension toward (Liddel and Scott, 1925: 1922–3; Klein 1966: 157). By experimenting with possible word choices, what becomes apparent are the minute differences between very similar words, a practice that exposes the limits of languages. That very exposure of limits and impossibilities also gives birth to new alternatives in a very gray area which is neither one language nor another, but a silent differing space not delimited by either one. By putting pen to paper, by choosing one possibility, what occurs is that the silent thought that seemed possible between the languages is deferred, delayed, erased by the delimiting chosen term.

Derrida's work suggests that translation theory might be the best "field of study" to begin to explore these unheard traces, these possibilities that are covered up as we speak. Translation theory is equipped, as Popovič has demonstrated, to follow the "dirty" play of all the mistakes, problems, accidents, insufficiencies, divergences, and differences. While still not what Derrida is referring to with his term *différance* – which is not to be maintained or grasped – such an analysis may be as close as one can come to revealing this silent property of language. To ignore such possibilities, as translation theory has historically done, only perpetuates its own inadequacy. Derrida prefers the term "regulated transformation" over that of translation, for he argues we will never have the transport of pure signifieds from one language to another:

> Difference is never pure, no more so is translation, and for the notion of translation we would have to substitute a notion of *transformation*: a regulated transformation of one language by

another, of one text by another. We will never have, and in fact
have never had, to do with some "transport" of pure signifieds
from one language to another, or within one and the same
language, that the signifying instrument would leave virgin
and untouched.

(Derrida 1981: 20)

Certainly such an approach would tend to break down the power
of the transcendental signified and free the field from evaluating
translations in terms of their proximity to pure equivalence. It
would perhaps also free literary scholars from the constrictions of
naming in order to listen and think – not in terms of just one
language or another, but in that gray area that as yet has no
boundaries, that is barely visible, that has no name and is not.

POST-DERRIDA DISCUSSION

The repercussions of the deconstructionist alternative to traditional approaches of translation are widespread and
accumulating, making them hard to characterize. In this section, I
want to touch briefly on four areas in which discussions are being
held: first from within *Tel Quel*; second, in Translation Studies;
third, in Anglo-American literary theory; and fourth, in language philosophy.

In French circles, much of the discussion of deconstruction,
translation, and the nature of language centers around writing by
James Joyce, and strategies preferred by his translators. Perhaps
the best example of the practice of "affirmative productivity" as
preferred by deconstructionists is James Joyce's own translation
of two passages from *Finnegans Wake*. The last thing he worked on
before he died, it demonstrates just how a translation illuminates
and elaborates upon the original, giving scholars a better sense of
the original's transitory nature. Jacqueline Risset, who first published Joyce's translation in the journal *Tel Quel* in 1973, suggests
that such a text demonstrates Derrida's thesis that translation
transforms the original as it brings it into a second language. She
argues that the Italian text of *Finnegans Wake* cannot be called a
translation at all, but speaks in terms of it being a "rewriting," an
"elaboration," which does not stand in opposition to the original,
but as a "work in progress" (Risset, 1984: 3). Clearly the "English"
text of *Finnegans Wake* is one example of the multiple linguistic
possibilities within (one) language in general, and thereby defies

translation as the Western world understands it. In some languages, *Finnegans Wake* has not been translated and is available only in the original, not merely because of the difficulty of translating it, but more because the text is not viewed as being English but plurilingual. Nearly every word in the book is so rich with foreign language reference that it pushes the parameters of monolingualism to the extreme. Theoretically, it already seems to represent an ultimate in terms of degrees of fragmentation of presentation; thus, any translation becomes senseless, or, in other terms, could only serve to telescope the free play of the lexical units into some sense producing and thereby limiting structure. The translation strategy employed by Joyce himself, however, exponentially increases the options for translation again, if that can be imagined, not by retaining the multilinguistic framework by importing foreign language morphemes, but by exploring the limits of language from within. Instead of coining new terms and neologisms, Joyce draws upon multiple levels already existing in the Italian language – various idioms, dialects, and archaisms – in order to achieve the multiple resonances of the original.

In an article called "Joyce Translates Joyce" (1984), Risset argues that Joyce did not seek hypothetical equivalents from the original, but extended the original to a new stage, "a more daring variation on the text in process" (Risset, 1984: 6). Not incidentally, Risset is a poet and translator herself, her most recent project being a translation of Dante's *Divine Comedy* into French, the first two volumes of which are complete and published by Flammarion. Her translation strategy seems to be to "deconstruct" the canonized Dante in France and, in her version, make the playful and colloquial Dante, one which every schoolchild in Italy can read and enjoy, accessible. Joyce, she argues, by resorting to the heterogeneous capabilities within one language, accomplishes similar allusory effects and levels of meaning in the Italian, yet without the obfuscation. Risset suggests that Joyce systematically eliminated all foreign language allusion, substituting instead a monolingual version in which all deformations are rendered in Italian. For example, in the phrase "Annona gebroren aroostokrat Nivia, dochter of Sense and Art, with Spark's pir-ryphlickathims funkling her fran," Joyce eliminates all reference to Latin, German, and Greek and writes "Annona genata arusticrata Nivea, laureolata in Senso e Arte, il ventaglio costellato di filgettanti" (Risset, 1984: 9). Because the length and depth of the history of Italian culture with all its aristocratic auras and classical airs are so well combined with the regional, uncultured, rural colors and tones, the Italian enjoys a resonance as rich as the foreign-distorted English. Such a strategy of radical Italianization reveals the pluralinguistic qualities inherent in any language somehow even more dramatically than even the original *Wake*. Risset concludes that Joyce's translation strategy reveals something about the nature of language and the "freedom of dialect." The creation of new words is always in process, and the study of dialect, thus, is seminal to better understanding translational phenomena. Joyce's strategy involves more than the use of and quotation of various dialects; instead, in Joyce's translation approach, "language itself" is "treated as dialect." Risset argues that in the "operation" of such a strategy, one becomes aware of "something else," i.e., "language whose field is disturbed, moved in accordance with a forgotten creativity" (Risset, 1984: 13). It is that something else that Risset wishes to "restore" to Dante in her own translations.

Joyce, in the activity of writing and in the activity of translation, has pushed the boundaries of language beyond margins hitherto contemplated. As the English moves outwards, the Italian moves inwards; yet both are always undoing and calling into question stability and definition as they create new terms and open up new avenues for thought. In his translation activity, however, Joyce emphasizes more strongly than in the original the sense of something disruptive about the nature of language that arises from within, not as something coming from a foreign source. As Derrida tends to make deliberate mistakes in order to create graphic disorder, so too Joyce deliberately deforms language within a colloquial and very much spoken context to achieve similar results, thereby delaying/deferring its own subsumation and silencing. This subversive aspect of language and of translation as employed by Joyce is dangerous politically and socially, which, perhaps, explains why the translation of Joyce has become the measuring device for assessing the degree of publishing freedom certain cultures enjoy. When and under what conditions Joyce gets translated is of historic relevance.

The political and institutional threat posed by such an alternative to any theory of translation based upon metaphysical dualism is fairly clear, which might explain why the Translation Studies scholars have been all but silent in response to the questions posed by deconstructionists. The only serious attempt in Translation Studies to talk about translation theory in post-Derridean terms has been Raymond Van den Broeck's article "Translation Theory after Deconstruction," published in 1988. Van den Broeck has read the pertinent sections from Derrida which deal with translation, and with the help of Jonathan Culler's 1983 text *On Deconstruction*, acknowledges that in every translation there is a substantial loss of meaning, leading to Derrida's substitution of the term transformation for translation. For Van den Broeck, in agreement with Culler, deconstruction is not an act of destruction, but an act of displacement, an act that challenges traditional oppositions, or even reverses such oppositions (Culler, 1983: 150; Broeck, 1988: 274). He quotes Derrida as saying that deconstruction must "through a double gesture, a double sentence, a double writing, put into practice a *reversal* of the classical opposition *and* a general *displacement* of the system" (Derrida, 1977: 195; Broeck, 1988: 278). This reversal and general displacement can be accomplished, according to Van den Broeck, by transforming the language of the target text through strong, forceful translation which experiments with and tampers with conventional usage. He quotes Derrida from "Living On" as saying that this sort of transference involves "the simultaneous transgression and reappropriation of a language" because "it forces the translator to transform the language into which he is translating" (Derrida, 1979: 87–9; qtd. by Broeck, 1988: 280–1). He then quotes Derrida from "Des Tours de Babel" on ensuring the survival of the original, arguing that Derrida claims the translator should employ an "abusive" translational strategy which "pursues the double move of both violating *and* sustaining the principles of usage" (Broeck, 1988: 283).

Van den Broeck then attempts to subsume Derrida under the Translation Studies approach by arguing that because Derrida subverts source-text oriented theories, he therefore must reinforce the claims of the target-text oriented approaches, i.e., that of Translation Studies. He sees the Translation Studies approach, especially the theory of Gideon Toury, developing parallel to and in fact preceding deconstruction theories. Just as deconstruction challenges theories of determinacy, theories which posit meaning as a given property of a text, so too, argues Van den Broeck, does Translation Studies account for diversity of translation modes and types (Broeck, 1988: 276). Van den Broeck goes so far as to say that Toury's *In Search of a Theory of Translation*, especially his insistence upon uncovering the norms governing translation, can better explain why Derrida's deconstructive approach calling for transgression and deformation has met with relatively small success. He argues that Derrida's theory is less a new theory of language, but merely an older and "highly prescriptive" one. "Deconstruction favours only the norm which in the classical opposition turns out to occupy the inferior position nowadays" (Broeck, 1988: 281). Van den Broeck does not "trust" Derrida's position because it does not provide an "objective basis" or a "point of departure for research" (Broeck, 1988: 281), as the Polysystem model does.

Van den Broeck's selective reading leads him to place Derrida only in the same metaphysical, faithful/free terms that traditionally govern translation theory. He concludes that: "Eventually deconstruction's theory of translation is not a theory the way we would like it. Very probably it is only a theory in the traditional sense of that term, viz. a theory that prescribes what translation *should* be" (Broeck, 1988: 286). To see Derrida as offering merely another prescription for better translation, i.e., one that imports estranging effects into the target language, is reductive and misleading. Derrida does advocate graphic displacement, but he also uses graphic disorder with care and precision in order to open up categorical thinking and to provide a space for thinking in other terms, as far as it may be possible. Van den Broeck has not attempted to follow Derrida's thinking or the play of the language into such frontiers, which is why he makes the mistake of suggesting that Derrida's calling for a reversal of traditional oppositions can be equated with a target-oriented approach. An empirical approach is an approach which reinforces dualistic conceptual thinking, which reinforces subject/object distinctions and perpetuates abstract/material distinctions that Derrida is constantly trying to break down. Derrida does more than write *différance* with an *a*; he also recalls a middle-voiced term that is neither subject nor predicate, that has been lost or repressed in the course of history, and that eludes empirical observation. Neither Van den Broeck nor any of the Translation Studies scholars have, to date, seriously considered the alternative, and such a silence impoverishes their systemic observations.

In Euro-American circles, the post-Derridean discussion about translation centers around an ongoing debate about Walter

Benjamin's "The Task of the Translator." Paul de Man in *Resistance to Theory* (1986) goes so far as to say "that you are nobody unless you have written about this text" (Man, 1986: 73). The first deconstructionist reading of Benjamin's essay can probably be located in Carol Jacobs' 1975 essay "The Monstrosity of Translation" in which she argues that mimetic theories, approaches which claim objectivity of knowledge, are not much help in reading Benjamin. Benjamin's concept of language, she argues, is based upon difference, and he has abandoned any belief that language refers to any objective reality. Translations, instead, are woven into a textual history that is always transforming terms, translating other translations. Benjamin's text "dislocates definitions" rather than establishing them, and for this reason, his writing is often ironic and deceptive, full of reverberations, but with an unlocatable source. She reads his essay itself less as a preface, less as a critical piece, and more as an act of translation itself – already in the paradigm of translations of translation.

In terms of Benjamin's strategy in such a (re)writing, Jacobs argues that in order to catch a glimpse of the nature of language as formed in the flux of intertextuality, we replace sentence and proposition as the fundamental unit with the word. What will result will not be natural, whole, and unified re-productions; instead the "monstrosity" of translation will rear its head. A heterogeneity emerges which "dismantles" all syntax and "dismembers" conventional, natural forms. Translation is not aimed at the reader – the concept of an ideal reader, according to Benjamin, is actually detrimental in the theoretical consideration of art. Translation "renders radically foreign that language we believe to be ours" (Jacobs, 1975: 756). Word-for-word translations are preferred to those which synthesize and unify. She quotes Benjamin as saying, "Literality thoroughly overthrows all reproduction of meaning with regard to the syntax and threatens directly to lead to incomprehensibility. In the eyes of the nineteenth century, Hölderlin's translations of Sophocles were 'monstrous examples of such literality'" (Jacobs, 1975: 761). Jacobs argues that this monstrosity is exactly what Benjamin praises.

Jacobs points out that this emphasis on differentiation rather than sameness, this focusing on words rather than on things or objects, has created problems for Benjamin's English translator Harry Zohn, whose less than literal version often reflected more of his own conception of language than Benjamin's. She offers her own translation of several passages, not as a criticism of Zohn or to establish a more "correct" version, but to offer an alternative reading in the play of the space between her translation and Zohn's. For example, she suggests that Zohn's logical but less than literal rendering of the metaphor about the fragment of an amphora (cited by Derrida above p. 165) may be misleading. Zohn's desire for unity, coherence, and logical connections causes him to suggest that the simile be read as follows: as fragments of a vessel can "be *glued* together must *match* in the smallest details" to form a larger, whole vessel, so too can translations be seen as fragments of a larger language (emphasis mine, Benjamin, trans. Zohn, 1969: 78). Jacobs' alternative suggests that as fragments, as the "*broken* parts" of a vessel "in order to be *articulated* together, must *follow* one another in the smallest detail," so too does translation make recognizable the *broken part* of a greater language (italics mine, Jacobs, 1975: 762). Not tempted by the urge for a consistent, whole "text," Jacobs translates literally, word for word, and thus her rendering leaves the passage incomplete in a Western sense. She does not join the translation and original, and instead offers the translation as a *Bruchstück*, consistent with not just Benjamin's metaphor, but also with what she sees as Benjamin's "strange" or "monstrous" mode of articulation. Jacobs understands but does not judge Zohn's historical conditioned reading; her essay offers an alternative, one which has engendered a plethora of subsequent Benjamin interpretations favorable to her own.

The best example of these is no doubt Paul de Man's essay "Conclusions: Walter Benjamin's 'The Task of the Translator,'" collected in *The Resistance to Theory* (1986). De Man clearly has followed Derrida's thinking as far as anyone, and has demonstrated his ability to confront the bottomless chessboard to which Derrida refers and to continue his work under such conditions. Yet whereas Derrida's reading plays affirmatively with the Benjamin text, de Man's deconstructive reading is largely couched in negative terminology and nihilism. Beginning, for example, with Hölderlin's translations from Sophocles praised so much by Benjamin for their radical alternative, de Man quotes Benjamin as arguing that Hölderlin's translations expanded language so much that they threatened to enclose the translator in silence and that meaning threatened to become lost in the "bottomless depths of language." De Man argues that translation so conceived gets drawn into something "essentially destructive," i.e., language itself. Whereas Derrida's conception of deconstruction is generally life-giving, positive, and regenerative, de Man's conception of the deconstruction project as articulated in the "Conclusion" is largely negative:

> All these activities – critical philosophy, literary theory, history – resemble each other in the fact that they do not resemble that from which they derive. But they are all intralinguistic: they relate to what in the original belongs to language, and not to meaning as an extralinguistic correlate susceptible of paraphrase and imitation. They disarticulate, they undo the original, they reveal that the original was already disarticulated. They reveal that their failure, which seems to be due to the fact that they are secondary in relation to the original, reveals an essential failure, an essential disarticulation which was already there in the original. They kill the original, by discovering that the original was already dead.
>
> (Man, 1986: 84)

One could effectively argue that the two conceptions are the same, just as life and death in Heidegger's formulation are so intertwined that they are to all intents and purposes indistinguishable. Yet in terms of the deconstruction project as a whole, the difference is not negligible. For de Man and other Euro-American deconstructionists, deconstruction has been used to attempt to displace an older, more conventional generation of scholars and critics and to establish themselves. Their treatment is occasionally merciless, and such an attitude often gets in the way of their argument. The de Man article, for example, is cruel in its treatment of the translator Harry Zohn. Unlike Jacobs, who historicized Zohn's work and offered alternatives, de Man treats Zohn and Maurice de Gandillac, Benjamin's French translator, like little schoolboys, arguing that they "don't seem to have the slightest idea of what Benjamin is saying" (Man, 1986: 79). De Man talks about the original being "absolutely unambiguous" in places and says that the translators have trouble following Benjamin, that they do not "get it." He cites examples not only of misplaced negatives, but also of "right" and "wrong" choices. "Nachreife," for example, from Benjamin's phrase "Nachreife des fremdes Wortes," an important concept in the argument, is translated by Zohn reasonably as "maturing process." This disturbs de Man, who feels the word carries connotations of melancholy, the feeling of exhaustion, rotten grapes, and the death of the original, that Zohn misses. Yet de Man's interpretation may have more to do with his own world view than the quality of the translation choice.

Most vivid in de Man's essay is his disparaging treatment of Zohn for his "mistranslation" of the fragments of the vessel metaphor. Comparing Jacobs' version to Zohn's, he argues that Zohn again gets it wrong, and that all you have to do, to see what Benjamin is saying, is "translate correctly, instead of translating like Zohn." De Man wants to demonstrate his understanding of metaphor and metonymy, the difference between "match" and "follow" (*gleichen* and *folgen*), a distinction which is useful for the preface's interpretation. De Man goes on to argue that fragments which follow one another will never constitute a totality. De Man sees every work as fragmented, and translations as fragments of fragments. Like Derrida, he denies knowledge of wholeness, of an intact vessel, or of any sense of original meaning. "Meaning," he writes, "is always displaced with regard to the meaning it ideally intended – that meaning is never reached" (Man, 1986: 91). While de Man's thinking about metaphor is useful and convincing with regard to the Benjamin essay, his insistence that he understands the "meaning" of Benjamin's piece better than Zohn or de Gandillac or others recalls reading strategies employed by I. A. Richards and the New Critics. The very notion of "getting it" and certainly "getting it better" actually contradicts de Man's main thesis, which suggests that no reader, de Man included, has access to original meaning. De Man's scholarly rhetoric, thus, is inconsistent with his theoretical claims. De Man's dismissive view of other readings, his condescending tone, and the belief that his view is "correct," serve merely to reveal his own ahistorical and subjective views. "Right" and "wrong" have ceased to be productive theoretical terms for Translation Studies scholars as well as deconstructionists.

In terms of a post-Derrida discussion of translation theory, the contributions of the post-Enlightenment language philosophers have been more productive than those by American literary critics. The most comprehensive text out so far is Andrew Benjamin's *Translation and the Nature of Philosophy* (1989). He, too, discusses Benjamin's "The Task of the Translator," but locates the discussion in a context that ranges from Enlightenment philosophy, residues of which still effect the discourse of this age, through a very thorough discussion of what Heidegger, Freud, and Derrida have contributed to our understanding of the nature of language in general and translation in particular. Benjamin's treatment of Heidegger, especially Heidegger's later writing about the nature of language and the problem of concealment, is particularly strong, and lays the foundation for his subsequent discussion of Derrida. While not agreeing with Derrida, Andrew Benjamin does very fairly present the possibilities of double readings, of *différance* in all its differing, delaying, and conflictual senses. Translation in a post-Derrida discussion, for Andrew Benjamin, ceases to be understood as any simple, definable single activity, but rather as a plurality of activities with a plurality of significations (A. Benjamin, 1989: 35). Andrew Benjamin's book begins with questions about the "ground" of difference, which he finds in the word "translation" itself, i. e., the term suggests both "ground" of the original and "ungrounded" difference. If there is no origin and there is nothing that is original, plurality is therefore "anoriginal." Andrew Benjamin's subsequent discussion looks at ways such anoriginality can be understood.

Andrew Benjamin does not agree with Derrida, nor with de Man, and instead finds a way out of the labyrinth via Donald Davidson. In a very useful discussion of Davidson's paper "On the Very Idea of a Conceptual Scheme," which studies translation as a way of focusing on criteria of identity for conceptual schemes, Andrew Benjamin argues that mutual understanding is "almost inescapable." A complex series of interconnected preconditions precedes the process of expressing equivalent "things" in another language. Benjamin quotes Davidson:

> The idea is then that something is a language, and associated with a conceptual scheme, whether we can translate it or not, if it stands in a certain relation predicating, organizing, facing, or fitting experience nature, reality, sensory promptings. The problem is to say what the relation is, and to be clear about the entities related.
>
> (Davidson, 1984: 191; qtd. by A. Benjamin, 1989: 65)

Davidson's approach thus mediates between the untouchable original and a movement of language that is intelligible, or at least indicates those "objects" that stand in relation to the source and target text and make communication possible. Davidson reaches back to concepts of Kantian universality which "overcome" the threat of the diversity of human languages and the questions posed by the deconstructionists. A humanistic concept of "nature" is posited which provides the ground which enables universality. "Man's rationality," argues Andrew Benjamin, "is a consequence of nature's endowment and consequently diversity and difference can be explained and accounted for as a digression and deviation away from the way that is proper to man in virtue of his being human" (A. Benjamin, 1989: 78–9).

At this point, Andrew Benjamin discusses Walter Benjamin's "The Task of the Translator." He agrees with de Man's reading that the fragments of a broken vessel do not presuppose an initial vessel, i.e., that original language is always already displaced language, and that therefore no original language exists. He then asks, however, how are we to understand the (postulated) futural vessel and what are the conditions (the totality) that implicitly causes us to think in terms of the "belonging together" of the fragments, and thereby the "belonging together" of languages. Andrew Benjamin and other post-Enlightenment philosophers think not about the abyss, not about the pre-ontological conditions, but about the pragmatic conditions which allow for interpretation and mutual understanding, which Andrew Benjamin calls ontological-temporal conditions. They seek to identify and describe the elements which allow for affirmative thinking about semantic and interpretive potential that are inherent in words; and they argue that one can think about translation without an origin to be or not to be retrieved. Meanings and interpretations emerge out of real conditions – they are actual as well as conflictual – and can be positively and empirically described. Andrew Benjamin argues, "Emergent meaning is the actualization of the potential for meaning and not the emergence out of non-meaning" (A. Benjamin, 1989: 180). In contrast to de Man and Derrida, he argues that there is never pure difference, but that difference always has a specificity. Walter Benjamin, argues Andrew Benjamin, locates "after-life," sur-vival, by locating the potential for afterlife within the text itself. Words incorporate a site of conflict, a site of unending after-life, which defers an end or a definitive interpretation. Interpreting Walter Benjamin's text against the grain of fashionable deconstruction readings, Andrew Benjamin argues that in Walter Benjamin, "the possibility of a different understanding of translation and philosophy is beginning to take place" (A. Benjamin, 1989: 108).

The possibility of a different understanding of translation in the post-deconstruction world will be the subject of the final chapter. In contrast to Van den Broeck, I suggest that Translation Studies need not try to subsume post-structural theories of translation under some target-oriented concept of empirical texts; instead, Translation Studies is already equipped to begin a study of writing about the differing and deferring "spaces" – of *différance* in action – and the theory needs to catch up to the possibilities of the methodology. Some scholars in Translation Studies seem to be on the threshold of making such a move, and the theoretical repercussions may be far-reaching.

Chapter 7

The future of Translation Studies

If, as Ted Hughes argued, the sixties was a period which experienced a boom in literary translation, the nineties might be characterized as experiencing a boom in translation theory. The process has already begun, Daniel Weissbort, editor of *Modern Poetry in Translation* (renamed *Poetry World*), a journal traditionally devoted to publishing literary translations and translation problems, added Romy Heylen, a scholar much influenced by Translation Studies and open to deconstructionist approaches, to the editorial board to incorporate a theoretical component in the journal. In a 1987 editorial titled "Translation Theory: A Challenge for the Future," Rainer Schulte, editor of *Translation Review*, a journal devoted to publishing literary translations and translation reviews, suggests that translation scholars and Euro-American literary translators can mutually help each other. He argues, for example, that the study of multiple translations of a single poem can enlarge the translator's understanding of the text and that translation theorists can learn from the literary translators' research into criteria for the evaluation of translations (Schulte, 1987: 2). Frederic Will has published the first two volumes – *Thresholds and Testimonies* (1988) and *A Portrait of John* (1990) – of a promised trilogy called *The Fall of the Gods* in which he suggests, not unlike Andrew Benjamin, that as man falls from original oneness, so too has translation fallen from claims of recovery of the original. Yet, Will suggests that both the learning of a new language and the activity of translation are attempts by fallen man to recover that original oneness. Minimally, at certain junctures or "thresholds" between languages, Will argues, lost portions of our cultural heritage seem to appear and a sense of continuity (and possible recuperation?) arises (Will, 1988: ix).

Douglas Robinson rises to the defense of the "atheoretical" American literary translator in *The Translator's Turn* (1991), arguing that the literary translator embodies an integration of feeling and thought, of intuition and systematization. In analyzing the "turn" that the translator takes from the source text to the target text, Robinson offers a "dialogical" model, one that analyzes the translator's dialogical engagement with the source language/original and with the ethics of the target language/receptor. Robinson allows for the translator to intervene, subvert, divert, even entertain, emphasizing the creative aspect of literary translation. The translation linguists, scientists, and philosophers have had their chance at translation theory; now it is time, he argues, for the literary translators to have their "turn."

In the field of the science of Translation, unusual approaches are being suggested; subjective factors are being incorporated into the objective science, including such unscientific rationale as "it sounds better" as a possible category (Jäger and Neubert, 1983: 110). New developments in psycholinguistics and socio-linguistics are having more and more influence on how translators are taught to translate in Germany. Mary Snell-Hornby's book *Translation Studies: Toward an Integrated Approach*, has pushed the text-typology approach to a point where the text is barely distinguishable in its network of cultural contextualizing information. In fact, she no longer defines translation as an activity that takes place between two languages, but views it as an interaction between two cultures. She understands culture as not just the "arts," but in a broader anthropological sense, as referring to all socially conditioned aspects of human life (Snell-Hornby, 1988: 39), a perspective that broadens the parameters normally considered by translation theorists, prescriptive or otherwise.

After a decade focused primarily upon the descriptive branch in Translation Studies and Polysystem theory, theory too seems on the return. In 1989, Lambert and Toury established a journal *Target* to provide a platform for discussion of theoretical, methodological, and descriptive ideas, and have been publishing work by translation theorists and scholars from the Low Countries, Germany, Israel, and Canada. In 1990, Even-Zohar published a new book, *Polysystem Studies*, revising certain concepts and better explaining others. While the book contains many essays previously published, including articles from *Papers in Historical Poetics* (1978a), further explanation of his concept of the "literary system" is elaborated in one chapter and a more detailed elaboration of "laws of literary interference" is formulated in another. Gideon Toury has begun thinking about other matters than better describing translation or further analyzing the system of norms governing translation. In a paper presented at the 1990 James Holmes Symposium on Translation in Amsterdam, he asks "What are Descriptive Studies into Translation Likely to Yield Apart from Isolated Descriptions?" (Toury, 1991). The issue of whether or not Translation Studies can or should control the reception and explanation of their own case studies will be one of the topics for the field in the immediate future. For the past couple of years, Toury has promised a book on the connection between descriptive research and the explanation of translational phenomena. Meanwhile, deconstruction strategies challenge from everywhere; both from outside Western discourse – by what we refer to as the Third World groups – and by subgroups – gays, blacks, women, and ethnic minorities – that challenge from within.

New and influential groups are forming, such as the well-endowed special research group in Göttingen, Germany, looking at translations from American literature into German, and a group in Canada, mostly from Montréal, Ottawa, and Québec, researching questions about translations in French-speaking Canada. Directed by Armin Paul Frank, the Göttingen Center for the Cooperative Study of Literary Translation, founded in 1985, has published four volumes in the series of *Göttinger Beiträge zur internationalen Übersetzungsforschung*, and two more are in press at the time of this writing. Although their approach is pair-bound and one-directional, i.e., from America into Germany, as they accumulate data and publish more, they provide Translation Studies scholars with valuable information that needs to be processed. Theoretically, the Göttingen group starts with definitions as laid out in Theo Hermans' *Manipulation of Literature* (1985) and undertakes a revaluation of certain assumptions, especially those regarding the interaction of systems and subsystems and the hierarchical nature of the polysystem in general. They arrive at a theory of translation which is transfer-oriented rather than target-oriented (Frank, 1990: 54), challenging Toury's definition on which Translation Studies is founded by making more allowances for each translator's individual and often creative choices regarding stylistic devices. They suggest that the evolution of the system may be more irregular than Polysystem theory hypothesizes. Epistemological questions are raised by the Göttingen group's claim that the translation of literature means the translation of a literary work's interpretation, one which is subject to the literary traditions in the target culture. Literary translation, according to the German group, is a part of a country's literary language, a cultural activity that is part of and contributes to a country's cultural heritage. Frank talks in terms of a translation culture in much the same way as one talks about a gourmet sampling the culinary delights of a particular town, region, or country (Frank, 1987: 86). Like Snell-Hornby, he too calls for an integrated theory of translation, one which is not derivative or speculative, but one "in the spirit of René Wellek and Austin Warren's *Theory of Literature*" (Frank, 1990: 55).

In Canada, a group of mostly feminists are researching political and theoretical problems of translating into "Québécois" (French from France as a language and culture bearer has been rejected). Annie Brisset raises ideological questions in "In Search of a Target Language: The Politics of Theatre Translation in Quebec" (1989). Barbara Godard raises theoretical questions about the nature of language, women's discourse, and feminist translation in "Theorizing Feminist Discourse/Translation" (1990). The complicated question of Canadian identity – problems of colonialism, bi-lingualism, nationalism, cultural heritage, weak literary system, and gender issues are involved – seems to provide a useful platform from which to begin raising questions about current translation theory.

The impact of American television, radio, music, and international advertising, bears more and more heavily upon any discussion of translation worldwide. Not only are Translation Studies scholars branching out to consider work in film and media studies (Delabastita, 1988; 1990), but film and media scholars are also turning to translation studies for insight and terminology (Cattrysse, 1991; 1992). Scholars from within what formerly could be termed a school or unified approach are changing, making generalizations about groupings more and more difficult. While many remain largely unaware of what fellow colleagues are doing in other parts of the world, within some groups a radical rethinking of positions is taking place.

One place where such a splintering is occurring is in the Belgian/Dutch group. This chapter will focus on new developments within this area and raise some questions about its future. Clearly there is a shift of focus occurring at this moment in Translation Studies; one might describe it as a move away from looking at translations as linguistic phenomena to looking at translations as cultural phenomena. José Lambert, who has been working outward from within a Polysystem theory framework, has been moving from microstructural descriptions to a focus on more global structures. His work should have wide-ranging repercussions for not only Translation Studies, but Comparative Literature in general. Susan Bassnett and André Lefevere, on the other hand, have, for some time now, been looking at macrostructural phenomena such as institutional power structures as well as at the microlevel shifts they induced. Bassnett and Lefevere argue that Translation Studies is taking an historic "Cultural Turn" as it propels itself into the nineties.

During the eighties, José Lambert expanded the field of investigation to include many aspects of translational phenomena not normally associated with interlingual translation and raised many questions about the nature of generic categories, definitions of texts in general, and definitions of translations in particular. As noted earlier, Lambert's descriptive research during the eighties made him more aware of the cultural complexities involved in defining and describing translations, which in turn served to reemphasize the need for systematic research. Yet his observations and initial conclusions are so far-reaching that one cannot classify them any longer as part of an applied or descriptive branch. In a co-authored article called "Translation" (forthcoming) to be published in the encyclopedia *Semiotics: A Handbook on the Sign-Theoretic Foundations of Nature and Culture* (edited by Roland Posner, Klaus Robering, and Thomas A. Seboek), Lambert, together with Clem Robyns, argues that no translation can be treated in isolation. Rather, translations are to be seen as the result of and the starting point from which to view semiotic processes at work in the formation of discursive practices. Translations, they argue, take place over a variety of systemic borders, not just between two languages. Finding himself theoretically closer to a Joycean position than he may dare admit, Lambert now also argues that every text, every word, contains "translated" elements. Lambert further points out that translated texts also contain many discursive elements which are not translated, and the category "non-translation" is becoming increasingly prominent in his descriptive work. Lambert's conception of Translation Studies for the nineties is conceived of as both a target-oriented empirical science and a transfer-oriented semiotic practice. How does he adopt both positions?

As an alternative for the nineties, Lambert and Robyns suggest that we view translations as one step in the ongoing process of an endless semiotic chain. This solves the traditional opposition between form and meaning by making it superfluous – any interpretation of the sign via translation becomes itself just another sign in the same evolving chain. Lambert and Robyns invoke Charles Sanders Peirce's concept of "final logical interpretant" to mediate between their target-oriented approach and a semiotic approach. Peirce's process of interpretation can actually halt the semiotic flux at a certain point for the interpretation of a specific sign, i.e., the final logical interpretant, which, in this case, is the translated text (see Gorlée, 1989, and forthcoming). This allows, for pragmatic reasons, not only for a target-text analysis, the cornerstone of Toury's theory, but also causes the source text to dissolve into a variety of sources, codes, and discourses. Translation, thus, is viewed by Lambert and Robyns less as an interlinguistic process and more as an intracultural activity. They also cite Umberto Eco, who views translation, according to Lambert and Robyns, as identical to culture (Eco, 1976: 71), which is conceived less as a static phenomenon and instead as the endless translation of signs into other signs. Translation gets redefined by Lambert and Robyns as the "migration-through-transformation of discursive elements (signs)" and as the "process during which they are interpreted (re-contextualized) according to different codes" (Lambert and Robyns, forthcoming). Translations thus take place not only between fixed languages and national literatures, but also between any sort of competing or varying discourses.

The implications of such a claim for Translation Studies, Comparative Literature, or for any single language department, such as English literature, are far-reaching. First it tends to explode the concept of national literature as a useful distinction; secondly, it breaks down distinctions between written and other discursive practices; and finally it opens up the possibility of exploring non-Western discursive practices that may impinge upon translation as defined in the West. Lambert has written about some of these implications in the essay "In Quest of Literary World Maps" published in *Interculturality and the Historical Study of Literary Translations*, edited by Harald Kittel and Armin Paul Frank (Lambert, 1991). In the article, Lambert demonstrates the uselessness of geographical categories for the study of languages, saying that most of us have an "indistinct, even medieval image of the literary world" (Lambert, 1991: 134), and instead suggests that we use linguistic maps, whose borderlines and territories produce many unexpected relations. The map is not only complicated by the fact that in certain countries such as India or Russia many languages are spoken (over 300 are reported in Nigeria), it is also ideologically tainted by Western conceptions – it shows only standard languages characterized by written traditions. A language needs to be institutionalized in order to be represented as such. There is no way of showing criss-crosses, interferences, or language stratifications (Lambert, 1991: 137).

This national reductionism, argues Lambert, is rooted in the institutional origins of literary research and has been propagated by those Western nations with strong literary traditions. Systems theory as posited by Even-Zohar and others tends to reduce explanation to languages and nations: large nations and small nations, primary literary centers and secondary systems. Lambert suggests that there are good reasons for testing other explanatory principles. It is not enough to posit hypotheses by theoretical explanation; more important to achieving better understanding of translational phenomena is historical-descriptive research. Lambert suggests we begin redefining our approach to literary studies by talking about literature *in* France, *in* Germany, *in* Italy (Lambert, 1991: 141). He raises questions about the types of literature we find in given socio-cultural contexts. He suggests that important literary phenomena are often not recognized as literature in certain cultures where they occur. By collecting canonized, non-canonized, and extraliterary texts published within a given society itself, by establishing repertories of cultural phenomena, scholars can make connections and see patterns that may be informative. Lambert asks questions about the connections between the literary phenomena – what are the contacts/non-contacts, unidirectional/multidirectional relations, and hierarchical relations? Especially important for Lambert are the norms and hierarchies of norms that exist in any given society or

language group. All of these questions stem from Translation
Studies research and Polysystem theory, but are having repercussions in fields such as comparative literature, national literary
studies, sociology, international relations, politics, and economics.
For Lambert, only the tip of the iceberg has been exposed; more
research and description, more observation of even the most
obvious phenomena needs to be done before one can begin to
theorize.

Susan Bassnett and André Lefevere come to a similar position,
yet from a different form of reasoning. Frustrated by the fact that
the analysis of "shifts" was becoming increasingly complicated and
the methods for analyzing them so detailed that readers could no
longer follow the explanations, Lefevere and Bassnett opted for a
different approach. They wanted to explain the shifts recorded
through empirical historical research, not just by the poetics and
the importation of poetic devices, but by looking at the images
and ideology represented as well. In the "Introduction: Proust's
Grandmother and the Thousand and One Nights; the 'Cultural
Turn' in Translation Studies" to their co-edited anthology *Translation, History and Culture* (1990), they suggest that the scholar use
terms such as "patronage," "refraction," and "ideology" in order
"to go into the vagaries and vicissitudes of the exercise of power in
a society, and what the exercise of power means in terms of the
production of culture, of which the production of translations is a
part" (Bassnett and Lefevere, 1990: 5). At the end of her contribution to the anthology, "Linguistic Transcoding or Cultural
Transfer? A Critique of Translation Theory in Germany," Mary
Snell-Hornby proposes that translation scholars abandon their
"scientistic" attitude and move from "text" as a translation unit to
"culture," a step that Bassnett and Lefevere see as "momentous,"
marking a "cultural turn" for the field. Taking a very materialist
position, Lefevere and Bassnett argue that Translation Studies
scholars have to deal not only with texts and/or repertories of texts
in historical paradigms, but also need to look at those institutions
which influence their production. They argue that "the student of
translation/rewriting is not engaged in an ever-lengthening and
ever more complex dance around the 'always already no longer
there,'" but that the student "deals with hard, falsifiable cultural
data, and the way they affect people's lives' (Bassnett and
Lefevere, 1990: 12).

As I suggested earlier, Lefevere has been moving to this position over a number of years. In 1987, for example, he published an article called "'Beyond Interpretation' or the Business of (Re)Writing," not only stealing/rewriting a title from Jonathan Culler for an essay in his *The Pursuit of Signs* (1981), but also asking questions about the purposes of literary/translation scholarship. Troubled by the "academization of criticism," the complexity of deconstructive criticism, the scientificity of translation analysis, the abstract nature of translation theory, Lefevere sees both literary criticism and translation criticism as perpetuating certain cultural values and as excluding and marginalizing others. He begins asking tough questions about Translation Studies" own social, political, and economic basis. To get "beyond interpretation," he argues that criticism is "no longer expected to produce interpretations, whether objective or definitive," but instead, interpretations "can be made use of to unravel the network of social, political, and economic factors which regulate both the production and the reception of literature" (Lefevere, 1987: 19). Lefevere argues that an analysis of literary texts, an analysis of how rewriting – translation being the most common form – insures the continuity of literature, must always consider not only the influence of poetics and literary systems, but also ideology and institutions of power. Any approach which foregrounds merely one or the other, according to Lefevere, will be insufficient.

In an article titled "Systems Thinking and Cultural Relativism" (1988–9), Lefevere talks more about how better to come to terms with the roles played by semiological systems of power in cultures. "To do so," he argues, "we could do worse than follow the examples of both Roland Barthes and Michel Foucault" (Lefevere, 1988–9: 57). He likes Barthes because he points out the arbitrariness and artificiality of semiological systems, and the vast and almost anonymous manner in which "deciding groups" in the establishment define our way of thinking, leaving the individual with little say. Semiological systems do not simply exist and evolve on their own, but are put into operation by force (Barthes, 1967: 31). Lefevere refers to Foucault, on the other hand, for reminding us of the positive role semiological systems of power can play. Foucault asks, "If power were never anything but repressive, if it never did anything but say no, do you really think one would be brought to obey it?" In keeping with deconstruction as an act of affirmative productivity, Foucault argues that power is not just a repressive force, but that "it traverses and produces things, it induces pleasure, forms knowledge, produces discourse" (Foucault, 1980: 119). By going beyond interpretation and looking at factors by which a culture shapes works of literature, Lefevere argues that we quickly arrive at the important role "rewriters" – critics, translators, anthologizers, and historiographers – play. Theo Hermans argued in 1985 that all translations can be seen as forms of manipulation of texts. In 1990, Lefevere argues that the study of all literary texts within any given culture can also be a study in manipulation. For rewriters are in charge of discourse, their function being "to preserve or reproduce discourse, but in order that it should circulate within a closed community, according to strict regulations" (Foucault, 1976: 225). Rewriters hold their position as experts after their sanctioning by social institutions through the awarding of degrees, publication of books and articles, invitations to conferences, and appointments at schools. Thus, to a large degree, rewriters indirectly conform to the values those institutions hold dear. Yet Lefevere argues that such writers are also aware of the restrictive nature of the poetics of their time. While never forgetting that all choices are invariably circumscribed by power, he does argue that "neither ideology nor poetics, neither patronage nor rewriters are monolithic entities. Those who feel unhappy with the ideology and/or poetics of their own system will plan to use (rewrite) elements taken from the other system to further their own ends" (Lefevere, 1988–9: 64). Using systems theory to study texts as they occur within culture would allow the scholar to describe literary phenomena without recourse to terms like "good" and "bad" or "right" and "wrong." Focusing on systems of power allows the scholar instead to describe such situations in a manner that does "justice to the relativity of all systems." Such an approach may, eventually, reverse a trend predominant in the West that has served only to isolate literary studies – Translation Studies included – from the rest of society.

Whereas Lefevere has arrived at a cultural relativism position by working within the field, primarily as a literary translator and Translation Studies scholar, Bassnett has enjoyed more of an insider/outsider relationship with Translation Studies. In addition to her work in Translation Studies (Bassnett, 1980; 1985), she has been very active in theatre criticism and women's studies. In the last several years she has published two books on Pirandello (Bassnett, 1983, 1989b), a book on three actresses (1988), a book on the women's movement in four different cultures (1986), books on Sylvia Plath and Elizabeth I (1987; 1988), and edited a book on Latin American Women's Writing (1990). Such a varied background has helped her remain open for differing approaches to the study of translation, and led her to organize a large international conference under the heading "Beyond Translation" held at the University of Warwick in 1988. In "Translation, Tradition, Transmission," her introduction to the Autumn 1989 edition of *New Comparison*, which collects some of the papers given at the conference, she argues that studying translation today means "being aware of the processes that shape a culture at a given point of time" (Bassnett, 1989a: 1). Such processes include the extraliterary: economic, political, social factors as well as metaphysical considerations. She concludes, "In short, the ideological dimension, so long ignored in investigations of translation processes, has been restored and our knowledge of cultural history has consequently been enriched" (Bassnett, 1989a: 1).

All of the approaches outlined in this book – from the American translation workshop and its emphasis on good taste and literary value, to the "science" of translations and its prescriptive focus on "quality," through early Translation Studies and its privileging literary devices which "function" artistically in the receiving culture, and Polysystem theory, which purports to "objectivity" in a very high-handed fashion, and finally deconstruction, which by its very scintillating performance distances itself from affecting real cultural exchange – threaten to become entrenched in academic systems and self-defeating battles over the same turf. Their claims for "correctness" or greater "objectivity," their often dogmatic attempts to build consensus at the expense of others, and their development of a very specific and often limiting jargon have merely led to much in-fighting, a lack of co-operation and intercultural exchange within the field, and further marginalization of the discipline. Yet something is changing now. Translation Studies seems to focus not solely on the source text, nor on the target text, but looks instead at how different discourses and semiotic practices are mediated through translation. In the wake of Heidegger's and Derrida's initiative, the philosophical problem of translation is studied as one of the central problems in philosophy. In the wake of Foucault, the political problem of translation within the academy and within society is becoming increasingly of interest to both literary critics and sociologists. In the nineties, those translation theorists who have worked through the contribution of deconstructionists will not only be at the forefront of their own field, but may begin to engage in meaningful exchanges with those from other fields.

Such a reassessment of definitions and erasure of boundaries that have previously constrained the field can only be positive, not only for Western theorists, but also for writers and translators of non-Western origin. In a series of lectures delivered as 1991 CERA Professor at the annual summer research seminar held at the University of Leuven, Susan Bassnett indicated that a slight opening in the cultural hegemony was about to occur. She argues that poets and translators Haroldo and Augusto de Campos from Brazil, for example, use Derrida to develop something like a postmodern and non-Eurocentric approach to translation. In their approach to literary translation, the de Campos brothers refuse any sort of preordained original, but instead view translation as a form of transgression. They use terms not part of any European approach or science, but come up with their own terms, one of which is translation as a form of "cannibalism." Yet this term is not to be understood as another form of possessing the original, but as a liberating form, one which eats, digests, and frees oneself from the original. Cannibalism is to be understood not in the Western sense, i.e., that of capturing, dismembering, mutilating, and devouring, but in a sense which shows respect, i.e., as a symbolic act of taking back out of love, of absorbing the virtues of a body through a transfusion of blood. Translation is seen as an empowering act, a nourishing act, an act of affirmative play that is very close to the Benjamin/Derrida position, which sees translation as a life-force that ensures a literary text's survival. The de Campos', according to Bassnett, are great admirers of Ezra Pound, arguing that his invention of Cathay was such a form of cannibalism inspired by love and reverence for a foreign culture. As early as 1952, the de Campos brothers founded the Grupo *Noigrandres*, and published a journal under the same name, leading a Brazilian movement in contemporary French and Anglo-American experimental verse and theory. "*Noigrandres*" is coined from Pound's Canto XX, in which Pound is struggling to decipher one Provençal term, "Noigandres, eh *noi* gandres / Now

what the DEFFIL can that mean!" (Pound, 1975: 90). By 1953, the
two had established a correspondence with Pound, and began
meeting with a group of painters and sculptors in São Paulo (de
Campos, Pignattari, and de Campos, 1965: 177). Ironically, it seems
that Pound's literary theory and its relation to sculpture and painting was better known in Brazil than it was in America. By avoiding
traditional notions of faithful/free, Bassnett argues, the de Campos
brothers' theory of translation not only does away with a sense of
loss, but also participates in a positive act of affirmation, of pleasure,
and of joy. The two have not only translated an anthology of Pound's
poems, Pound's *The Cantos*, and Pound's *ABC of Reading*, but also
Joyce's *Finnegans Wake*, as well as work by e. e. cummings, Stéphane
Mallarmé, and Vladimir Mayakóvski.

While a "cannibalistic" theory of translation may be disturbing
to the Western translation scholar, it is not inconsistent with the
approach implicitly advocated throughout this book. Language is
never reducible to a formal system, nor to a static concept, be it
literary or linguistic, and translations, invariably demonstrate the
inherent instability of language in their every act – in other words,
the all too human desire for unification and closure that tends to
engender only further mistranslation and misrecognition. Historically, translation criticism has valorized translations which
measure up to some ideal by smoothing over contradictions, and
has ignored or dismissed those which do not cohere. Such a
practice in turn affects that which gets produced, and the self-
perpetuating nature of the phenomenon should be clear. While
traditionally translation theories made certain metaphysical
claims, translations themselves often fail to conform to the claims
being made about them. For in the act of reproducing the textual
relations (of the original text), a double constitution becomes
quite lucid: the language restraints imposed by the receiving
culture are enormous, yet the possibility of creating new relations
in the present are also vivid – not just the old relations transported
to a new time and place, but also a myriad of signifying practices
which both reinforce and alter present signifying practices. In
fact, the process of translation and the process of the construction
of our own selves may be analogous: as translations are subjected
to at least two semiotic systems (source and target languages), but
are nevertheless capable of changing those very structures, so are
we as humans the subjects of a variety of discourses, but also free
to change those relations that condition our existence.

Walter Benjamin, in his essay "The Task of the Translator," understood this double constitution very well. Translation is viewed as a "mode" of its own, one which offers a way of "coming to terms with the foreignness of languages" (W. Benjamin, trans. Zohn, 1969: 75), yet a way frequently unrealized. Benjamin speaks in terms of a "recreation" which "must lovingly and in detail" transform and renew something living, i.e., the original text, as it supplements and ensures the survival of the existing language. Benjamin's essay not only breaks down any reified concept of the inviolable original, but also argues that our own language, our own generic categories, our own concept of text, and our own concept of sacrosanct, should not be reified. This is why Benjamin, like Pound, asks that we translate not by using whole or unified categories, which invariably reinforce existing generic distinctions, but instead proceed word-by-word or image-by-image. Only then can foreign cultural elements enter our own discourse and begin to break down our limited cultural conceptions, ensuring our growth. Benjamin argues against translations which turn foreign language into German, and instead advocates the kind of translation which allows itself to be affected by the foreign language, allows itself, in his words, to pursue "its own course according to the laws of fidelity in the freedom of linguistic flux" (W. Benjamin, trans. Zohn, 1969: 80). Derrida talks about redefining translation as "regulated transformation." The entire essay can be read as an attempt to define the laws specific to translation alone, this "mode" of writing which owes no allegiance to its source, nor to its receiver, but enjoys its own unique kind of freedom. Benjamin's theory is clearly liberating and empowering, allowing one not only to "liberate the language imprisoned in a work," but also to escape from the "spell" of one's own language (W. Benjamin, trans. Zohn, 1969: 80). In addition to reporting on the various approaches governing translation theory today, I have tried in the course of this book to point out how each particular translation theory may help us better understand this double movement, this "interpellation" which simultaneously interrupts our own constructed identities and propels them forward.

While the process of interpellation is active in every act of reading, writing, and communication, it is often obscured and performed unconsciously, thus often difficult to observe. Perhaps the single greatest asset of Translation Studies – the one most important for the field's survival and growth – is the increasing awareness by scholars in other fields that, in the analysis of translation, elements of the functioning of the unconscious can be seen. In her essay "Taking Fidelity Philosophically," Barbara Johnson argues, "In the process of translation from one language to another, the scene of linguistic castration – which is nothing other than a scene of impossible but unavoidable translation and normally takes place out of sight – is played on center stage" (Johnson, 1985: 144). Because translation "is played out on center stage," certain misrecognitions and "shifts," from the source text, can be identified and analyzed. Using translated texts to better understand subjective translation strategies, Holmes, Popovič, and Lefevere suggest examining precisely those shifts to pursue such an investigation. Because of its unique nature, translation gives us access to those very unconscious and "out of sight" manipulations which result in mistranslation and misrecognition. Derrida suggests that "recovering" that out of sight place may be possible, or at least as far as it may be possible, translation will be the place where it may become visible.

Certain Translation Studies scholars seem to be on the verge of doing precisely that. The field's descriptive methodology, based on actual texts, documents such shifts as they occur in the history of the life of one "original" text. Such translation histories can be "used" to reveal how the literary mind under real historical circumstances interprets the world. By examining actual translated texts instead of hypothetical models, Even-Zohar and Toury have exposed an horizon of real cultural and institutional manipulation affecting the process of literary and cultural evolution. By going beyond interpretation, the theorist can read these case studies symptomatically for the unconscious manipulations which are also a part of every literary text. Hidden entities become visible in the translated text. That silence does not necessarily tell us anything, but it does inform us, as literary theorists, of the conditions necessary for particular utterances, and, ironically, dispels any notion of truth or literal meaning. In such an approach, the very concept of "meaning" is altered. What becomes visible instead is an unstable entity, cohering to a degree in the *relation* between the implicit and the explicit. If in translation the *non-dit* is brought out into the open, we can measure that which is said against that which cannot be said in a particular context and begin to unveil another kind of "meaning" of any given text.

In contrast to most other kinds of literary texts, translated works, because they can be compared to other translations in different cultural contexts and different historical periods, lend themselves well to such an analysis. Bassnett and Lefevere argue that the methodology for such an analysis is in place. Because research has already shown that translations have proven a major factor in the development of culture worldwide, and because Translation Studies as a discipline already has developed a methodology that can show the relationships between literary evolution and other developing cultural systems, Bassnett and Lefevere claim that our notions of Comparative Literature need to be rethought and that perhaps Comparative Literature should be redefined as a "subcategory of Translation Studies" (Bassnett and Lefevere, 1990: 12).

For the scholar who works "monolinguistically," however, such relations tend to remain out of sight and thus become very difficult to grasp in a concrete way. Freudian slips and idiosyncrasies may give us clues, but in general there is not much *material* to base a such a reading on. As a result, literary criticism is dominated by "correct" interpretation or rearticulation of that which has already been said. The advantage of working with overt translated literature begins to emerge: with careful study, the shifts, the misrecognitions, and the relations which constitute them become even more visible than the one-to-one correspondences. Traditional translation theory, based upon notions governing traditional monolinguistic criticism, tended to dismiss such shifts as "errors" and "mistakes." As I have suggested, such standards imply notions of substantialism and textual equivalence that limit certain other possibilities of translation practice, marginalize unorthodox translations, and impinge upon real intercultural exchange. Current translation criticism, however, is beginning to compare the nature of the "mistake" to the original, analyze the relation, and identify the causes.

Whether one proceeds inductively, like Lambert, or deductively, like Lefevere and Bassnett, to identify such causes, the results are much the same. What becomes apparent when analyzing the evolution of one text in history, viewing its multiple forms and the processes of reintegration into different historical epochs, are not the eternal verities of the original, but the mechanisms of history which mask any sense of the original at all. By recognizing the limits imposed by the receiving culture, by problematizing those discursive constraints, critics can hope not only to open up the discourse of translation theory for its own possible transformation, but to help open the receiving culture for possible social change (through the practice of translation). Translation Studies scholars no doubt can learn much from scholars of ethnic minorities, women, minor literatures, and popular literatures. Much of the most exciting work in the field is already being produced by scholars from the "smaller" countries – Belgium, the Netherlands, Israel, Czechoslovakia, and French-speaking Canada.

In their 1990 anthology *Translation, History and Culture*, Bassnett and Lefevere offer a space for such alternative discourse. Barbara Godard, who has published both on Quebec writers and on feminist critical theory, gives a good introduction to the correlation between translation theory based upon notions of difference and theories of feminist discourse in "Theorizing Feminist Discourse/Translation." Whereas difference or non-equivalence has been judged negatively by traditional translation theorists, difference becomes a positive aspect in a feminist framework. Nine of the thirteen contributors to the Bassnett and Lefevere collection are women, which is in itself an historical turn for the field. Maria Tymoczko, an Irish studies scholar, opens up the thorny problem of translations in oral traditions, subverting any translation theory based upon a notion of a fixed text, be it source or target, in her article "Translation in Oral Tradition as a Touchstone for Translation Theory and Practice" (Tymoczko, 1990). In "Translation and the Consequences of Scepticism," Anne Mette Hjort from Montréal talks about the problem of reference, and the consequences for translation if one accepts Quine's claim that the referents of terms are inscrutable (Hjort, 1990). Elzbieta Tabakowska from Poland further explores the problem of Bakhtinian polyphony and internal dialogism in "Linguistic Polyphony as a Problem in Translation" (Tabakowska, 1990). Although the actual business of translation tends to be female dominated, the theorizing of the activity has traditionally been commandeered by men. Polysystem theory and Translation Studies have to a large degree continued the trend, and their very scientific discourse and claims of objectivity have perhaps served to further exclude women. One difference between recent Translation Studies and Bassnett/Lefevere's position is precisely that the latter has opened a space for discussion of the feminist challenge that the former has largely ignored.

As the French-Canadian and other women are well aware, a bond exists between feminist theory and translation theory. As women's discourse has been repressed by more dominant forms in Western culture, so too have some approaches to translation theory been subsumed by more dominant forms of literary theory. The theoretical insights gained by the feminist contributors should prove not only valuable in terms of gaining insight into the nature of language, but also in terms of Translation Studies' struggle to gain acceptance within the larger institution of comparative literature and literary theory. The field has gained only a small degree of institutionalization in Europe, and it remains largely excluded from American academic centers. Theoretically, Walter Benjamin's suggestion that literary translation be considered neither as source or target text oriented, but as a mode of its own – subject to its own laws – is alien to the current reception-oriented trend in Translation Studies and Anglo-American literary theory. Yet such a marginalization may be an asset. Perhaps because of its being a minor discourse within larger institutions, the study of literary translation has been able to gain valuable insights into the nature of language and into cross-cultural communication. Translation Studies scholars are achieving a theoretical basis which enables them to engage as equal partners in discussions with professionals from any number of fields – media studies, sociology, linguistics, anthropology, psychology, cultural studies, literary theory, literary history, and philosophy – and this very lack of entrenchment and potential for interdisciplinary investigation may have its advantages. Some radical rethinking of certain positions is taking place, and certain surprising risks are being taken as definitions within the field get called into question. If the field had a more permanent status within the institution, chances are fewer risks would be taken.

I hope this book serves to aid future collaboration, to break down misconceptions of competing viewpoints, and to further open the door for new, alternative approaches. Much work still needs to be done. The deconstruction of the authorities governing the field of translation, of literary criticism, of culture in general, is merely a first step. Although modern translation theory has evolved a long way since its structuralist beginnings, it now stands on the threshold of a very exciting new phase, one which can begin to unpack the relations in which meaning is constituted, and thus better inform our post-structuralist conception of language and literary discourse, as well as our selves. With such insight, perhaps we will be less likely to dismiss that which does not fit into or measure up to our standards, and instead open our selves to alternative ways of perceiving – in other words, to invite real intra- and intercultural communication.

References

Apter, Ronnie (1984) *Digging for the Treasure: Translation After Pound*, New York: Peter Lang.

Arnauld, Antoine (1964) *The Art of Thinking: Port-Royal Logic*, trans. James Dickoff and Patricia James, Indianapolis: Bobbs-Merrill.

Austin, J. L. (1962) *How to Do Things with Words*, Cambridge: Harvard University Press.

Bakhtin, Mikhail (1981) *The Dialogic Imagination*, trans. and ed. Michael Holquist, Austin: University of Texas Press.

Bann, Stephen (1984) "The Career of *Tel Quel* : *Tel Quel* becomes *L'Infini*," in E. S. Shaffer (ed.) *Comparative Criticism* 6, Cambridge: Cambridge University Press.

Bann, Stephen and John Bowlt (eds) (1973) *Russian Formalism: A Collection of Articles and Texts in Translation*, Edinburgh: Scottish Academy Press.

Barry, Elaine (ed.) (1973) *Robert Frost on Writing*, New Brunswick: Rutgers University Press.

Barthes, Roland (1964) "Criticism as Language," in *The Critical Moment: Essays on the Nature of Literature*, London: Faber & Faber.

——(1967) *Elements of Semiology*, trans. Annette Lavers and Colin Smith, New York: Hill & Wang.

Bassnett, Susan (1980) *Translation Studies*, London: Methuen.

——(1983) *Luigi Pirandello*, London: Macmillan.

——(1985) "Ways Through the Labyrinth; Strategies and Methods for Translating Theatre Texts," in Theo Hermans (ed.) *The Manipulation of Literature*, New York: St. Martins Press.

——(1986) *Feminist Experiences: The Woman's Movement in Four Cultures*, London: Allen & Unwin.

——(1987) *Sylvia Plath*, London: Macmillan.

——(1988) *Elizabeth I: A Feminist Biography*, Oxford: Berg.

——(1989a) "Translation, Tradition, Transmission," in Susan Bassnett (ed.) *Beyond Translation, New Comparison* 8 (Autumn): 1–2.

——(1989b) *File on Pirandello*, London: Methuen.

Bassnett, Susan (ed.) (1989) *Beyond Translation, New Comparison* 8 (Autumn).

——(1990) *Knives and Angels: Latin American Women's Writing*, London: Zed.

Bassnett, Susan, P. Bono, R. Duranti, A. Goldoni, and M. V. Tessitore (eds) (1988) *The Actress in her Time: Bernhardt, Terry, Duse*, Cambridge: Cambridge University Press.

Bassnett, Susan and André Lefevere (eds) (1990) *Translation, History and Culture*, London: Pinter.

Belloc, Hilaire (1931) *On Translation*, Oxford: Clarendon Press.

Bender, Karl-Heinz, Klaus Berger, and Mario Wandruszka (eds) (1977) *Imago linguae; Beiträge zu Sprache, Deutung und Übersetzen: Festschrift zum 60. Geburtstag von Fritz Päpcke*, Munich: W. Fink.

Benjamin, Andrew (1989) *Translation and the Nature of Philosophy; A New Theory of Words*, London and New York: Routledge.

Benjamin, Walter (1955) *Illuminationen*, Frankfurt: Suhrkamp.

——(1969) *Illuminations*, trans. Harry Zohn, New York: Schocken Books.

Berlin, Brent, Dennis E. Breedlove, and Peter H. Raven (1974) *Principles of Tzeltal Plant Classification*, New York: Academic Press.

Bernasconi, Robert (1985) *The Question of Language in Heidegger's History of Being*, Atlantic Highlands, NJ: Humanities Press.

Biemel, Walter (1973) *Heidegger*, Reinbek bei Hamburg: Rowohlt Taschenbuch Verlag.

——(1976) *Heidegger*, trans. J. L. Mehta, New York: Harcourt Brace Jovanovich.

Bishop, Elizabeth and Emanuel Brasil (eds) (1971) *An Anthology of Twentieth Century Brazilian Poetry*, Middletown, CT: Wesleyan University Press.

Bloom, Harold, Paul de Man, Jacques Derrida, Geoffrey Hartman, and J. Hillis Miller (1979) *Deconstruction and Criticism*, New York: The Seabury Press.

Bly, Robert (1984) "The Eight Stages of Translation," in William Frawley (ed.) *Translation: Literary, Linguistic and Philosophical Perspectives*, Newark: University of Delaware Press.

Bonnefoy, Yves (1968) *On the Motion and Immobility of Douve*, trans. Galway Kinnell, Athens: Ohio University Press.

Borges, Jorge Luis (1962) "Pierre Menard, Author of *Don Quixote*," trans. Anthony Bonner, in Anthony Kerrigan (ed.) *Ficciones*, New York: Grove Press.

——(1972) *Selected Poems*, trans. Alistair Reid, Ben Belitt, and others, New York: Delacorte Press.

Bragt, Katrin Van (1982) "The Tradition of a Translation and its Implications: 'The Vicar of Wakefield' in French Translation," in André Lefevere and Kenneth David Jackson (eds) *The Art and Science of Translation, Dispositio* (19-21): 63-76.

Brisset, Annie (1989) "In Search of a Target Language: The Politics of Theatre Translation in Quebec," *Target* 1(1): 9–28.

Broeck, Raymond Van den (1978) "The Concept of Equivalence in Translation Theory: Some Critical Reflections," in James S. Holmes, José Lambert, and Raymond Van den Broeck (eds) *Literature and Translation*, Leuven, Belgium: Acco.

——(1981) "The Limits of Translatability Exemplified by Metaphor Translation," in Itamar Even-Zohar and Gideon Toury (eds) *Translation Theory and Intercultural Relations, Poetics Today* 2(4): 73–88.

——(1985) "Second Thoughts on Translation Criticism: A Model of its Analytic Function," in Theo Hermans (ed.) *The Manipulation of Literature: Studies in Literary Translation*, New York: St. Martins Press.

——(1988) "Translation Theory after Deconstruction," *Linguistica Antverpiensia* 22: 266–88.

Broeck, Raymond Van den, and André Lefevere (1979) *Uitnodiging tot de vertaalwetenschap*, Muiderberg: Coutinho.

Bühler, Hildegund (ed.) (1985) *Proceedings from X. Weltkongress der FIT*, Vienna: Wilhelm Braumüller.

Bühler, Karl (1965) *Sprachtheorie*, Stuttgart: Fischer.

Campos, Augusto de (1965) "Pound (made new) in Brazil," in *Ezra Pound*, vol. 1, Paris: L"Herne.

Campos, Augusto de, Décio Pignatari, and Haroldo de Campos (1965) *Teoria da Poesia Concreta; Textos Críticos e Manifestos 1950–1960*, São Paulo: Edições Invenção.

Campos, Haroldo de (1969) *A Arte No Horizonte do Provável*, São Paulo: Editôra Perspectiva S.A.

Carroll, John B. (ed.) (1962) *Selected Writings of Benjamin Lee Whorf*, Cambridge, MA: Technology Press of Massachusetts Institute of Technology.

Catford, J. C. (1969) *A Linguistic Theory of Translation: An Essay in Applied Linguistics*, London: Oxford University Press.

Cattrysse, Patrick (1991) "De Semi-Documentaire: een analyse in termen van normen en systemen," *Communicatie* 20 (3): 11-32.

——(1992) "Film (Adaptation) as Translation: Some Methodological Proposals," *Target* 4 (1):53–70.

Chomsky, Noam (1957) *Syntactic Structures*, The Hague: Mouton.

——(1965) *Aspects of the Theory of Syntax*, Cambridge, MA: The MIT Press.

——(1966) *Cartesian Linguistics*, New York: Harper & Row.

——(1968) "Quine's Empirical Assumptions," *Synthese* 19: 53–68.

——(1972) *Language and Mind*, 2nd ed., New York: Harcourt Brace Jovanovich.

——(1980) *The Logical Structure of Linguistic Theory*, New York and London: Plenum Press.

Chomsky, Noam, and Michel Foucault (1974) "Human Nature: Justice Versus Power," in Fons Elders (ed.) *Reflexive Water*, London: Souvenir Press.

Congrat-Butler, Stefan (1979) *Translation and Translators: An International Directory and Guide*, New York: R. R. Bowker Company.

Culler, Jonathan D. (1981) *Pursuit of Signs – Semiotics, Literature, Deconstruction*, Ithaca: Cornell University Press.

——(1983) *On Deconstruction: Theory and Criticism after Structuralism*, London: Routledge.

cummings, e.e. (1960) *Dez Poemas de e.e. cummings*, trans. Augusto de Campos, Rio de Janeiro: Serviço de Documentaçao-MEC.

Davidson, Donald (1984) *Inquiries into Truth and Interpretation*, Oxford: Clarendon Press.

Davie, Donald (1964) *Ezra Pound; Poet as Sculptor*, New York: Oxford University Press.

——(1975) *Pound*, Glasgow: Fontana.

Delabastita, Dirk (1988) "Translation and Mass-Communication: Film and T.V. – Translation as Evidence of Cultural Dynamics," Preprint, no. 10, Leuven: Departement Literatuurwetenschap.

——(1990) "Translation and the Mass Media," in Susan Bassnett and André Lefevere (eds) *Translation, History and Culture*, London: Pinter.

Derrida, Jacques (1974) *Of Grammatology*, trans. Gayatri Chakravorty Spivak, Baltimore: Johns Hopkins University Press.

——(1977) "Signature Event Context," *Glyph* 1: 172–97.

——(1978) *Writing and Difference*, trans. Alan Bass, Chicago: University of Chicago Press.

——(1979) "Living On" and "Border Lines," trans. James Hulbert, in Harold Bloom, Paul de Man, Jacques Derrida, Geoffrey Hartman, and J. Hillis Miller, *Deconstruction and Criticism*, New York: The Seabury Press.

——(1981) *Positions*, trans. Alan Bass, Chicago: University of Chicago Press.

——(1982) *Margins of Philosophy*, trans. Alan Bass, Chicago: University of Chicago Press.

——(1985a) "Des Tours de Babel," trans. Joseph F. Graham, in Joseph F. Graham (ed.) *Difference and Translation*, Ithaca: Cornell University Press.

——(1985b) *The Ear of the Other: Texts and Discussions with Jacques Derrida*, ed. Christie McDonald, trans. Peggy Kamuf, Lincoln: University of Nebraska Press.

——(1987) *Glas*, trans. J. P. Leavy, Lincoln: University of Nebraska Press.

Descartes, René (1955) "Notes Directed against a Certain Programme," trans. E. S. Haldane and G. T. Ross, in *The Philosophical Works of Descartes*, vol. 1, New York: Dover.

D'Hulst, Lieven (1982) "The Conflict of Translation Models in France (End of 18th – Beginning of 19th Century)," in André Lefevere and Kenneth David Jackson (eds) *The Art and Science of Translation, Dispositio* 7(19–21): 41–52.

——(1987) *L'Evolution de la poésie en France (1780–1830): Introduction à une analyse des interférences systémiques*, Leuven: University Press (Symbolai, series D literaria, 1).

D'Hulst, Lieven, José Lambert, and Katrin van Bragt (1979) *Littérature et traduction en France, 1800–1850; Etat des travaux*, Leuven: Preprint, Department of General Literary Studies, University of Leuven.

Doran, Marci Nita and Marilyn Gaddis Rose (1981) "The Economics and Politics of Translation," in Marilyn Gaddis Rose (ed.) *Translation Spectrum: Essays in Theory and Practice*, Albany: State University of New York Press.

Dressler, Wolfgang U. (ed.) (1978) *Current Trends in Textlinguistics*, Berlin: W. de Gruyter.

Eagleton, Terry (1985) "Ideology and Scholarship," in Jerome J. McGann (ed.) *Historical Studies and Literary Criticism*, Madison: University of Wisconsin Press.

Eco, Umberto (1976) *A Theory of Semiotics*, Bloomington: Indiana University Press.

Èjxenbaum, Boris M. (1978) "The Theory of the Formal Method," trans. I. R. Titunik, in Ladislav Matejka and Krystyna Pomorska (eds) *Readings in Russian Poetics: Formalist and Structuralist Views*, Ann Arbor: Michigan Slavic Publications.

Elston, Angela (1980) "The Golden Crane Anthology of Translation," *Modern Poetry in Translation*, 39 (Spring): 11–36.

Engle, Paul and Hualing Nieh Engle (1985) Foreword to *Writing from the World: II*, Iowa City: International Books and the University of Iowa Press.

Erlich, Victor (1981) *Russian Formalism: History – Doctrine*, 3rd ed., New Haven: Yale University Press.

Even-Zohar, Itamar (1978a) *Papers in Historical Poetics*, in Benjamin Hrushovski and Itamar Even-Zohar (eds) *Papers on Poetics and Semiotics* 8, Tel Aviv: University Publishing Projects.

——(1978b) "The Position of Translated Literature within the Literary Polysystem," in James S. Holmes, José Lambert, and Raymond Van den Broeck (eds) *Literature and Translation: New Perspectives in Literary Studies with a Basic Bibliography of Books on Translation Studies*, Leuven, Belgium: Acco. Also in (1978a) *Papers in Historical Poetics*, in Benjamin Hrushovski and Itamar Even-Zohar (eds) *Papers on Poetics and Semiotics* 8, Tel Aviv: University Publishing Projects.

——(1981) "Translation Theory Today: A Call for a Transfer Theory," in Itamar Even-Zohar and Gideon Toury (eds) *Translation Theory and Intercultural Relations*, *Poetics Today* 2:4 (Summer–Autumn): 1–8.

——(1990) *Polysystems Studies*, *Poetics Today*, 11:1 (Spring).

Even-Zohar, Itamar and Gideon Toury (eds) (1981) *Translation Theory and Intercultural Relations*. *Poetics Today* 2:4 (Summer–Autumn).

Felsteiner, John (1980) *Translating Neruda: The Way to Macchu Picchu*, Stanford: Stanford University Press.

——(1989) "Kafka and the Golem: Translating Paul Celan," in Daniel Weissbort (ed.) *Translating Poetry: The Double Labyrinth*, Iowa City: University of Iowa Press.

Fenollosa, Ernest (1936) *The Chinese Written Character as a Medium for Poetry*, ed. Ezra Pound, San Francisco: City Lights.

Filipec, J. (1973) "Der Äquivalenzbegriff und das Problem der Übersetzen," in Walter Graul, Otto Kade, Karl Kokoschko, and Hans Zikmund (eds) *Neue Beiträge zu Grundfragen der Übersetzungswissenschaft* vols 5, 6, *Beihefte zur Zeitschrift Fremdsprachen*, Leipzig: Enzyklopädie.

Follain, Jean (1979) *The Transparence of the World*, trans. W. S. Merwin, New York: Atheneum.

Foucault, Michel (1973) *The Order of Things*, trans. anonymous, New York: Vintage Books.

——(1976) *The Archeology of Knowledge and The Discourse on Language*, trans. A. M. Sheridan Smith, New York: Harper & Row.

——(1977) *Language, Counter-memory, Practice*, trans. Donald F. Bouchard and Sherry Simon, Ithaca: Cornell University Press.

——(1980) *Power/Knowledge; Selected Interviews and Other Writings 1972–1977*, ed. Colin Gordon, trans. Colin Gordon, Leo Marshall, John Mepham, and Kate Soper, New York: Pantheon.

Foucault, Michel, Roland Barthes, Jacques Derrida, Jean-Louis Baudry, and Phillipe Sollers (1968) *Théorie d'ensemble*, Paris: Seuil.

Frank, Armin Paul (1987) "Einleitung," in Brigitte Schultze (ed.) *Die literarische Übersetzung. Fallstudien zu ihrer Kulturgeschichte, Göttinger Beiträge zur Internationalen Übersetzungsforschung*, vol. 1, Berlin: Erich Schmidt Verlag.

——(1989) "'Translation as System' and *Übersetzungskultur*: On Histories and Systems in the Study of Literary Translation," *New Comparison* 8 (August): 85–98.

——(1990) "Systems and Histories in the Study of Literary Translations: A Few Distinctions," in Roger Bauer and Douwe Fokkema (eds) *Proceedings of the XIIth Congress of the International Comparative Literature Association*, vol. 1, Munich: Iudicium.

Frawley, William (ed.) (1984) *Translation: Literary, Linguistic and Philosophic Perspectives*, Newark: The University of Delaware Press.

Frost, Robert (1973) "Conversations on the Craft of Poetry," in Elaine Barry (ed.) *Robert Frost on Writing*, New Brunswick: Rutgers University Press.

Frow, John (1986) *Marxism and Literary History*, Oxford: Basil Blackwell.

Galan, F. W. (1985) *Historic Structures: The Prague School Project, 1928–1946*, Austin: University of Texas Press.

Godard, Barbara (1990) "Theorizing Feminist Discourse/Translation," in Susan Bassnett and André Lefevere (eds) *Translation, History and Culture*, London: Pinter.

Gorlée, Dinda (1989) "Wittgenstein, Translation and Semiotics," *Target* 1(1): 69–94.

——(forthcoming) *Translation after Jakobson after Peirce*.

Graehs, Lillebil, Gustav Korlén, and Bertil Malmberg (eds) (1978) *Theory and Practice of Translation*, Nobel Symposium 39, Bern: Lang.

Graham, Joseph F. (1981) "Theory for Translation," in Marilyn Gaddis Rose (ed.) *Translation Spectrum: Essays in Theory and Practice*, Albany: State University of New York Press.

Graham, Joseph F. (ed.) (1985) *Difference in Translation*, Ithaca: Cornell University Press.

Graves, Robert (1955) *The Crowning Privilege*. London: Cassell.

Guillevic, Eugene (1969) *Selected Poems*, trans. Denise Levertov, New York: New Directions.

Gumperz, John (1982) *Discourse Strategies*, Cambridge: Cambridge University Press.

Gumperz, John and Dell Hymes (eds) (1972) *Directions in Sociolinguistics: The Ethnography of Communication*, New York: Holt, Rinehart & Winston.

Hamburger, Michael (1989) "Brief Afterthoughts on Versions of a Poem by Hölderlin," in Daniel Weissbort (ed.) *Translating Poetry: The Double Labyrinth*, Iowa City: University of Iowa Press.

Harman, Gilbert (ed.) (1974) *On Noam Chomsky: Critical Essays*, Garden City, NY: Anchor Books.

Harris, Zellig (1940) "Review of Louis H. Gray, *Foundations of Language*," *Language* 16: 227.

Heidegger, Martin (1962) *Being and Time*, trans. John Macquarrie and Edward Robinson, New York: Harper & Row.

——(1969) *Identity and Difference*, bilingual ed., trans. Joan Stambaugh, New York: Harper & Row.

——(1971a) *On the Way to Language*, trans. Peter D. Hertz, New York: Harper & Row.

——(1971b) *Poetry, Language, Thought*, trans. Albert Hofstadter, New York: Harper & Row.

——(1972a) *Sein und Zeit*, 12th ed., Tübingen: Max Niemeyer Verlag.

——(1972b) *On Time and Being*, trans. Joan Stambaugh, New York: Harper & Row.

——(1975) *Early Greek Thinking*, trans. David Farrell Krell and Frank A. Capuzzi, New York: Harper & Row.

——(1977a) *Basic Writings*, ed. David Farrell Krell, New York: Harper & Row, 1977.

——(1977b) *Holzwege. Gesamtausgabe*, vol. 5, Frankfurt-on-Main: Vittorio Klostermann.

Hermans, Theo (1985) "Introduction: Translation Studies and a New Paradigm," in Theo Hermans (ed.) *The Manipulation of Literature: Studies in Literary Translation*, New York: St. Martins Press.

——(1991) "The Question of Norms," in Kitty Van Leuven-Zwart and Tom Naaijkens (eds) *Translation Studies: The State of the Art*, Amsterdam: Rodopi.

Hermans, Theo (ed.) (1985) *The Manipulation of Literature: Studies in Literary Translation*, New York: St. Martins Press.

Holmes, James S. (1969) "Poem and Metapoem: Poetry from Dutch to English," *Linguistica Antverpiensia* 3: 101–15.

——(1970) "Forms of Verse Translation and the Translation of Verse Form," in James S. Holmes, Frans de Haan and Anton Popovič (eds) *The Nature of Translation*, The Hague: Mouton.

——(1972/75) *The Name and Nature of Translation Studies*, Amsterdam: Translation Studies Section, Department of General Studies.

——(1973–4) "On Matching and Making Maps: From a Translator's Notebook," *Delta* 16 (4): 67–82.

——(1978) "Describing Literary Translation: Models and Methods," in James S. Holmes, José Lambert, and Raymond Van den Broeck (eds) *Literature and Translation: New Perspectives in Literary Studies with a Basic Bibliography of Books on Translation Studies*, Leuven, Belgium: Acco.

——(1985) "The State of Two Arts: Literary Translation and Translation Studies in the West Today," in Hildegund Bühler (ed.) *Proceedings from X. Weltkongress der FIT*, Vienna: Wilhelm Braumüller.

——(1988) *Translated! Papers on Literary Translation and Translation Studies*, Approaches to Translation Studies 7, Amsterdam: Rodopi.

——(1989) "Translating Martial and Vergil: Jacob Lowland among the Classics," in Daniel Weissbort (ed.) *Translating Poetry: The Double Labyrinth*, Iowa City: University of Iowa Press.

Holmes, James S., Frans de Haan, and Anton Popovič (eds) (1970) *The Nature of Translation*, The Hague: Mouton.

Holmes, James S., José Lambert, and Raymond Van den Broeck (eds.) (1978) *Literature and Translation: New Perspectives in Literary Studies with a Basic Bibliography of Books on Translation Studies*, Leuven, Belgium: Acco.

Honig, Edwin (1985) *The Poet's Other Voice: Conversations on Literary Translation*, Amherst: University of Massachusetts Press.

Hughes, Ted (1983) Introduction to *Modern Poetry in Translation: 1983*, New York: MPT/Persea.

——(1989) "Postscript to János Csokits' Note," in Daniel Weissbort (ed.) *Translating Poetry: The Double Labyrinth*, Iowa City: University of Iowa Press.

Humboldt, Wilhelm von (1988) *On Language: The Diversity of Human Language-structure and its Influence on the Mental Development of Mankind*, trans. Peter Heath, Cambridge: Cambridge University Press.

Hymes, Dell (1974) *Foundations in Sociolinguistics*, Philadelphia: University of Pennsylvania Press.

Jacobs, Carol (1975) "The Monstrosity of Translation," *Modern Language Notes* 90.6 (December): 755–66.

Jackson, Robert Louis and Stephen Rudy (eds) (1985) *Russian Formalism: A Retrospective Glance*, New Haven: Yale Center for International and Area Studies.

Jakobson, Roman (1959) "On Linguistic Aspects of Translation," in Reuben A. Brower (ed.) *On Translation*, Cambridge, MA: Harvard University Press.

——(1976) "What is Poetry?" trans. M. Heim, in Ladislav Matejka and Irwin R. Titunik (eds), *Semiotics of Art: Prague School Contributions*, Cambridge, MA: The MIT Press.

Jäger, Gert and Albrecht Neubert (eds) (1983) *Semantik und Übersetzungswissenschaft: Materialien der III. Internationalen Konferenz "Grundfragen der Übersetzungswissenschaft,"* Leipzig: Enzyklopädie.

Johnson, Barbara (1987) *A World of Difference*, Baltimore: Johns Hopkins University Press.

——(1985) "Taking Fidelity Philosophically," in Joseph F. Graham (ed.) *Difference and Translation*, Ithaca: Cornell University Press.

Joyce, James (1962) *Panaroma do Finnegans Wake*, trans. Augusto de Campos and Haroldo de Campos, São Paulo: Comissão Estadual de Literature.

Juarroz, Roberto (1977) *Vertical Poems*, trans. W. S. Merwin, Santa Cruz: Kayak.

Kade, Otto (1964) "Ist alles übersetzbar?" *Fremdsprachen*, 84–100.

——(1968) *Zufall und Gesetzmässigkeit in der Übersetzung*, Leipzig: Enzyklopädie.

Katz, Jerrold J. (1972) *Semantic Theory*, New York: Harper & Row.

Keeley, Edmund (1981) "The State of Translation," *Modern Poetry in Translation* 41–2: 7–18.

Kenner, Hugh (1954) Introduction to Ezra Pound's *Translations*, New York: New Directions.

——(1971) *The Pound Era*, Berkeley and Los Angeles: University of California Press.

Kittel, Harald (ed.) (1988) *Die literarische Übersetzung: Stand und Perspektiven ihrer Erforschung. Göttinger Beiträge zur Internationalen Übersetzungsforschung*, vol. 2, Berlin: Schmidt.

Klein, Ernest (1966) *A Comprehensive Etymological Dictionary of the English Language*, Amsterdam: Elsevier.

Klöpfer, Rolf (1967) *Die Theorie der literarischen Übersetzung. Freiburger Schriften zur Romanishen Philogie*, vol. 12, Munich: Wilhelm Fink Verlag.

——(1981) "Intra- and Intercultural Translation," in Itamar Even-Zohar and Gideon Toury (eds) *Translation Theory and Intercultural Relations, Poetics Today* 2:4 (Summer–Autumn): 29–38.

Koller, Werner (1979) *Einführung in die Übersetzungswissenschaft*, Uni-Taschenbücher 819, Heidelberg: Quelle & Mayer.

Korn, Marianne (1983) *Ezra Pound, Purpose, Form, Meaning*, London: Middlesex Polytechnic Press.

Koschmieder, Erwin (1965) *Beiträge zur allgeminen Syntax*, Heidelberg: C. Winter.

Kramer, G. (1973) "Zum Begriff der syntaktischen Invarianz in der Translation," in Walter Graul, Otto Kade, Karl Kokoschko, and Hans Zikmund (eds) *Neue Beiträge zu Grundfragen der Übersetzungswissenschaft* vols 5, 6, *Beihefte zur Zeitschrift Fremdsprachen*, Leipzig: Enzyklopädie.

Krell, David Farrell (1986) *Intimations of Mortality: Time, Truth and Finitude in Heidegger's Thinking of Being*, University Park: The Pennsylvania State University Press.

Kristeva, Julia (1973) "The Ruin of a Poetics," trans. Vivienne Mylne, in Stephen Bann and John E. Bowlt (eds) *Russian Formalism*, Edinburgh: Scottish Academic Press.

——(1980) *Desire in Language: A Semiotic Approach to Literature and Art*, ed. Leon S. Roudiez, trans. Thomas Gora, Alice Jardine, and Leon S. Roudiez, New York: Columbia University Press.

——(1983) "Mémoire," *L'Infini* (Winter): 39–54.

——(1984) *Revolution in Poetic Language*, trans. Margaret Waller, New York: Columbia University Press.

Kundera, Milan (1988) "Key Words, Problems Words, Words I Love," *The New York Times Book Review*, 6 March: 1 and 24–6.

Lakoff, George (1970) *Irregularity in Syntax*, New York: Holt, Rinehart & Winston.

Lakoff, Robin (1972) "Language in Context," *Language*, 48(4): 907–27.

Lambert, José (1982) "How Emile Deschamps Translated Shakespeare's Macbeth, or Theatre System and Translation System in French," in André Lefevere and Kenneth David Jackson (eds) *The Art and Science of Translation, Dispositio* (19–21): 53–62.

——(1986) "Les Relations littéraires internationales comme problème de réception," *Oeuvres et Critiques* 11(2): 173–89. Also in Janos Riez (ed.) (1986) *Festschrift für Henry Remak*, Tübingen: Gunther Narr.

——(1988) "Twenty Years of Research on Literary Translation at the Katholieke Universiteit Leuven," in Armin Paul Frank (ed.) *Die Liter-*

arische Übersetzung, Göttinger Beiträge zur internationalen Übersetzungsforschung, vol. 2, Berlin: Erich Schmidt.

——(1989a) "Translation Studies and (Comparative) Literary Studies in 1989," in *Os Estudios literarios (entre) Ciencia e hermeneutica*, Actes do I. Congresso da APLC, Lisbon: Associaçao Portuguesa da Literatura Comparada.

——(1989b) "La Traduction, les langues et la communication de masse: Les ambiguïtés du discours international," *Target* 1(2): 215–37.

——(1991) "In Quest of Literary World Maps," in Harald Kittel and Armin Paul Frank (eds) *Interculturality: the Historical Study of Literary Translations*, Berlin: Erich Schmidt.

Lambert, José and Hendrik Van Gorp (1985) "On Describing Translations," in Theo Hermans (ed.) *The Manipulation of Literature*, New York: St. Martins Press.

Lambert, José, Lieven D"Hulst, and Katrin Van Bragt (1985) "Translated Literature in France, 1800–1850," in Theo Hermans (ed.) *The Manipulation of Literature: Studies in Literary Translation*, New York: St. Martins Press.

Lambert, José and Clem Robyns (forthcoming) "Translation," in Roland Posner, Klaus Robering, and Thomas A. Sebeok (eds) *Semiotics: A Handbook on the Sign–Theoretic Foundations of Nature and Culture*, Berlin and New York: W. de Gruyter.

Larson, Mildred L. (1984) *Meaning-Based Translation: A Guide to Cross-Language Equivalence*, Lanham, Maryland: University Press of America.

Lefevere, André (1975) *Translating Poetry: Seven Strategies and a Blueprint*, Assen/Amsterdam: Van Gorcum.

——(1977a) *Literary Knowledge: A Polemical and Programmaic Essay on its Nature, Growth, Relevance and Transmission*, Assen/Amsterdam: Van Gorcum, 1977.

——(1977b) *Translating Literature: The German Tradition: From Luther to Rosenzweig*, Assen/Amsterdam: Van Gorcum.

——(1978a) "Translation: The Focus of the Growth of Literary Knowledge," in James S. Holmes, José Lambert, and Raymond Van den Broeck (eds) *Literature and Translation*, Leuven, Belgium: Acco.

——(1978b) "Translation Studies: The Goal of the Discipline," in James S. Holmes, José Lambert, and Raymond Van den Broeck (eds) *Literature and Translation: New Perspectives in Literary Studies with a Basic Bibliography of Books on Translation Studies*, Leuven, Belgium: Acco.

——(1979) "What Kind of Science Should Comparative Literature Be?" *Dispositio* 4: 10.

——(1981a) "Beyond the Process: Literary Translation in Literature and Literary Theory," in Marilyn Gaddis Rose (ed.) *Translation Spectrum: Essays in Theory and Practice*, Albany: State University of New York Press.

——(1981b) "Translated Literature: Towards an Integrated Theory," *Bulletin: Midwest MLA*, 14:1 (Spring): 68–78.

——(1981c) "Programmatic Second Thoughts on 'Literary' and 'Translation'," in Itamar Even-Zohar and Gideon Toury (eds) *Translation*

Theory and Intercultural Relations, Poetics Today 2:4 (Summer–Autumn): 39–50.

——(1982a) "Literary Theory and Translated Literature," in André Lefevere and Kenneth David Jackson (eds) *The Art and Science of Translation, Dispositio* 7(19–21).

——(1982b) "Mother Courage's Cucumbers: Text, System and Refraction in a Theory of Literature," *Modern Language Studies* 12: 4 (Fall): 3–20.

——(1984) "That Structure in the Dialect of Man Interpreted," in E. S. Shaffer (ed.) *Comparative Criticism* 6, Cambridge: Cambridge University Press.

——(1987) "'Beyond Interpretation' or the Business of (Re)Writing," *Comparative Literature Studies* 24(1): 17–39.

——(1988–9) "Systems Thinking and Cultural Relativism," *Jadavpur Journal of Comparative Literature* 26–7: 55–68.

——(1990) "Translation: Its Genealogy in the West," in Susan Bassnett and André Lefevere (eds) *Translation, History and Culture*, London: Pinter.

Lefevere, André and Susan Bassnett (1990) "Introduction: Proust's Grandmother and the Thousand and One Nights. The 'Cultural Turn' in Translation Studies," in Susan Bassnett and André Lefevere (eds) *Translation, History and Culture*, London: Pinter.

Lefevere, André and Kenneth David Jackson (eds) (1982) *The Art and Science of Translation, Dispositio* 8(19–21).

Leibniz, Gottfried Wilhelm (1949) *New Essays Concerning Human Understanding*, trans. A. G. Langley, LaSalle, IL: Open Court.

Lenneberg, Eric H. (1967) *Biological Foundations of Language*, New York: Wiley.

Lentricchia, Frank (1980) *After the New Criticism*, Chicago: University of Chicago Press.

Leuven-Zwart, Kitty M. Van (1984) *Vertailing en origineel*, Dordrecht: Foris.

——(1989) "Translation and Original: Similarities and Dissimilarities, I," *Target* 1(2): 151–82.

——(1990) "Translation and Original: Similarities and Dissimilarities, II," *Target* 2(1): 69–96.

Leuven-Zwart, Kitty M. Van and Tom Naaijkens (eds) (1991) *Translation Studies: The State of the Art*, Amsterdam: Rodopi.

Levý, Jiří (1965) "Will Translation Theory be of Use to Translators?" *Übersetzen: Vorträge und Beiträge vom Internationalen Kongress literarischer Übersetzer in Hamburg*, Frankfurt-on-Main.

——(1967) "Translation as a Decision Making Process," *To Honor Roman Jakobson*, vol. 2: 1171–82, The Hague: Mouton.

——(1969) *Die literarische Übersetzung: Theorie einer Kunstgattung*, trans. Walter Schamschula, Frankfurt-on-Main: Athenäum.

——(1976) "The Translation of Verbal Art," trans. Susan Larson, in Ladislav Matejka and Irwin Titunik (eds) *Semiotics of Art: Prague School Contributions*, Cambridge, MA: The MIT Press.

Liddell, Henry George and Robert Scott (eds) (1925) *A Greek–English Lexicon*, Oxford: Clarendon.

Lloyd, David (1982) "Translator as Refractor: Towards a Re-reading of James Clarence Mangan as Translator," in André Lefevere and Kenneth David Jackson (eds) *The Art and Science of Translation, Dispositio* 7(19–21): 141–62.

——(1987) *Nationalism and Minor Literature: James Clarence Magnan and the Emergence of Irish Cultural Nationalism*, Berkeley: University of California Press.

Lowell, Robert (1961) *Imitations*, New York: Farrar, Straus & Giroux.

McCawley, James D. (1976) *Grammar and Meaning: Papers on Syntactic and Semantic Topics*. New York: Academic Press.

Machado, Antonio (1983) *Times Alone: Selected Poems of Antonio Machado*, trans. Robert Bly, Middletown, CT: Wesleyan University Press.

Macherey, Pierre (1978) *A Theory of Literary Production*, trans. Geoffrey Wall, London: Routledge & Kegan Paul.

Macura, Vladimír (1990) "Culture as Translation," in Susan Bassnett and André Lefevere (eds) *Translation, History and Culture*, London: Pinter.

Mallarmé, Stéphane (1974) *Mallarmé*, trans., Augusto de Campos, Haroldo de Campos and Décio Pignattari, São Paulo: Editora Perspectiva.

Man, Paul de (1986) "Walter Benjamin's 'The Task of the Translator,'" *The Resistance to Theory*, Minneapolis: University of Minnesota Press.

Mandelbaum, D. (ed.) (1949) *Selected Writings in Language, Culture and Personality by Edward Sapir*, Berkeley: University of California Press.

Matejka, Ladislav (1976) "Prague School Semiotics," in Ladislav Matejka and Irwin R. Titunik (eds) *Semiotics of Art: Prague School Contributions*, Cambridge, MA: The MIT Press.

——(1978) "The Formal Method and Linguistics," in Ladislav Matejka and Krystyna Pomorska (eds) *Readings in Russian Poetics: Formalist and Structuralist Views*, Ann Arbor: Michigan Slavic Publications.

Matejka, Ladislav and Irwin R. Titunik (eds) (1976) *Semiotics of Art: Prague School Contributions*, Cambridge, MA: The MIT Press.

Matejka, Ladislav and Krystyna Pomorska (eds) (1978) *Readings in Russian Poetics: Formalist and Structuralist Views*, Michigan Slavic Contributions 8, Ann Arbor: Michigan Slavic Publications.

Mathesius, Vilém (1913) "O problémch českého přakladatelství [Über die Probleme des tschechischen Übersetzerwesens] ," *Přehled* 11.

Mayakóvski, Vladimir (1968) *Poemas de Maiacóvski*, trans. Augusto de Campos, Haroldo de Campos, and Boris Schnaiderman, Rio de Janeiro: Editora Tempo Brasileiro.

Medvedev, Pavel (1976) *Die formale Methode in der Literaturwissenschaft*, ed. and trans. Helmut Glück, Stuttgart: J.B. Metzler.

——(1985) *The Formal Method in Literary Scholarship: A Critical Introduction to Sociological Poetics*, trans. Albert J. Wehrle, Cambridge, MA: Harvard University Press.

Mette Hjort, Anne (1990) "Translation and the Consequences of Scepticism," in Susan Bassnett and André Lefevere (eds) *Translation, History and Culture*, London: Pinter.

Merwin, W.S. (1979) *Selected Translations, 1968–1978*, New York: Atheneum.

——(1989) "Translating Juarroz and Noren: Working Papers," in Daniel Weissbort (ed.) *Translating Poetry: The Double Labyrinth*, Iowa City: University of Iowa Press.

Miko, František (1969) *Estetika výrazu. Teória vyrazu a štýl*, Bratislava.

——(1970) "La Théorie de l'expression et la traduction," in James S. Holmes, Frans de Haan, and Anton Popovič (eds) *The Nature of Translation*, The Hague: Mouton.

Miko, František and Anton Popovič (1978) *Tvorba a recepcia: Estetická kommunikácia a metakomunikácia*, Tatran.

Mukařovský, Jan (1976a) "Art as a Semiotic Fact," trans. I. R. Titunik, in Ladislav Matejka and Irwin R. Titunik (eds) *Semiotics of Art: Prague School Contributions*, Cambridge, MA: The MIT Press.

——(1976b) "Poetic Reference," trans. S. Janecek, in Ladislav Matejka and Irwin R. Titunik (eds) *Semiotics of Art: Prague School Contributions*, Cambridge, MA: The MIT Press.

Neubert, Albrecht (1973) "Invarianz und Pragmatik," in Walter Graul, Otto Kade, Karl Kokoschko, and Hans Zikmund (eds) *Neue Beiträge zu Grundfragen der Übersetzungswissenschaft*, vols 5, 6, *Beihefte zur Zeitschrift Fremdsprachen*, Leipzig: Enzyklopädie.

——(1985) *Text and Translation*, Übersetzungswissenschaftliche Beiträge 8, Leipzig: Enzyklopädie.

——(1986) "Translatorische Relativität," in Mary Snell-Hornby (ed.) *Übersetzungswissenschaft – eine Neuorientierung: Zur Integrierung von Theorie und Praxis*, Tübingen: Franke Verlag.

Nida, Eugene A. (1952) *God's Word in Man's Language*, New York: Harper & Brothers.

——(1960) *Message and Mission; The Communication of the Christian Faith*, New York: Harper & Brothers.

——(1964) *Toward a Science of Translating: With Special Reference to Principles and Procedures Involved in Bible Translating*, Leiden: E.J. Brill.

——(1969) "Science of Translation," *Language* 47: 483–98.

——(1974) "Translation," in Thomas A. Sebeok (ed.) *Current Trends in Linguistics*, vol. 12: 1045–66, The Hague: Mouton.

——(1976) "A Framework for the Analysis and Evaluation of Theories of Translation," in Richard W. Brislin (ed.) *Translation: Applications and Research*, New York: Gardner Press.

——(1982) *Translating Meaning*, San Dimas, California: English Language Institute.

Nida, Eugene A. and William D. Reyburn (1981) *Meaning Across Cultures*, American Society of Missiology Series, Maryknoll, NY: Orbis Books.

Nida, Eugene A. and Charles R. Taber (1969) *The Theory and Practice of Translation*, Leiden: E.J. Brill.

Nietzsche, Friedrich (1954) *Thus Spoke Zarathustra*, in *The Portable Nietzsche*, trans. Walter Kaufman, New York: Viking.

Norris, Christopher (1982) *Deconstruction: Theory and Practice*, London: Methuen.

Peachy, Frederic and Richard Lattimore (1919) *The Pound Newsletter* 5; and *The New Age* (27 November).

Peirce, Charles Sanders (1931–1966) *Collected Papers*, ed. Charles Hartshorne, Peter Weiss, and Arthur W. Burks, Cambridge, MA: Belknap Press of Harvard University Press.

Pomorska, Krystyna (1978) "Russian Formalism in Retrospect," in Ladislav Matejka and Krystyna Pomorska (eds) *Readings in Russian Poetics: Formalist and Structuralist Views*, Ann Arbor: Michigan Slavic Publications.

Popovič, Anton (1970) "The Concept 'Shift of Expression' in Translation Analysis," in James S. Holmes, Frans de Haan, and Anton Popovič (eds) *The Nature of Translation*, The Hague: Mouton.

——(n.d.) *Dictionary for the Analysis of Literary Translation*, The University of Alberta, Edmonton: Department of Comparative Literature.

——(1976) "Aspects of Metatext," *Canadian Review of Literature/Revue Canadienne de Littérature Comparée* 3(3): 225–35.

——(1984) "From J. Levý to Communicational Didactics of Literary Translation," in Wolfram Wilss and Gisela Thome (eds) *Translation Theory and its Implementation in the Teaching of Translating and Interpreting*, Tübingen: Gunther Narr.

Pound, Ezra (1911–12) "I Gather the Limbs of Osiris," in *The New Age* 10 (November–February).

——(1913) "How I Began," in *T. P.'s Weekly* 21 (June 6).

——(1914) "Vortex," in *BLAST* 1 (June 20): 153–4.

——(1915) *Cathay*, London: E. Mathews.

——(1917) *Lustra of Ezra Pound, with earlier poems*, New York: Knopf.

——(1937) *Polite Essays*, London: Faber & Faber.

——(1950) *Letters 1907–1941*, ed. D.D. Paige, New York: Harcourt, Brace.

——(1951) *ABC of Reading*, London: Faber & Faber.

——(1954) *Literary Essays of Ezra Pound*, ed. T. S. Eliot, London: Faber & Faber.

——(1957) *Selected Poems of Ezra Pound*, New York: New Directions.

——(1960) *Cantares de Ezra Pound*, trans. Augusto de Campos, Haroldo de Campos, and Décio Pignattari, Rio de Janeiro: Serviço de Documentação-MEC.

——(1963) *Translations*, New York: New Directions.

——(1968) *Antologia Poética de Ezra Pound*, trans. Augusto de Campos, Haroldo de Campos, *et al.*, Lisbon: Ulisséia.

——(1970a) *Gaudier-Brzeska: A Memoir*, New York: New Directions.

——(1970b) *ABC da Literatura*, trans. Augusto de Campos and José Paulo Paes, São Paulo: Cultrix.

——(1975) *The Cantos*, London: Faber & Faber.

——(1976) *Collected Early Poems of Ezra Pound*, ed. Michael John King, New York: New Directions.

Pound, Ezra and Marcella Spann (eds) (1964) *Confucius to Cummings*, New York: New Directions.

Quine, Willard V. O. (1951) "Two Dogmas of Empiricism," *Philosophical Review* 60.

——(1959) "Meaning and Translation," in Reuben A. Brower (ed.) *On Translation*, Cambridge, MA: Harvard University Press.

——(1960) *Word and Object*, Cambridge, MA: The MIT Press.

——(1968) "Replies," *Synthese* 19: 264–80.

——(1974) "Methodological Reflections on Current Linguistic Theory," in Gilbert Harman (ed.) *On Noam Chomsky: Critical Essays*, Amherst: University of Massachusetts Press.

Rabate, Jean-Michel (1986) *Language, Sexuality and Ideology in Ezra Pound's Cantos*, Albany: State University of New York Press.

Ransom, John Crowe (1941) *The New Criticism*, Norfolk, CT: New Directions.

Raffel, Burton (1988) *The Art of Translating Poetry*, University Park: The Pennsylvania State University Press.

Reck, Michael (1967) *Ezra Pound: A Close-up*, New York: MacGraw-Hill.

Reiss, Katharina (1971) *Möglichkeiten und Grenzen der Übersetzungskritik*, Munich: Max Hueber Verlag.

——(1976) *Texttyp und Übersetzungsmethode: Der operative Text*, Kronsberg: Scriptor Verlag.

Reiss, Katharina and Hans J. Vermeer (1984) *Grundlegung einer allgemeinen Translationstheorie*, Tübingen: Max Niemeyer Verlag.

Richards, I. A. (1929) *Practical Criticism*, New York: Harcourt Brace.

——(1953) "Toward a Theory of Translating," in Arthur F. Wright (ed.) *Studies in Chinese Thought*, Chicago: University of Chicago Press.

Risset, Jacqueline (1984) "Joyce Translates Joyce," trans. Daniel Pick, in E.S. Shaffer (ed.) *Comparative Criticism* 6, Cambridge: Cambridge University Press.

——(1985) Introduction to *La Divine Comédie: L'Enfer* by Dante, trans. Jacqueline Risset, Paris: Flammarion.

Robinson, Douglas (1991) *The Translator's Turn*, Baltimore: Johns Hopkins University Press.

Rosch, Eleanor (1973) "Natural Categories," *Cognitive Psychology* 4: 328–50.

Rose, Marilyn Gaddis (ed.) (1981) *Translation Spectrum: Essays in Theory and Practice*, Albany: State University of New York Press.

Sapir, Edward (1949) *Selected Writings in Language, Culture and Personality of Edward Sapir*, ed. D. Mandelbaum, Berkeley: University of California Press.

Schulte, Rainer (1987) "Translation Theory: A Challenge for the Future," *Translation Review* 23: 1–2.

——(1988) "Poet as Translator: Correspondences and Renewal," *Translation Review* 26: 12–22.

Schultze, Brigitte (ed.) (1987) *Die literarische Übersetzung: Fallstudien zu ihrer Kulturgeschichte. Göttinger Beiträge zur Internationalen Übersetzungsforschung*, vol. 1, Berlin: Erich Schmidt Verlag.

Scott, Charles E. (1987) *The Language of Difference*, Atlantic Highlands, NJ: Humanities Press International.

Searle, John R. (1969) *Speech Acts: An Essay in the Philosophy of Language*, London: Cambridge University Press.

——(1982) "Chomsky's Revolution in Linguistics," in Gilbert Harman (ed.) *On Noam Chomsky: Critical Essays*, Amherst: The University of Massachusetts Press.

Shaffer, E. S. (ed.) (1984) *Comparative Criticism* 6, Cambridge: Cambridge University Press.

Shavit, Zohar (1981) "Translation of Children's Literature as a Function of Its Position in the Literary Polysystem," in Itamar Even-Zohar and Gideon Toury (eds) *Translation Theory and Intercultural Relations, Poetics Today* 2:4 (Summer–Autumn): 171–80.

Smith, Barbara Herrnstein (1978) *On the Margins of Discourse: The Relation of Literature to Language*, Chicago: The University of Chicago Press.

Snell-Hornby, Mary (1988) *Translation Studies: An Integrated Approach*, Amsterdam/Philadelphia: John Benjamins.

——(1990) "Linguistic Transcoding or Cultural Transfer? A Critique of Translation Theory in Germany," in Susan Bassnett and André Lefevere (eds) *Translation, History and Culture*, London: Pinter.

Snell-Hornby, Mary (ed.) (1986) *Übersetzungswissenschaft – eine Neuorientierung: Zur Integrierung von Theorie und Praxis*, Tübingen: Franke Verlag.

Sollers, Philippe (1968) "Le Réflex de réduction," in Michael Foucault, Roland Barthes, Jacques Derrida, Jean-Louis Baudry, and Philippe Sollers, *Théorie d'ensemble*, Paris: Seuil.

Sollers, Philippe and David Hayman (1981) *Vision à New York*, Paris: Bernard Grasset.

Stein, Dieter (1980) *Theoretische Grundlagen der Übersetzungswissenschaft*, Tübingen: Gunther Narr.

Steiner, George (1975) *After Babel*, London/Oxford: Oxford University Press.

——(1978) *On Difficulty and Other Essays*, New York/Oxford: Oxford University Press.

Strand, Mark and Charles Simic (eds) (1976) *Another Republic: 17 European and South American Writers*, New York: Ecco Press.

Sullivan, J. P. (1964) *Ezra Pound and Sextus Propertius: A Study in Creative Translation*, Austin: University of Texas Press.

Tabakowska, Elzbieta (1990) "Linguistic Polyphony as a Problem in Translation," in Susan Bassnett and André Lefevere (eds) *Translation, History and Culture*, London: Pinter.

Todorov, Tzvetan (1966) *Théorie de la littérature; Textes des formalistes russes réunis*, Paris: Seuil.

——(1973) "Some Approaches to Russian Formalism," in Stephen Bann and John E. Bowlt (eds) *Russian Formalism*, Edinburgh: Scottish Academic Press.

Tomlinson, Charles (ed.) (1980) *Oxford Book of Verse in English Translation*, Oxford: Oxford University Press.

Toury, Gideon (1977) *Normot šel tirgum ve-ha-tirgum ha-sifruti le-ivrit ba-šanim* 1930–1945, Tel Aviv: The Porter Institute for Poetics and Semiotics.

——(1978) "The Nature and Role of Norms in Literary Translation," in James S. Holmes, José Lambert, and Raymond van den Broeck (eds) *Literature and Translation: New Perpectives in Literary Studies with a Basic Bibliography of Books on Translation Studies*, Leuven, Belgium: Acco, 1978. Also in (1980) *In Search of a Theory of Translation*, Tel Aviv: The Porter Institute for Poetics and Semiotics.

——(1980) *In Search of a Theory of Translation*, Tel Aviv: The Porter Institute for Poetics and Semiotics.

——(1981) "Translated Literature: System, Norm Performance: Toward a TT-Oriented Approach to Literary Translation," in Itamar Even-Zohar and Gideon Toury (eds) *Translation Theory and Intercultural Relations, Poetics Today* 2:4 (Summer–Autumn): 9–29. Also in (1980) *In Search of a Theory of Translation*, Tel Aviv: The Porter Institute for Poetics and Semiotics.

——(1982) "A Rationale for Descriptive Translation Studies," in André Lefevere and Kenneth David Jackson (eds) *The Art and Science of Translation, Dispositio* 7(19–21): 23–40. Also in (1985) Theo Hermans (ed.) *The Manipulation of Literature: Studies in Literary Translation*, New York: St. Martins Press.

——(1984) "Translation, Literary Translation and Pseudotranslation," in E. S. Shaffer (ed.) *Comparative Criticism* 6, Cambridge: Cambridge University Press.

——(1986) "Translation: A Cultural-Semiotic Perspective," in Thomas Sebeok and Paul Bouissac (eds) *Dictionary of Semiotics*, 1111–24, Berlin/New York/Amsterdam: Mouton de Gruyter.

——(1988) "Translating English Literature via German – and Vice Versa: A Symptomatic Reversal in the History of Modern Hebrew Literature," in Armin Paul Frank (ed.) *Die Literarische Übersetzung. Göttinger Beiträge zur internationalen Übersetzungsforschung*, vol. 2, Berlin: Erich Schmidt.

——(1991) "What are Descriptive Studies in Translation Likely to Yield Apart from Isolated Descriptions?" in Kitty Van Leuven-Zwart and Tom Naaijkens (eds) *Translation Studies: The State of the Art*, Amsterdam: Rodopi.

Transtroemer, Tomas (1971) *Twenty Poems of Tomas Transtroemer*, trans. Robert Bly, Madison, MN: Seventies Press.

Trakl, Georg (1961) *Twenty Poems of Georg Trakl*, trans. James Wright, John Knoepfle, and Robert Bly, Madison, MN.: Sixties Press.

Tymoczko, Maria (1982) "Strategies for Integrating Irish Epics into European Literature," in André Lefevere and Kenneth David Jackson (eds) *The Art and Science of Translation, Dispositio* 7(19–21): 123–40.

——(1985) "How Distinct are Formal and Dynamic Equivalence?" in Theo Hermans (ed.) *The Manipulation of Literature: Studies in Literary Translation*, New York: St. Martins Press.

——(1986) "Translation as a Force for Literary Revolution in the Twelfth-Century Shift from Epic to Romance," *New Comparison* 1 (Summer): 7–27.

——(1990) "Translation in Oral Tradition as a Touchstone for Translation Theory and Practice," in Susan Bassnett and André Lefevere (eds) *Translation, History and Culture*, London: Pinter.

Tynjanov, Jurij (1921) *Dostoevskij: Gogol*, Opajaz.

——(1978a) "The Meaning of the Word in Verse," trans. M. E. Suino, in Ladislav Matejka and Krystyna Pomorska (eds) *Readings in Russian Poetics: Formalist and Structuralist Views*, Ann Arbor: Michigan Slavic Publications.

——(1978b) "On Literary Evolution," trans. C. A. Luplow, in Ladislav Matejka and Krystyna Pomorska (eds) *Readings in Russian Poetics:*

Formalist and Structuralist Views, Ann Arbor: Michigan Slavic Publications.

Tynjanov, Jurij and Roman Jakobson (1978) "Problems in the Study of Literature and Language," in Ladislav Matejka and Krystyna Pomorska (eds) *Readings in Russian Poetics: Formalist and Structuralist Views*, Ann Arbor: Michigan Slavic Publications.

Vance, Eugene (1985) "Translation in the Past Perfect," in Christie McDonald (ed.) *The Ear of the Other: Texts and Discussions with Jacques Derrida*, trans. Peggy Kamuf, Lincoln: University of Nebraska Press.

Vanderauwera, Ria (1982) "Review: Gideon Toury *In Search of a Theory of Translation*," in André Lefevere and Kenneth David Jackson (eds) *The Art and Science of Translation, Dispositio* 7(19–21): 177–80.

Verhaar, J. W. M. (1980) "J. M. Edie: Speaking and Meaning. The Phenomenology of Language," *Language* 56: 211–14.

Weissbort, Daniel (1983) Foreword to *Modern Poetry in Translation*, New York: MPT/Persea.

Weissbort, Daniel (ed.) (1989) *Translating Poetry: The Double Labyrinth*. Iowa City: University of Iowa Press.

Wellek, René (1969) *The Literary Theory and Aesthetics of the Prague School*. Michigan Slavic Contributions, ed. Ladislav Matejka. Ann Arbor: Department of Slavic Languages and Literature, University of Michigan.

——(1986) *A History of Modern Criticism: 1750–1950*, vol. 5, New Haven: Yale University Press.

Wellek, René and Austin Warren (1949) *Theory of Literature*, New York: Harcourt Brace.

Whorf, Benjamin Lee (1962) *Selected Writings of Benjamin Lee Whorf*, ed. John B. Carroll, Cambridge, MA: Technology Press of Massachusetts Institute of Technology.

Will, Frederic (1966) *Literature Inside Out*, Cleveland: Western Reserve University Press.

——(1973) *The Knife in the Stone*, The Hague: Mouton.

——(1984) *Shamans in Turtlenecks*, Amsterdam: Rodopi.

——(1988) *Thresholds and Testimonies*, Detroit: Wayne State University Press.

——(1990) *A Portrait of John*, Detroit: Wayne State University Press.

Wilss, Wolfram (1977) *Übersetzungswissenschaft. Probleme und Methoden*, Stuttgart: Ernst Klett Verlag.

——(1982) *The Science of Translation: Problems and Methods*, trans. Wolfram Wilss, Tübingen: Gunter Narr.

——(1988) *Kognition und Übersetzen: Zu Theorie und Praxis der menschlichen und der maschinellen Übersetzen*, Tübingen: Max Niemeyer Verlag.

——(1989) "Towards a Multi-facet Concept of Translation Behavior," *Target* 1(2): 129–50.

——(forthcoming) "Was ist fertigkeitsorientiertes Übersetzen?" *Lebende Sprachen*.

Wittgenstein, Ludwig (1968) *Philosophical Investigations*, trans. G. E. M. Anscombe, Oxford: Basil Blackwell.

Wollen, Peter (1982) *Readings and Writings: Semiotic Counter-Strategies*, London: Verso and NLB.

Yahalom, Shelly (1981) "Le Système littéraire en état de crise: Contacts inter-systémiques et comportement traductionnel," in Itamar Even-Zohar and Gideon Toury (eds) *Translation Theory and Intercultural Relations, Poetics Today* 2:4 (Summer–Autumn): 143–60.

Yip, Wai-lim (1969) *Ezra Pound's Cathay*, Princeton: Princeton University Press.

Zdanys, Jonas (1987) "Teaching Translation: Some Notes Toward a Course Structure," *Translation Review*, 23: 9–11.

Index